DRAFTING ARTICLES OF ASSOCIATION

To Susan

DRAFTING ARTICLES OF ASSOCIATION

NEIL SINCLAIR

Solicitor and Partner,
Berwin Leighton

LAW & TAX

© Neil Sinclair 1996

Neil Sinclair has asserted his right under the
Copyright, Designs and Patents Act 1988 to be identified
as the author of this work

ISBN 075200 1809

Published by
FT Law & Tax
21–27 Lamb's Conduit Street,
London WC1N 3NJ

A Division of Pearson Professional Limited

Associated offices
Australia, Belgium, Canada, Hong Kong, India, Japan, Luxembourg,
Singapore, Spain and USA

A CIP catalogue record for this book is available from the British Library.

Printed and bound in Great Britain by Bell & Bain, Glasgow

Contents

Draft Articles

Appendices

TABLE OF CASES

TABLE OF CASES

TABLE OF STATUTES

TABLE OF STATUTORY INSTRUMENTS

Glossary

ABI	Association of British Insurers
ARTICLE (ART)	An article in one of the Appendices
CA	Companies Act
LONDON STOCK EXCHANGE	London Stock Exchange Limited
OLD TABLE A	Table A in the First Schedule to CA 1948
REGULATION (REG)	A regulation in Table A or Old Table A
TABLE A	Table A in the Schedule to the Companies (Tables A to F) Regulations 1985 (SI No 805)

1

Introduction

Table A

The legislation provides little guidance as to what constitutes articles of association. Every company is deemed to have articles in the form of Table A except insofar as articles are registered which exclude or modify Table A (CA 1985, s 8). Whilst it is clear, therefore, that Table A provides a precedent for the matters to be covered by articles, it would appear to be open to a company to exclude Table A in its entirety without replacing it.

The contents of Table A fall into a number of categories:

(1) Some regulations repeat provisions of the legislation which bind a company whether or not included in the articles. Examples are reg 6, which confirms the entitlement of shareholders to certificates for their shares (CA 1985, s 185), and reg 38, dealing with the periods of notice required for the convening of meetings (CA 1985, s 369). Any attempt by the articles to modify these requirements will be ineffective.

(2) The legislation contains numerous provisions which apply except to the extent that they are modified by the articles. An example is CA 1985, s 370 which states that, except insofar as the articles otherwise provide, the quorum at meetings of the members is two and members have one vote for each share they hold. The quorum requirements are invariably modified in the case of joint venture companies (see Appendix C, art 17) and companies where special protection is provided for minority shareholders (as in Appendix D, art 23). Voting rights are also normally altered in those cases (see Appendix C, art 20

and Appendix D, art 24) and preference shares will generally not confer voting rights unless the preferred dividends are in arrear.

(3) The legislation specifies a number of powers which a company may elect to take in its articles, such as the ability to pay commissions to a person subscribing for shares (CA 1985, s 97 and Table A, reg 4) and to alter the company's share capital (CA 1985, s 121 and Table A, reg 32).

(4) Some of the regulations of Table A confirm rules derived from the common law rather than express legislation. Examples are the power of the directors to manage the company and to pay dividends (see the comments on Table A, regs 72 and 102 in Chapter 2).

(5) A wide range of the regulations in Table A deals with matters which facilitate, but are not essential for, the operation of the company. It is, for example, generally convenient for the directors to be able to appoint alternates to represent them at board meetings from which they will be absent (see Table A, regs 65–69) and to give the chairman the power to resolve questions as to the voting entitlements of directors who have an interest in the subject matter of a resolution (see Table A, reg 98).

(6) Other provisions of Table A are included to protect the interests of shareholders. These include the requirement for non-executive directors to be subject to retirement by rotation (see Table A, regs 73–80) and the disenfranchisement of directors in relation to resolutions where they have an interest (see Table A, reg 94). This category of regulation is the one that is most subject to amendment in articles which do not simply adopt Table A in its entirety.

Because Table A has statutory force, a regulation which it contains cannot be invalid (see *Lock v Queensland Investment and Mortgage Co* [1896] AC 461) and it may therefore be followed, either in detail or in principle, with confidence as to its effectiveness.

The contents of articles

It is most unusual for a company to adopt Table A without any amendment. This is partly because some of the regulations, such as those relating to the powers of the directors to vote on resolutions in respect of which they have an interest, are rarely acceptable without change. Most private companies simply omit restrictions which are perceived to fulfil no relevant purpose whilst others retain the regulations but in amended form. There are also areas which are not adequately covered by Table A and where experience has shown the value of including new powers and rights in the articles. An example is an article (such as art 57 in Appendix A) which permits the directors to hold board meetings by conference telephone.

In the case of private companies, there are few restraints as to what the articles may provide. As mentioned above, certain statutory rules cannot be overridden whilst others are inherent elements of the common law relating to companies. In relation to listed companies, the contents of articles are constrained by the Listing Rules of the London Stock Exchange (see Chapter 6, p 173) and by the expectations of the investing community (see Chapter 6, p 179).

Despite the freedom that private companies enjoy, articles are normally closely based on Table A. Deviations are generally in matters of detail or to cover the particular requirements which arise, for example, in the case of joint venture companies. Whilst Table A works satisfactorily in practice, it suffers a number of imperfections and these should be rectified when detailed articles are drafted.

The structure of this book

The main part of this book is a detailed analysis of Table A. Chapter 2 reviews each regulation and indicates the extent to which changes are permitted or desirable. Subsequent chapters discuss the form of articles that are appropriate in a number of special cases. In the case of private companies, informality and freedom from administrative minutiae are of prime importance. Apart from this, shareholders of private companies will generally wish to have the ability to prevent unwelcome third parties from acquiring shares. This control is achieved through the use of pre-emption provisions which are complex and variable. A large part of Chapter 3 is devoted to a review of the important considerations in drafting pre-emption articles.

It is necessary to give particularly careful consideration to the rights of the different parties in joint venture companies, which commonly have a deadlock voting structure, and those companies where special protection is given to minority shareholders (see Chapter 5, p 163). At the other extreme are wholly-owned subsidiaries where the objective is to ensure that the parent company can exercise its control without delay and with minimum formality (see Chapter 4, p 128).

The last set of articles is that for a listed company. A number of special considerations apply to these companies (see Chapter 6). The format and content of Table A has been followed as much as possible in this case as it is not the purpose of this book to make purely cosmetic drafting changes. As a result, there will be a degree of overlap between the various articles contained in the appendices in order to avoid relying on extensive cross-references.

The law is stated as at 31 December 1995.

2

Commentary on Table A

Introduction

Section 8(2) of CA 1985 provides that Table A applies to a company limited by shares if and to the extent that it is not excluded or modified by the articles registered by the company. For private companies it is standard practice to adopt Table A with a limited number of omissions and amendments which merely modify Table A. An appropriate article for this purpose would be as follows:

2.1 Table A modified

The regulations contained in Table A in the Schedule to the Companies (Tables A to F) Regulations 1985, apart from regulations ... , apply to the company except insofar as they are inconsistent with these articles.

In the case of public companies, however, it is the usual procedure to disapply Table A in its entirety and to adopt full length articles. Suitable wording is:

2.2 Table A excluded

The regulations contained in Table A in the Schedule to the Companies (Tables A to F) Regulations 1985 do not apply to the company.

In both cases it should be borne in mind that, as discussed in Chapter 1, many of the regulations in Table A repeat statutory rules which apply in any event. These offer no, or little, scope for amendment and, when proposing an alteration to Table A, a check should always be made to see if the regulation which is to be altered embodies any statutory wording and, if so, whether and to what extent amendments are permitted.

Long form articles generally follow Table A in the order of the matters covered and will adopt many of the Table A regulations either verbatim or in paraphrase. When drafting full length articles the opportunity should be taken, in the case of regulations which closely follow Table A, to improve upon some of the rather stilted drafting that Table A adopts. By way of example, there are set out below the first five regulations of Table A, followed by an alternative, and, it is suggested, improved, version.

> 1   In these regulations[1]—
>
> 'the[2] Act' means the Companies Act 1985 including any[3] statutory modification or re-enactment thereof[4] for the time being in force[5].
>
> 'the articles'[6] means the articles of the company.
>
> 'clear days' in relation to the period of a notice means that period excluding the day when the notice is given or deemed to be given and the day for which it is given or on which it is to take effect.
>
> 'executed' includes any mode of execution.
>
> 'office' means the registered office of the company.
>
> 'the[2] holder'[7] in relation to shares means the member whose name is entered in the register of members as the holder of the shares.
>
> 'the seal' means the common seal of the company.
>
> 'secretary' means the secretary of the company or any[3] other person appointed to perform the duties of the secretary of the company[8], including a joint, assistant or deputy secretary.

---

[1]   The use of the word 'regulations' is curious having regard to the defined term 'the articles'.

[2]   It is generally better to omit 'the' from the defined term. If 'the' is kept in the definition consistency would require that this is done in every case—including, in the present context, in the definitions of 'office' and 'secretary'.

[3]   It is often better to replace 'any' with 'the', 'a' or 'an' or simply to omit it.

[4]   Legal archaisms should be avoided. They can generally be replaced by simple language without difficulty.

[5]   The words 'for the time being in force' are redundant.

[6]   This definition is barely necessary as references in the text to 'the articles' could hardly be taken to be referring to some other articles of association. This would be even clearer if all references in the text were to '*these* articles'.

[7]   It is good practice to put definitions in alphabetical order.

[8]   The repetition of the phrase 'of the company' is unnecessary.

'the[2] United Kingdom' means Great Britain and Northern Ireland. Unless the context otherwise requires, words or expressions contained in these regulations[9] bear the same meaning as in the Act but excluding any[3] statutory modification thereof[4] not in force when these regulations[9] become[10] binding on the company.

2   Subject to the provisions of the Act and without prejudice to any[3] rights attached to any[3] existing shares, any[3] share may be issued with such[11] rights or restrictions as the company may[12] by ordinary resolution determine.

3   Subject to the provisions of the Act, shares may be issued which are to be redeemed[13] or are liable to be[14] redeemed at the option of the company or the holder[13] on such terms and in such manner as may[12] be provided by the articles.

4   The company may exercise the powers of paying commissions conferred by the Act. Subject to the provisions of the Act, any[3] such[11] commissions may be satisfied by the payment of cash or by the allotment of fully or partly paid shares or partly in one way and partly in the other[15].

5   Except as required by law no[16] person shall be recognised by the company as holding any[3] share upon trust and (except as

---

[9]   As 'the articles' is a defined term, those words should replace 'these regulations'.

[10]   'Became' is preferred. It is also more usual—and probably clearer—to refer to the date of adoption of the articles, or the formation of the company if the articles are in their original form, rather than the date on which the articles became binding on the company.

[11]   'Such' is often unnecessarily legalistic and should be avoided. It can usually be omitted, except where (as in reg 2) the relevant phrase is 'such ... as ...', or is replaced with 'the'.

[12]   It is preferable to use the indicative mood instead of the subjunctive.

[13]   The absence of punctuation leads to a mild ambiguity. Does the phrase 'on such terms and in such manner as may be provided by the articles' qualify both shares 'which are to be redeemed' and shares which 'are liable to be redeemed'?

[14]   Purely from a drafting point of view, this wording is unduly legalistic. It would be preferable to replace 'or are liable to be redeemed' with the simpler 'may be redeemed'. The wording in reg 3, however, follows that used in CA 1985, s 159, on which the authority to issue redeemable shares is based. To avoid any argument as to whether the statutory requirement has been satisfied, it is better to track the section accurately.

[15]   This drafting is excessively wordy. There is no need to refer to commissions being payable in cash as that would be the natural procedure unless cash was expressly prohibited.

[16]   The way in which negatives are expressed can be confusing.

otherwise provided by the articles or by law) the company shall not be bound by or recognise any[3] interest in any[3] share except an absolute right to the entirety thereof[4] in the holder.

The following is a suggested reformulation of these regulations:

1   In these articles—

'Act' means the Companies Act 1985 including statutory modifications or re-enactments.

'clear days' in relation to the period of a notice means that period excluding the day when the notice is given or deemed to be given and the day for which it is given or on which it is to take effect.

'executed' includes any mode of execution.

'holder' in relation to shares means the member whose name is entered in the register of members as holder of them.

'office' means the registered office of the company.

'seal' means the common seal of the company.

'secretary' means the secretary of the company or other person appointed to perform the duties of secretary, including a joint, assistant or deputy secretary.

'United Kingdom' means Great Britain and Northern Ireland. Unless the context otherwise requires, words or expressions contained in these articles bear the same meaning as in the Act but excluding statutory modifications not in force when these articles were adopted.

2   Subject to the provisions of the Act and without prejudice to the rights attached to existing shares, a share may be issued with such rights or restrictions as the company by ordinary resolution determines.

3   Subject to the provisions of the Act, shares may be issued which are to be redeemed, or are liable to be redeemed, at the option of the company or the holder, on such terms and in such manner as are provided by these articles.

4   The company may exercise the powers of paying commissions conferred by the Act. Subject to the provisions of the Act,

commissions may be satisfied wholly or partly by the allotment of fully or partly paid shares.

5   Except as required by law, a person shall not be recognised by the company as holding a share on trust. Except as otherwise provided by these articles or by law, the company shall not be bound by or recognise an interest in a share except the holder's absolute right to the entirety of it.

Another tiresome feature of Table A is its tendency to use unduly long sentences. An example is reg 21:

> A person any of whose shares have been forfeited shall cease to be a member in respect of them and shall surrender to the company for cancellation the certificate for the shares forfeited but shall remain liable to the company for all moneys which at the date of forfeiture were presently payable by him to the company in respect of those shares with interest at the rate at which interest was payable on those moneys before the forfeiture or, if no interest was so payable, at the appropriate rate (as defined in the Act) from the date of forfeiture until payment but the directors may waive payment wholly or in part or enforce payment without any allowance for the value of the shares at the time of forfeiture or for any consideration received on their disposal.

This would be much easier to follow if broken down into short sentences and properly punctuated:

> A person, any of whose shares have been forfeited, shall cease to be a member in respect of them. He shall surrender to the company for cancellation the certificate for the shares forfeited. He shall nevertheless remain liable to the company for all moneys which at the date of forfeiture were presently payable by him to the company in respect of those shares. Interest shall be charged on the moneys at the rate at which interest was payable on the moneys before the forfeiture or, if no interest was so payable, at the appropriate rate (as defined in the Act). The interest shall be payable from the date of forfeiture until payment. The directors may waive payment of the interest wholly or in part. They may also enforce payment without any allowance for the value of the shares at the time of forfeiture or for any consideration received on their disposal.

Apart from detailed drafting points such as the above, the regulations of Table A form a good basis for the articles of most ordinary companies. In amending Table A, there are broadly three techniques which can be adopted. The first of these is to make the minimum change that is required to give effect to the alteration. As an example, reg 46 of Table

A provides that at least two members can join together to demand that a poll is taken at a meeting. An amendment which would increase the minimum to three members would be:

> Regulation 46 of Table A is amended by replacing 'two' with 'three'.

Whilst this way of achieving the desired change is satisfactory in technical terms and makes the necessary change briefly and unambiguously, it suffers from the very considerable disadvantage of being totally obscure without a careful reading of the regulation.

The second approach is to state the objective of the amendment and to leave it to general words to bring the change into effect. The following would achieve this:

> A poll may be demanded by not less than three members having the right to vote at the meeting and regulation 46 of Table A is modified accordingly.

The advantage of this approach is that it makes it very clear what the intention is in relation to the amendment but, as it leaves the detailed drafting unspecified, there is a risk that the precise form of the amended regulation may be ambiguous.

Finally, a precise wording change can be made which duplicates enough of the amended regulation for its new sense to be readily understood. This would be done as follows:

> Regulation 46 of Table A is amended by replacing 'by at least two members having the right to vote at the meeting' with 'by at least three members having the right to vote at the meeting'.

Each of these is acceptable although, unless the alternatives would, in a particular case, be readily intelligible, the third is best. Whilst it makes the amendments wordier, this is more than compensated for by the increased clarity. In general it is the technique adopted in this commentary and it is recognised that in a number of cases amendments could be made considerably shorter with only a marginal reduction in clarity.

A different approach may be appropriate if a change is made which effectively introduces a completely new feature. An example is the common clause which treats telephone board meetings as being as effective as meetings at which the participants are physically present in the same place (see Chapter 3, p 125 (Appendix A, art 57)). The article may either be added as an additional independent clause or may be appended, by way of amendment, to the most suitable regulation of Table A (in this case, reg 88 or 89). If the new regulation has little connection with an existing regulation, the former procedure is to be preferred.

Review of Table A

The following discussion reviews the contents of Table A, each regulation being reprinted at the start of the commentary relating to it.

Interpretation

Regulation 1

In these regulations—

'the Act' means the Companies Act 1985 including any statutory modification or re-enactment thereof for the time being in force.

'the articles' means the articles of the company.

'clear days' in relation to the period of a notice means that period excluding the day when the notice is given or deemed to be given and the day for which it is given or on which it is to take effect.

'executed' includes any mode of execution.

'office' means the registered office of the company.

'the holder' in relation to shares means the member whose name is entered in the register of members as the holder of the shares.

'the seal' means the common seal of the company.

'secretary' means the secretary of the company or any other person appointed to perform the duties of the secretary of the company, including a joint, assistant or deputy secretary.

'the United Kingdom' means Great Britain and Northern Ireland.

Unless the context otherwise requires, words or expressions contained in these regulations bear the same meaning as in the Act but excluding any statutory modification thereof not in force when these regulations become binding on the company.

A number of points arise in relation to the defined terms:

(1) as mentioned above, it is barely necessary to introduce 'the articles' as a defined term;

(2) the definition of 'clear days' is a confirmation of the common law meaning attached to those words (*Re Hector Whaling Co* [1936] Ch 208) but, as it is important to make sure that the correct amount of notice is given, the definition is administratively convenient;

(3) the definition of 'executed' is circular and can, without loss, be omitted;

(4) the reference in the definition of 'secretary' to assistant and deputy secretaries reflects the provisions of CA 1985, s 283(3); and

(5) by expressly defining the 'United Kingdom' it is made clear that the Channel Islands and the Isle of Man are not included.

It should be noted that this regulation adopts definitions which are contained in CA 1985 as in force at the time that the articles are adopted by the company. Conversely, references to the 'Act' are treated as references to the version current at any particular time. This difference of approach is unsatisfactory and it is, in any case, convenient to refer to the current edition of the Companies Act when identifying the meaning of defined terms rather than having to locate a copy of the Act as it applied on the date of adoption of the articles. If the approach is preferred of adopting the definitions applicable from time to time, the last paragraph of reg 1 should be amended as follows:

2.3 Statutory references

> The last sentence of regulation 1 of Table A is amended by deleting the words 'but excluding any statutory modification thereof not in force when these regulations become binding on the company'.

There is another point to be considered in relation to a simple adoption of the statutory definitions. This is the fact—which Table A disregards—that some terms have different definitions for different parts of the Act. For example, the term 'company' generally means a company formed under the 1985 Act or its predecessors (CA 1985, s 735). However, in s 736 (which defines 'subsidiary' and 'holding company'), 'company' includes any body corporate. Another example is 'shadow director', which in certain cases excludes parent companies (CA 1985, s 741). A particularly dangerous example of a special definition is 'group', which is defined in CA 1985, s 262(1) as being a company and its subsidiary undertakings. This is contrary to the usual understanding that a group comprises only a company and its subsidiaries, thus excluding subsidiary undertakings which are not also subsidiaries.

An article such as reg 1 which adopts statutory definitions generally would, it is suggested, be treated in cases where there are variations in the meanings of the terms as having adopted the definition which is most widely applicable. This could be made clearer by the following amendment to reg 1:

2.4 Statutory definitions

> Regulation 1 of Table A is amended by adding at the end of the last sentence the words 'but, if a particular word or expression has more than one definition in the Act, the definition to be adopted is that which has the most general application in the Act'.

A number of other definitions which are commonly adopted are:

'Auditors'	The auditors of the company. (This definition is really redundant as the articles can hardly be referring to the auditors of a different company when using the word.)
'Board'	The board of directors of the company or a quorum of the directors present at a board meeting. (As with 'auditors', this definition serves little purpose—references to the 'board' in the articles must relate to the board of the company. Alternatively, it is perfectly acceptable to refer to the 'directors'—which also needs no definition.)
'London Stock Exchange'	London Stock Exchange Limited. (This definition will generally be relevant only in the case of listed companies.)
'Member'	A member of the company.
'paid up'	Includes credited as paid up. (Shares are credited as paid up when reserves are capitalised. The distinction between shares which are paid up or credited as paid up is one without a difference.)
'Register'	The register of members.

'Subsidiary'   A subsidiary undertaking of the company. (The meaning of 'subsidiary undertaking' does not have to be spelled out if, as is generally the case, definitions in CA 1985 are adopted by the articles. The use of the well-recognised and fairly narrowly defined term 'subsidiary' to encompass the much wider scope of 'subsidiary undertaking' is unwise as it might easily be overlooked that, what appears to be a word with a standard meaning, is being used in an exceptionally wide sense. This could be of considerable importance, for example, in relation to borrowing limits.)

'Writing'   Includes any method of representing or reproducing words in a legible and non-transitory form. (A definition of 'writing' was included in Old Table A but does not appear in the current version. The definition is strictly not required because a similar one appears in the Interpretation Act 1978 and that applies to Table A and to special articles used with Table A. An express statement as to the scope of the word is, nevertheless, helpful and is generally included in long form articles.)

A definition to the following effect is also often found:

> Words in the singular include the plural and vice versa; words importing one gender only include all genders; and a reference to a person includes a body corporate and an unincorporated body of persons.

This is, however, technically unnecessary, although convenient, because the Law of Property Act 1925, s 61 implies the following in deeds, documents and other instruments unless the context otherwise requires:

> 'person' includes a corporation;
> the singular includes the plural and vice versa; and
> the masculine includes the feminine and vice versa.

Note that the statutory definition does not refer to the neuter gender but it is unlikely that the construction of a document would be affected by this omission. In addition, 'person' does not expressly include an unincorporated body of persons but, as the singular is deemed to include the plural, references to 'person' will include 'persons'. This should suffice to cover persons who constitute an unincorporated association.

Share capital

Regulation 2

> Subject to the provisions of the Act and without prejudice to any rights attached to any existing shares, any share may be issued with such rights or restrictions as the company may by ordinary resolution determine.

This provides that the rights and restrictions attached to new shares are to be determined by an ordinary resolution of the shareholders. It is, in many cases, convenient to give the directors the power to determine the rights and restrictions provided that they do not have the power to override the express provisions of any applicable resolution. This can be achieved by the following:

2.5   Share rights determined by directors

> Regulation 2 of Table A is amended by adding at the end 'or, if there is no relevant resolution or so far as the resolution does not make specific provision, as the directors determine'.

It may be appropriate, where the protection of minority rights is important, to replace the requirement of an ordinary resolution with one for a special resolution (see Appendix D, art 6).

Regulation 3

> Subject to the provisions of the Act, shares may be issued which are to be redeemed or are liable to be redeemed at the option of the company or the holder on such terms and in such manner as may be provided by the articles.

The authority to issue redeemable shares is given in accordance with CA 1985, s 159. Redemption may be obligatory or at the option of either the company or the holders of the shares. The last few words of this regulation—'on such terms and in such manner as may be provided by the articles'—are in accordance with s 160(3)[17] which requires that the terms and conditions of redemption must be specified in the articles.

Regulation 4

> The company may exercise the powers of paying commissions conferred by the Act. Subject to the provisions of the Act, any such commissions may be satisfied by the payment of cash or by the allotment of fully or partly paid shares or partly in one way and partly in the other.

Section 97 of CA 1985 permits the company to pay commissions to a person for subscribing or agreeing to subscribe (or finding another person to do so) for shares if the articles authorise the payment. It is invariable practice to give this authority even where, as in most private companies, it is unlikely to be used.

Regulation 5

> Except as required by law no person shall be recognised by the company as holding any share upon trust and (except as otherwise provided by the articles or by law) the company shall not be bound by or recognise any interest in any share except an absolute right to the entirety thereof in the holder.

This embodies the principle, supported by CA 1985, s 360, that the company treats the shareholder as the absolute owner of his shares even if given notice to the contrary. Where the company issues, or might issue, bearer shares, the principle can be extended to apply to the share warrants by the following amendment:

> Regulation 5 of Table A is amended by adding at the end 'or, in the case of a bearer warrant, in the bearer of the warrant'.

Share certificates

Regulation 6

> Every member, upon becoming the holder of any shares, shall be entitled without payment to one certificate for all the shares

---

[17] This is due to be replaced, at a date which is currently undetermined, by a new and more comprehensive s 159A.

of each class held by him (and, upon transferring a part of his holding of shares of any class, to a certificate for the balance of such holding) or several certificates each for one or more of his shares upon payment for every certificate after the first of such reasonable sum as the directors may determine. Every certificate shall be sealed with the seal and shall specify the number, class and distinguishing numbers (if any) of the shares to which it relates and the amount or respective amounts paid up thereon. The company shall not be bound to issue more than one certificate for shares held jointly by several persons and delivery of a certificate to one joint holder shall be a sufficient delivery to all of them.

A member has a right to a share certificate in respect of his holding under CA 1985, s 185 and the Listing Rules of the London Stock Exchange amplify this entitlement as detailed in Chapter 6, p 173. The statutory right requires that the share certificate is available within two months after allotment of the shares or the lodging of the relevant transfer form, unless the issue of the shares otherwise provides. It is a helpful reminder in the case of a company with a large number of shareholders to spell out this time limit with the following article.

2.6 Time limit for issue of share certificate

The first sentence of regulation 6 of Table A is amended by replacing 'upon becoming the holder of any shares' with 'within two months after the allotment, or lodgment of a duly stamped transfer, to him of the shares (or within such other period as the terms of issue provide)'.

An exception to the right to a certificate is provided in s 185 in the case of an allotment or transfer to, or to the nominee of, a 'recognised clearing house' or to the nominee of a 'recognised investment exchange' within the meaning of the Financial Services Act 1986.

Since the coming into force of CA 1985, s 36A, which was introduced by CA 1989, it is no longer necessary for a share certificate to be sealed with the common seal, as specified in reg 6. Section 36A(4) provides that a document signed by a director and the secretary, or by two directors, has the same effect as if executed under the common seal. Although the position could be clearer, it is suggested that a share certificate which is signed by two directors or by a director and the secretary has the same effect as one that is sealed and therefore complies with the article. To avoid any confusion, however, reg 6 can be amended as follows:

2.7   Execution of share certificates

Regulation 6 of Table A is amended by adding after 'Every certificate shall be sealed with the seal' the words 'or executed in such other manner as the directors authorise, having regard to the Act (and the regulations of the London Stock Exchange)'.

The words in brackets will not be required if the shares of the company are not listed.

Regulation 7

If a share certificate is defaced, worn out, lost or destroyed, it may be renewed on such terms (if any) as to evidence and indemnity and payment of the expenses reasonably incurred by the company in investigating evidence as the directors may determine but otherwise free of charge, and (in case of defacement or wearing-out) on delivery up of the old certificate.

As mentioned in Chapter 6, p 174, the Listing Rules of the London Stock Exchange restrict slightly the expenses which the company may charge for a replacement share certificate.

Lien

A remarkably large part of Table A is taken up with provisions relating to the creation of liens on the company's shares, the enforcement of calls and the forfeiture of shares on which calls remain unpaid. In practice, partly-paid shares, which are those mainly affected by these regulations, are comparatively unusual and the ability of a private company to take advantage of a lien or a right of forfeiture is restricted by the absence of a market for the shares. The comments which follow should be considered with that in mind.

Regulation 8

The company shall have a first and paramount lien on every share (not being a fully paid share) for all moneys (whether presently payable or not) payable at a fixed time or called in respect of that share. The directors may at any time declare any share to be wholly or in part exempt from the provisions of this regulation. The company's lien on a share shall extend to any amount payable in respect of it.

The company is given a first and paramount lien on shares for sums payable on them. This confers priority for the company over liens claimed by other parties. In the case of private companies the lien is often extended to cover all sums owed to the company by the holder of the shares. Section 150 of CA 1985 prohibits this extension in the case of listed companies and the Listing Rules of the London Stock Exchange repeat the prohibition.

The lien conferred by reg 8 extends to amounts 'payable' in respect of the share. It is not clear that this would cover distributions *in specie* made on the share and, to avoid the doubt, the wording can be amended by the following article:

2.8   Lien to extend to distributions

Regulation 8 of Table A is amended by replacing 'any amount payable in respect of it' with 'all distributions of money and other assets attributable to it'.

Regulation 9

The company may sell in such manner as the directors determine any shares on which the company has a lien if a sum in respect of which the lien exists is presently payable and is not paid within fourteen clear days after notice has been given to the holder of the share or to the person entitled to it in consequence of the death or bankruptcy of the holder, demanding payment and stating that if the notice is not complied with the shares may be sold.

This is in satisfactory form apart from a drafting error whereby reference is sometimes made to a 'share' and on other occasions to 'shares'.

Regulation 10

To give effect to a sale the directors may authorise some person to execute an instrument of transfer of the shares sold to, or in accordance with the directions of, the purchaser. The title of the transferee shall not be affected by any irregularity in or invalidity of the proceedings in reference to the sale.

Although this regulation provides for the execution of a transfer of the shares sold as a result of an exercise of a lien, it does not deal with the registration of the transfer. A further point is that reg 10 differs from reg 22 in that it does not contain an express statement that the purchaser of the shares is not concerned with the application of the sale proceeds. An amendment to reg 10 to cover these matters is as follows:

2.9   Transferee of lien shares

Regulation 10 of Table A is amended by adding at the end the following sentence:

'The transferee shall be registered as the holder of the shares comprised in the transfer (whether the share certificate has been produced or not) and he shall not be bound to see to the application of the purchase consideration.'.

Regulation 11

The net proceeds of the sale, after payment of the costs, shall be applied in payment of so much of the sum for which the lien exists as is presently payable, and any residue shall (upon surrender to the company for cancellation of the certificate of the shares sold and subject to a like lien for any moneys not presently payable as existed upon the shares before the sale) be paid to the person entitled to the shares at the date of the sale.

This provides for the excess of the proceeds of sale over amounts payable to the company to be paid to 'the person entitled to the shares at date of sale'. To avoid the rather far-fetched argument that it is the purchaser who is entitled to the shares at the date of sale and who should therefore receive the excess sum, the wording could be modified as follows:

Regulation 11 of Table A is amended by replacing 'to the person entitled to the shares at the date of the sale' with 'to the person entitled to the shares immediately prior to the sale'.

Calls on shares and forfeiture

Regulation 12

Subject to the terms of allotment, the directors may make calls upon the members in respect of any moneys unpaid on their shares (whether in respect of nominal value or premium) and each member shall (subject to receiving at least 14 clear days' notice specifying when and where payment is to be made) pay to the company as required by the notice the amount called on his shares. A call may be required to be paid by instalments. A call may, before receipt by the company of any sum due thereunder, be revoked in whole or in part. A person on whom a call is made shall remain liable for calls made upon him notwithstanding the subsequent transfer of the shares in respect whereof the call was made.

This deals with the procedure for making calls and is curiously drafted in referring to the member receiving, rather than being given, the specified period of notice. This could be significant because reg 115 deals with the time at which notice is deemed to be given but not the time at which it is deemed to be received. Furthermore, there seems to be no good reason why the call may be revoked only if no payment has been received—it would be better to permit revocation whilst any amount remains unpaid. Both of these points can be covered by amending reg 12 as follows:

(a) by replacing 'subject to receiving at least fourteen clear days' notice' with 'subject to being given at least fourteen clear days' notice'; and

(b) by replacing 'before receipt by the company of any sum due thereunder' with 'before receipt by the company of the sum due thereunder'.

Regulation 13

A call shall be deemed to have been made at the time when the resolution of the directors authorising the call was passed.

The effect of this regulation is to make the call effective at the earliest possible moment. The lien created by reg 8 will attach immediately the directors authorise the call as it applies whether the sums are presently payable or not. This is in contrast to the position where the lien is restricted to debts 'due and payable' (*Re British Provident Life and Fire Insurance Society, Orpen's Case* (1863) 9 Jur NS 615).

Regulation 14

The joint holders of a share shall be jointly and severally liable to pay all calls in respect thereof.

This confirms the joint and several liability which joint shareholders have in respect of calls.

Regulation 15

>   If a call remains unpaid after it has become due and payable the person from whom it is due and payable shall pay interest on the amount unpaid from the day it became due and payable until it is paid at the rate fixed by the terms of allotment of the share or in the notice of the call or, if no rate is fixed, at the appropriate rate (as defined by the Act) but the directors may waive payment of the interest wholly or in part.

Interest is payable on late calls at the rate fixed by the terms of allotment or in the notice of call or, if none, at the 'appropriate rate'. This is defined in CA 1985, s 107 and is currently 5 per cent per annum. This rate is probably unduly low and a higher minimum rate can be specified as follows:

2.10   Rate of interest on unpaid calls

>   Regulation 15 of Table A is amended by adding after 'at the appropriate rate (as defined by the Act)' the words 'or, if higher, at the rate of [15]% per annum'.

The references to calls being 'due and payable' appear to be the same as the calls simply being 'payable' (*Re Stockton Malleable Iron Co* (1875) 2 ChD 101). An appropriate change in the drafting can be made in the case of long form articles but it is not worth altering reg 15 in this minor respect if Table A is generally being adopted.

Regulation 16

>   An amount payable in respect of a share on allotment or at any fixed date, whether in respect of nominal value or premium or as an instalment of a call, shall be deemed to be a call and if it is not paid the provisions of the articles shall apply as if that amount had become due and payable by virtue of a call.

Unless the articles so provide, payments made on applications for shares or on allotment are not 'calls' for the purposes of the regulations relating to liability to interest and forfeiture (*Croskey v Bank of Wales* (1863) 4 Giff 314). The purpose of reg 16 is to deem all payments on shares to be calls.

Regulation 17

Subject to the terms of allotment, the directors may make arrangements on the issue of shares for a difference between the holders in the amounts and times of payment of calls on their shares.

In accordance with CA 1985, s 119(*a*), the directors are given power to differentiate between shareholders in relation to calls because, in the absence of an express entitlement, the directors may not make calls on some shareholders and not others (*Galloway v Halle Concerts Society* [1915] 2 Ch 233). In most companies it will be inappropriate to give the directors power to discriminate between shareholders and reg 17 is likely to be of use only where the shareholders are a cohesive group who are prepared to see special arrangements made for some members but not for others. Regulation 17 may therefore generally be omitted but, as the issue of partly paid shares is unusual, it can in practice be ignored.

Regulation 18

If a call remains unpaid after it has become due and payable the directors may give to the person from whom it is due not less than fourteen clear days' notice requiring payment of the amount unpaid together with any interest which may have accrued. The notice shall name the place where payment is to be made and shall state that if the notice is not complied with the shares in respect of which the call was made will be liable to be forfeited.

This is similar to reg 9 but provides that, if after the period of notice the call remains unpaid, the shares may be forfeited rather than sold. Forfeiture gives rise to a reduction of capital and the power to make the reduction is confined to cases where calls or other amounts payable in respect of shares are not paid (*Hopkinson v Mortimer, Harley & Co Ltd* [1917] 1 Ch 646). The articles may provide that a share can be surrendered instead of being forfeited, but surrender is permitted only in circumstances justifying a forfeiture and no payment may be made in return for the surrender as this would amount to a purchase by the company of its own shares (*Hope v International Financial Society* (1876) 4 ChD 327). Regulation 18 of Table A can be amended by adding at the end the following sentence:

2.11 Surrenders

The directors may accept the surrender of a share which is liable to be forfeited. In that event, references in these articles to 'forfeiture' include 'surrender'.

The notice given under reg 18 as the first step to a forfeiture requires the holder to pay amounts unpaid on the share together with accrued interest. Although the forfeiture procedure is rarely exercised in practice, it is nevertheless quite common to extend the shareholder's obligation to cover expenses incurred by the company. A suitable alteration is to add to reg 18 after 'together with any interest which may have accrued' the words 'and all expenses incurred by the company as a result of the non-payment'.

Regulation 19

If the notice is not complied with any share in respect of which it was given may, before the payment required by the notice has been made, be forfeited by a resolution of the directors and the forfeiture shall include all dividends or other moneys payable in respect of the forfeited shares and not paid before the forfeiture.

This regulation, which deals with the forfeiture, refers to the forfeiture as including all dividends and other moneys 'payable' in respect of the forfeited share. As mentioned in relation to reg 8, 'payable' may have a narrow meaning and the regulation could be clarified by replacing 'all dividends and other moneys payable in respect of the forfeited shares' with 'all distributions attributable to the forfeited share'.

A small drafting error in the regulation should be mentioned. The clause begins by referring to a share being forfeited but then refers to the forfeited shares. As has been done in the clarification suggested above, the opportunity can be taken to replace the reference to 'shares' with 'share'.

Regulation 20

Subject to the provisions of the Act, a forfeited share may be sold, re-allotted or otherwise disposed of on such terms and in such manner as the directors determine either to the person who was before the forfeiture the holder or to any other person and

at any time before sale, re-allotment or other disposition, the
forfeiture may be cancelled on such terms as the directors think
fit. Where for the purposes of its disposal a forfeited share is to
be transferred to any person the directors may authorise some
person to execute an instrument of transfer of the share to that
person.

Whilst this regulation covers the procedure for selling the forfeited
shares, unlike Old Table A it does not in terms deal with the receipt of
the sale proceeds and the registration of the transfer. For this purpose
reg 20 of Table A could be amended by adding at the end the following
sentence:

2.12 Transfer of forfeited shares

'The directors may receive the consideration given for the share on its
disposal and, if the share is in registered form, may register the transferee
as the holder.'.

Regulation 21

A person any of whose shares have been forfeited shall cease
to be a member in respect of them and shall surrender to the
company for cancellation the certificate for the shares forfeited
but shall remain liable to the company for all moneys which at
the date of forfeiture were presently payable by him to the
company in respect of those shares with interest at the rate at
which interest was payable on those moneys before the
forfeiture or, if no interest was so payable, at the appropriate
rate (as defined in the Act) from the date of forfeiture until
payment but the directors may waive payment wholly or in part
or enforce payment without any allowance for the value of the
shares at the time of forfeiture or for any consideration received
on their disposal.

The holder of a forfeited share remains liable for sums payable at the
date of forfeiture, together with interest, even though he ceases to be a
member in respect of the share. The interest is charged at the rate at
which interest was payable on the outstanding sums or, if there was no
rate of interest, at the 'appropriate rate'. If this phrase is changed in
relation to reg 15, the amendment which is suggested above in the
commentary on reg 15 should be extended so that it applies also to reg
21. This would be achieved as follows:

2.13   Rate of interest on unpaid calls

Regulations 15 and 21 of Table A are amended by adding after 'at the appropriate rate (as defined in the Act)' the words 'or, if higher, at the rate of [15]% per annum'.

Regulation 22

A statutory declaration by a director or the secretary that a share has been forfeited on a specified date shall be conclusive evidence of the facts stated in it as against all persons claiming to be entitled to the share and the declaration shall (subject to the execution of an instrument of transfer if necessary) constitute a good title to the share and the person to whom the share is disposed of shall not be bound to see to the application of the consideration, if any, nor shall his title to the share be affected by any irregularity in or invalidity of the proceedings in reference to the forfeiture or disposal of the share.

This inordinately long sentence covers the following:
   (1) A statutory declaration regarding the forfeiture will be conclusive.
   (2) The declaration will constitute title to the share.
   (3) The purchaser will not be concerned as to the application of the purchase consideration.
   (4) The purchaser's title will not be affected by an invalidity in the forfeiture proceedings.

The regulation is satisfactory in its operation although, if long form articles are being adopted, the opportunity should be taken to break it down into separate sentences.

Transfer of shares

Regulation 23

The instrument of transfer of a share may be in any usual form or in any other form which the directors may approve and shall be executed by or on behalf of the transferor and, unless the share is fully paid, by or on behalf of the transferee.

Section 182(1)(*b*) of CA 1985 states that shares are transferable in the manner provided in the company's articles and it is therefore necessary to include a provision dealing with this. Regulation 23, which provides for the form of share transfer to be as approved by the directors, is satisfactory for this purpose.

Regulation 24

The directors may refuse to register the transfer of a share which is not fully paid to a person of whom they do not approve and they may refuse to register the transfer of a share on which the company has a lien. They may also refuse to register a transfer unless—

(a) it is lodged at the office or such other place as the directors may appoint and is accompanied by the certificate for the shares to which it relates and such other evidence as the directors may reasonably require to show the right of the transferor to make the transfer;

(b) it is in respect of only one class of shares; and

(c) it is in favour of not more than four transferees except in the case of executors or trustees of a deceased member.

Section 183 of CA 1985 provides that it is not lawful for a company to register a transfer of shares unless a proper instrument of transfer has been delivered to it.

The directors are given power to refuse to register the transfer of a partly-paid share if they do not approve of the transferee. It is almost invariably the practice to change the powers to reject transfers except in the case of listed companies or companies with large numbers of shareholders. For most private companies, either the right will be extended to all shares, whether partly- or fully-paid, or will be replaced entirely by pre-emption rights. There is, in particular, no reason to limit the directors' right of refusal to cases where they do not approve of the proposed transferee. It is common practice with private companies to disapply reg 24 and to give the directors the right to reject any transfers, as does the following article:

2.14 Right to reject share transfers

The directors may, at their discretion and without giving a reason for doing so, decline to register a transfer of a share, whether it is fully-paid or not.

The same effect is sometimes achieved by keeping reg 24 as a whole and simply replacing the first sentence with the wording set out above.

This is, however, pointless as the remaining provisions of reg 24 deal with special cases where the directors may reject transfers. If they are free to reject any transfers the special cases do not need to be mentioned.

In many cases of private company articles, detailed pre-emption provisions are adopted, as discussed in Chapter 3.

If reg 24 is retained, it may be found helpful to provide a reminder that transfers cannot be registered unless they are properly stamped (this reflects the prohibition in the Stamp Act 1891, s 17 against registering inadequately stamped share transfers). The following article would be suitable:

> Regulation 24 of Table A is amended by adding in paragraph (a) after 'it is lodged' the words 'duly stamped (if stampable)'.

Regulation 25

> If the directors refuse to register a transfer of a share, they shall within two months after the date on which the transfer was lodged with the company send to the transferee notice of the refusal.

This repeats CA 1985, s 183(5). The period of two months for the giving of notice of rejection of a share transfer may be excessive in the case of private companies and a shorter period of, say, 14 days might be more suitable. The following article makes the change:

> Regulation 25 of Table A is amended by replacing 'two months' with 'fourteen days'.

Regulation 26

> The registration of transfers of shares or of transfers of any class of shares may be suspended at such times and for such periods (not exceeding 30 days in any year) as the directors may determine.

Section 358 of CA 1985 entitles a company to close the registrar of members for up to 30 days a year, subject to giving notice by advertisement. This right, and the corresponding one given by reg 27, are generally inappropriate for private companies. It would be reasonable to disapply reg 26 but this would leave the s 358 position unchanged. The wording of the regulation is satisfactory although it is strictly not necessary to refer both to transfers of shares and to transfers of any class of shares—if registration may be suspended in respect of any class, it may be suspended for all classes.

Regulation 27

> No fee shall be charged for the registration of any instrument of transfer or other document relating to or affecting the title to any share.

It would not be acceptable generally, and is specifically prohibited for listed companies by the Listing Rules of the London Stock Exchange (see Chapter 6, p 174), for a fee to be charged for registering transfers. Regulation 27 is therefore normally adopted without amendment.

Regulation 28

> The company shall be entitled to retain any instrument of transfer which is registered, but any instrument of transfer which the directors refuse to register shall be returned to the person lodging it when notice of the refusal is given.

The obligation to return to the transferor the transfer of a share which is rejected by the directors may be modified so that it does not apply in the case of fraud. This is effected by the following:

2.15 Retention of instrument of transfer

> Regulation 28 of Table A is amended by replacing 'shall be returned to the person lodging it' with 'shall (except in the case of fraud) be returned to the person lodging it'.

Transmission of shares

Regulation 29

> If a member dies the survivor or survivors where he was a joint holder, and his personal representatives where he was a sole holder or only surviving holder, shall be the only persons recognised by the company as having any title to his interest in the shares, but nothing in this article shall release the estate of a deceased joint holder from any liability in respect of any share jointly held by him.

This regulation accords with CA 1985, s 183(2) which provides that an instrument of transfer is not required to effect the registration of a person to whom the right to any shares has been transmitted by operation of law. The wording is acceptable.

Regulation 30

> A person becoming entitled to a share in consequence of the death or bankruptcy of a member may, upon such evidence being produced as the directors may properly require, elect either to become the holder of the share or to have some person nominated by him registered as the transferee. If he elects to become the holder he shall give notice to the company to that effect. If he elects to have another person registered he shall execute an instrument of transfer of the share to that person. All the articles relating to the transfer of shares shall apply to the notice or instrument of transfer as if it were an instrument of transfer executed by the member and the death or bankruptcy of the member had not occurred.

This regulation is in accordance with CA 1985, s 183(2) which provides an exception to the general rule that a transfer of shares cannot be registered without a proper instrument of transfer (CA 1985, s 184(1)). A transfer is not required to register as shareholder a person to whom the right to shares has been transmitted by operation of law. The reference in the regulation to the person claiming entitlement by transmission producing such evidence as the directors 'properly' require relates to CA 1985, s 187 which specifies that production of any document which is by law sufficient evidence of probate or letters of administration is sufficient evidence of the grant.

The regulation provides no sanction if the person entitled to the share by transmission simply makes no decision as to whether to take the shares in his own name or to transfer them to a third party. This is discussed further in relation to art 15 in Appendix D (see Chapter 5, p 167).

Regulation 31

> A person becoming entitled to a share in consequence of the death or bankruptcy of a member shall have the rights to which he would have been entitled if he were the holder of the share, except that he shall not, before being registered as the holder of the share, be entitled in respect of it to attend or vote at any meeting of the company or at any separate meeting of the holders of any class of shares in the company.

Although the regulation makes it clear that the person entitled by transmission has the same rights as if he were the holder of the share, there is no express statement as to the rights of the deceased or bankrupt registered holder. An article to cover this is the following:

2.16   Cessation of rights of former shareholder

Regulation 31 of Table A is amended by adding at the end the following sentences:
'When a person becomes entitled to a share by transmission, the rights of the holder in relation to it cease. The person entitled by transmission may give a good discharge for dividends and other distributions in respect of the share.'.

If reg 30 is amended so that the directors can require the person entitled by transmission to make the election to take or transfer the shares, reg 31 should be amended to make it clear that the rights of the person entitled by transmission are suspended whilst he is in default of an obligation to make the election. The appropriate amendment is:

2.17   Suspension of rights of successor

Regulation 31 of Table A is amended by replacing 'shall have the rights' with 'shall (unless he has failed to comply with a notice requiring him to elect under regulation 30) have the rights'.

Although reg 31 does not deal with the giving of notices to persons entitled by transmission, they are entitled to notices as if they were holders because that is one of the rights which the regulation confers. This is confirmed by the specific provisions contained in reg 116.

Alteration of share capital

Regulation 32

The company may by ordinary resolution:
  (a) increase its share capital by new shares of such amount as the resolution prescribes;
  (b) consolidate and divide all or any of its share capital into shares of larger amount than its existing shares;
  (c) subject to the provisions of the Act, sub-divide its shares, or any of them, into shares of smaller amount and may determine that, as between the shares resulting from the

sub-division, any of them may have any preference or
advantage as compared with the others; and

(d) cancel shares which, at the date of the passing of the
resolution, have not been taken or agreed to be taken by any
person and diminish the amount of its share capital by the
amount of the shares so cancelled.

This substantially repeats CA 1985, s 121 except that it does not refer
to the conversion of share capital into stock. The introduction in CA
1948 of the ability to determine not to number shares made the use of
stock of reduced interest and, although lengthy regulations relating to
stock were included in Old Table A, they are omitted in the current
version. If it is felt desirable to include these provisions, reference
should be made to the long form articles in Appendix E.

The regulation contains a minor drafting defect in para (c). The
second half of the paragraph, referring to the right to determine the
relative rights of the shares resulting from the sub-division, is an
addition to the corresponding paragraph in s 121(2). The use of the word
'may' in the middle of para (c) strictly means that the words 'by ordinary
resolution' which appear after 'may' at the beginning of the regulation
do not qualify the last half of para (c). It would thus appear that the
determination of the relative entitlements of the shares arising from the
sub-division can be made without an ordinary resolution and,
presumably, can be fixed by the directors.

Regulation 33

Whenever as a result of a consolidation of shares any members
would become entitled to fractions of a share, the directors may,
on behalf of those members, sell the shares representing the
fractions for the best price reasonably obtainable to any person
(including, subject to the provisions of the Act, the company)
and distribute the net proceeds of sale in due proportion among
those members, and the directors may authorise some person to
execute an instrument of transfer of the shares to, or in
accordance with the directions of, the purchaser. The transferee
shall not be bound to see to the application of the purchase
money nor shall his title to the shares be affected by any
irregularity in or invalidity of the proceedings in reference to
the sale.

This deals with the disposal of fractions of shares arising on a consolidation and is of theoretical interest in the case of most private companies. This is because care would normally be taken to ensure that fractions do not arise and, furthermore, it would generally not be possible to sell the fractions in the absence of a market in the shares.

Regulation 34

> Subject to the provisions of the Act, the company may by special resolution reduce its share capital, any capital redemption reserve and any share premium account in any way.

Section 135 of CA 1985 permits a company to reduce capital by special resolution if the articles permit. Although in practice taking advantage of this power cannot be taken without the implementation of numerous procedural steps, it is nevertheless common practice to include the power in the articles.

Purchase of own shares

Regulation 35

> Subject to the provisions of the Act, the company may purchase its own shares (including any redeemable shares) and, if it is a private company, make a payment in respect of the redemption or purchase of its own shares otherwise than out of distributable profits of the company or the proceeds of a fresh issue of shares.

Under CA 1985, s 162 a company has power to purchase its own shares, subject to the provisions of Chapter VII of the Act, if authorised by its articles. This regulation is perhaps given undue prominence in Table A by having its own heading and it is usual in long form articles to move it into the section dealing with the share capital as a whole.

General meetings

Regulation 36

> All general meetings other than annual general meetings shall be called extraordinary general meetings.

This regulation is merely declaratory and is acceptable.

Regulation 37

> The directors may call general meetings and, on the requisition of members pursuant to the provisions of the Act, shall forthwith proceed to convene an extraordinary general meeting for a date not later than eight weeks after receipt of the requisition. If there are not within the United Kingdom sufficient directors to call a general meeting, any director or any member of the company may call a general meeting.

An extraordinary general meeting may be requisitioned by members holding not less than one-tenth of the paid-up voting share capital of the company (CA 1985, s 368). To avoid the directors abusing their obligation to convene the meeting by issuing a notice for a deferred date, CA 1985, s 368(8) was introduced by CA 1989. The effect is that not only must the directors send out the notice of meeting within 21 days of receipt of the requisition but, in addition, the meeting must be convened for a date which is not more than 28 days after the date of the notice. The eight week period referred to in reg 37 as the maximum between the date of the receipt of the requisition and of the date of the meeting should now strictly be seven weeks.

Notice of general meetings

Regulation 38

> An annual general meeting and an extraordinary general meeting called for the passing of a special resolution or a resolution appointing a person as a director shall be called by at least twenty-one clear days' notice. All other extraordinary general meetings shall be called by at least fourteen clear days' notice but a general meeting may be called by shorter notice if it is so agreed—
>
> > (a) in the case of an annual general meeting, by all the members entitled to attend and vote thereat; and
> >
> > (b) in the case of any other meeting by a majority in number of the members having a right to attend and vote being a majority together holding not less than ninety-five per cent in nominal value of the shares giving that right.
>
> The notice shall specify the time and place of the meeting and the general nature of the business to be transacted and, in the case of

an annual general meeting, shall specify the meeting as such. Subject to the provisions of the articles and to any restrictions imposed on any shares, the notice shall be given to all the members, to all persons entitled to a share in consequence of the death or bankruptcy of a member and to the directors and auditors.

This complex regulation covers a number of points:

(1) An annual general meeting requires 21 clear days' notice.

(2) An extraordinary general meeting also requires 21 clear days' notice if the business includes the passing either of a special resolution or of a resolution to appoint a director.

(3) Other meetings require 14 clear days' notice.

(4) The period of notice may be reduced in the case of an annual general meeting with the agreement of all the members entitled to attend and vote.

(5) The period of notice may be reduced in the case of other meetings with the consent of the holders of shares giving 95 per cent of the votes.

(6) The notice must state the time and place of the meeting and the general nature of the business to be transacted.

(7) The notice of an annual general meeting must specify the meeting as such.

(8) The notice must be sent to (a) all the members; (b) persons entitled by transmission on the death or bankruptcy of a member; (c) the directors; and (d) the auditors.

A large part of this regulation deals with the requirements of CA 1985, s 369. This invalidates a provision in the articles requiring less than 21 days' notice for an annual general meeting or 14 days' for other meetings. Section 369(3) sets out the levels of shareholder agreement required for shorter periods as summarised in paras 4 and 5.

The requirement of 21 days' notice to be given for a meeting to consider a resolution to appoint a person as a director was not included in Old Table A and may perfectly well be deleted, as follows:

2.18 Notice period for resolution to appoint director

The first sentence of regulation 38 of Table A is amended by deleting 'or a resolution appointing a person as a director'.

A further difference in Old Table A was the distinction that was made between 'special' and other business. Special business was business transacted at an extraordinary general meeting and any business at an annual general meeting apart from declaring a dividend; the consideration of the accounts, balance sheets and reports of the directors and the auditors; the election of directors in place of those retiring; and the appointment of, and fixing the remuneration of, the auditors. The reason for the distinction was that the notice of the meeting was required, in respect of special business, to specify the general nature of that business. It is not considered to be really necessary to make this distinction any longer since business which would have fallen outside the 'special' category will be adequately described by the briefest terms.

The regulation imposes an obligation to give the notice not only to the shareholders but also to the directors and auditors. The first of these is not a statutory requirement and, although in practice the directors will invariably receive notice of meetings, the need to give them notice is a technical matter which, if overlooked, could cause difficulties. Regulation 38 can be amended to deal with this as follows:

2.19 Notice to directors regarding meetings

> Notice of meetings need not be given to the directors as such and regulation 38 of Table A is modified accordingly.

The requirement to give notice to the auditors reflects the provisions of CA 1985, s 390 and cannot be reversed.

Regulation 39

> The accidental omission to give notice of a meeting to, or the non-receipt of notice of a meeting by, any person entitled to receive notice shall not invalidate the proceedings at that meeting.

This reverses the common law rule that failure to give notice to each person entitled to receive it invalidates the meeting (*Smyth v Darley* (1849) 2 HLC 789).

Proceedings at general meetings

Regulation 40

> No business shall be transacted at any meeting unless a quorum is present. Two persons entitled to vote upon the business to be transacted, each being a member or a proxy for a member or a duly authorised representative of a corporation, shall be a quorum.

This regulation requires that a quorum exists not just when the meeting proceeds to business—which was the approach adopted in Old Table A—but also when the business is transacted. The advantage of the wording in the Old Table A is that a dissatisfied shareholder has a reduced ability in a company with a small number of shareholders to prevent business being transacted by walking out of the meeting. An article which restores the Old Table A position, whilst using slightly different wording, is:

2.20 Quorum required at commencement of business

Regulation 40 of Table A is amended by replacing 'unless a quorum is present' with 'unless a quorum is present when the meeting commences business'.

Section 370 of CA 1985 provides that, subject to any contrary provisions in the company's articles, two members 'personally present' are a quorum. Regulation 40 is more flexible in that it takes into account members who are represented by proxies.

It is now possible to have single-member companies and, in that event, the quorum at shareholders' meetings is one, regardless of any contrary provision in the articles of the company (CA 1985, s 370A, inserted by the Companies (Single Member Private Limited Companies) Regulations 1992). It would seem to be the case that it is possible to have meetings at which the quorum is a single person in the case of companies with more than one member as the legislation in a number of places recognises implicitly that a meeting can take place although only one person is present (eg, CA 1985, ss 367(2) and 371(2)). Whilst it is not essential to amend reg 40 even where it is known or expected that there will be only one member, as with a wholly-owned subsidiary company, it is potentially confusing to leave the reference to a two member quorum unchanged. A suitable amendment to reg 40 is:

2.21 Quorum of one at general meeting

Regulation 40 of Table A is amended by replacing the second sentence with:
'One person entitled to vote on the business to be transacted, being a member or a proxy for a member or a duly authorised representative of a corporation, shall be a quorum.'.

Regulation 41

> If such a quorum is not present within half an hour of the time appointed for the meeting, or if during a meeting such a quorum ceases to be present, the meeting shall stand adjourned to the same day in the next week at the same time and place or to such time and place as the directors may determine.

As mentioned in relation to reg 40, Table A differs from Old Table A in requiring that a quorum is present not just at the beginning of the meeting but also when business is transacted. There is no legal principle which necessitates anything more than the presence of the quorum at the start of the meeting (*Re Hartley Baird* [1955] Ch 143), unless the departure leaves only one member present (*Re London Flats Ltd* [1969] 2 All ER 744). If, therefore, the approach discussed in the commentary on reg 40 is adopted and the Old Table A procedure applied, a consequential amendment to reg 41 is needed, as follows:

2.22 Absence of quorum

> Regulation 41 of Table A is amended by deleting 'or if during a meeting such a quorum ceases to be present'.

The regulation does not make any special provision for a reduced number of members to constitute a quorum at the adjourned meeting. This is to be contrasted with reg 54 of Old Table A which, until it was amended by CA 1989, provided that the members present at the adjourned meeting would be a quorum. The amendment was made at the same time that the minimum quorum for all companies was reduced from three to two. At that level, it is rather inappropriate to refer to the 'members' present at the adjourned meeting being a quorum as, if the meeting is inquorate, it must be because only one member is present.

Regulation 41 as a whole is rather unsophisticated and an article which provides for a single member to be a quorum at an adjourned meeting and also deals with a number of other points is as follows:

2.23 Quorum at adjourned meeting

> If, within 15 minutes (or such longer time not exceeding one hour as the chairman of the meeting decides) from the time appointed for the meeting, a quorum is not present or if during the meeting a quorum ceases to be present, the meeting, if convened on the requisition of members, shall be dissolved. It shall otherwise stand adjourned to the same day in the next week, at the same time and place, or to such other day and at

such time and place as the chairman or, failing him, the directors, shall determine. At the adjourned meeting, the quorum shall be a single member present in person or by proxy.

If the intention is that the quorum should never be less than two, the last sentence should be omitted. This will then accord with Table A. If reg 40 is amended, so that a quorum is required only at the start of the meeting, the words 'or if during the meeting a quorum ceases to be present' should be excluded.

Regulation 42

The chairman, if any, of the board of directors or in his absence some other director nominated by the directors shall preside as chairman of the meeting, but if neither the chairman nor such other director (if any) be present within fifteen minutes after the time appointed for holding the meeting and willing to act, the directors present shall elect one of their number to be chairman and, if there is only one director present and willing to act, he shall be chairman.

Instead of giving the directors the right to nominate a chairman of the meeting if the chairman of the board is not present, it would be reasonable to give the power of nomination to the chairman of the board. As he is elected to that position by the directors, it would seem sensible to allow him to appoint a director to take his place if he knows that he will not be present at a meeting. The directors could retain their power as a fall-back in case the director nominated by the chairman also misses the meeting. An article making these changes is:

2.24 Nomination of chairman of general meeting

Regulation 42 of Table A is amended by replacing 'or in his absence some other director nominated by the directors' with 'or a director nominated by the chairman or, in the absence of the chairman or of the director (if any) nominated by the chairman, some other director nominated by the directors'.

Another point for consideration here is whether the 15 minutes given for the directors to turn up at the meeting before an alternative chairman is selected is the correct period for the particular company whose articles are being drafted.

Regulation 43

> If no director is willing to act as chairman, or if no director is present within fifteen minutes after the time appointed for holding the meeting, the members present and entitled to vote shall choose one of their number to be chairman.

Rather curiously, this regulation—by use of the word 'shall'—requires the members present to appoint a chairman in the absence of directors. It would seem preferable to replace 'shall' with 'may' as follows:

2.25   Members' right to appoint chairman

> Regulation 43 of Table A is amended by replacing 'the members present and entitled to vote shall choose' with 'the members present and entitled to vote may choose'.

Regulation 44

> A director shall, notwithstanding that he is not a member, be entitled to attend and speak at any general meeting and at any separate meeting of the holders of any class of shares in the company.

This regulation deals satisfactorily with the right of a director who is not a shareholder to attend and speak at meetings.

Section 390 of CA 1985 gives the auditors the right to attend general meetings and to speak on any part of the business which concerns them as auditors. It may also be helpful, in certain circumstances, for a person who is not a member or director of the company to be invited to attend a general meeting. An article covering both these is the following, which would replace reg 44:

2.26   Persons entitled to attend general meeting

> The persons entitled to attend and speak at general meetings and at separate class meetings are the directors (even if they are not members), the auditors (but their right to speak is limited to business which concerns them as auditors) and any other person invited to do so by the chairman.

Regulation 45

> The chairman may, with the consent of a meeting at which a quorum is present (and shall if so directed by the meeting),

adjourn the meeting from time to time and from place to place, but no business shall be transacted at an adjourned meeting other than business which might properly have been transacted at the meeting had the adjournment not taken place. When a meeting is adjourned for 14 days or more, at least seven clear days' notice shall be given specifying the time and place of the adjourned meeting and the general nature of the business to be transacted. Otherwise it shall not be necessary to give any such notice.

In the case of listed companies, and perhaps also with other companies where there is a large number of shareholders, it is helpful to extend the provisions relating to adjournments to deal in particular with the possibility of the meeting becoming disorderly. Reference should be made to the discussion of Appendix E, art 57 in Chapter 6.

Regulation 46

A resolution put to the vote of a meeting shall be decided on a show of hands unless before, or on the declaration of the result of, the show of hands a poll is duly demanded. Subject to the provisions of the Act, a poll may be demanded—

(a) by the chairman; or

(b) by at least two members having the right to vote at the meeting; or

(c) by a member or members representing not less than one-tenth of the total voting rights of all the members having the right to vote at the meeting; or

(d) by a member or members holding shares conferring a right to vote at the meeting being shares on which an aggregate sum has been paid up equal to not less than one-tenth of the total sum paid up on all the shares conferring that right;

and a demand by a person as proxy for a member shall be the same as a demand by the member.

Section 373 of CA 1985 invalidates provisions in the articles which increase beyond the stated levels the number or category of shareholders who may join in demanding a poll. Regulation 46 follows s 373 in two respects, namely paras (c) and (d), but differs in relation to para (b) by giving the right to any two shareholders rather than the statutory maximum of five. Until CA 1989 amended the equivalent regulation in

Old Table A, the number of members who could demand a poll regardless of the number of shares they held was three. This was then reduced to the present level of two but the wording of the remaining paragraphs of the regulation was adopted without making the appropriate consequential change. The references to 'members' in paras (c) and (d) are unnecessary because, if it needs more than a single member to aggregate the specified voting or shareholding levels, they will in any case be able to demand the poll under para (b) regardless of their holdings. The point is, however, of no significance and there is no need to delete 'members' from these paragraphs.

As s 373 does not require any particular number to be stated as having the right to demand a poll, as long as it does not exceed five, it is possible to alter para (b) by replacing 'two' with 'three' (a common change), 'four' or 'five'. The other difference is that reg 46, unlike s 373, gives the chairman a right to demand a poll. In addition, s 373 states that the instrument appointing a proxy to vote at a meeting is deemed also to confer authority to demand or join in demanding a poll. This is referred to in rather different terms at the end of reg 46. If full articles are adopted, it would be preferable either to omit the reference to proxies or to include it in the same terms as are used in s 373.

It should also be noted that s 373(1) invalidates a provision in the articles which would have the effect of excluding the right to demand a poll on any question other than the election of the chairman of the meeting or the adjournment of the meeting.

Regulation 47

> Unless a poll is duly demanded a declaration by the chairman that a resolution has been carried or carried unanimously, or by a particular majority, or lost, or not carried by a particular majority and an entry to that effect in the minutes of the meeting shall be conclusive evidence of the fact without proof of the number or proportion of the votes recorded in favour of or against the resolution.

In the absence of a poll, a resolution is deemed conclusively to have been carried or lost if, first, the chairman declares that result and, secondly, an entry to that effect is made in the minutes of the meeting. The second requirement is sometimes omitted. In addition, the wording of the regulation can be improved as it makes the chairman's ruling, with the appropriate minute, conclusive, 'unless a poll is duly demanded'.

This fails to deal with the case where the demand for a poll is withdrawn. These points may be covered as follows:

2.27   Declaration of result of vote
Regulation 47 of Table A is amended:
(a) by adding after 'Unless a poll is duly demanded' the words 'and the demand is not withdrawn before the poll is taken'; and
(b) by deleting 'and an entry to that effect in the minutes of the meeting'.

Regulation 48
The demand for a poll may, before the poll is taken, be withdrawn but only with the consent of the chairman and a demand so withdrawn shall not be taken to have invalidated the result of a show of hands declared before the demand was made.

This requires that the chairman consents to the demand for a poll being withdrawn. The regulation is sometimes amended by removing the need for the chairman to give his approval, as follows:

2.28   Withdrawal of demand for poll
Regulation 48 of Table A is amended by deleting 'but only with the consent of the chairman'.

The amendment is, however, unlikely to be of significance as, in practice, the chairman will exercise a right to proceed with the poll which is no longer demanded only in the most special circumstances.

Regulation 49
A poll shall be taken as the chairman directs and he may appoint scrutineers (who need not be members) and fix a time and place for declaring the result of the poll. The result of the poll shall be deemed to be the resolution of the meeting at which the poll was demanded.

This may be amended so that, instead of the chairman merely having the right to appoint scrutineers if he chooses, he must do so if the meeting requires. An article to effect this is:

2.29   Appointment of scrutineers
The chairman shall appoint scrutineers if required to do so by the meeting. Regulation 49 of Table A is modified accordingly.

Regulation 50

> In the case of an equality of votes, whether on a show of hands or on a poll, the chairman shall be entitled to a casting vote in addition to any other vote he may have.

The wording of this regulation, in referring to the chairman having a casting vote 'in addition to any other vote he may have' if there is an equality of votes, is not consistent with the corresponding wording in reg 88. This gives the chairman a 'second or casting vote' at meetings of the board. The reason for the difference is not obvious as, in both cases, the chairman may have multiple votes in his own right. This could arise at a shareholders' meeting because of his own shareholding or because he holds proxies for other shareholders. In the case of a board meeting, the chairman could have additional votes by virtue of being an alternate for one or more of the other directors. The point is of no real significance as there can be no doubt in practice that the two regulations work in the same way.

Regulation 51

> A poll demanded on the election of a chairman or on a question of adjournment shall be taken forthwith. A poll demanded on any other question shall be taken either forthwith or at such time or place as the chairman directs not being more than thirty days after the poll is demanded. The demand for a poll shall not prevent the continuance of a meeting for the transaction of any business other than the question on which the poll was demanded. If a poll is demanded before the declaration of the result of a show of hands and the demand is duly withdrawn, the meeting shall continue as if the demand had not been made.

The arrangements specified in this regulation for the taking of polls are satisfactory.

Regulation 52

> No notice need be given of a poll not taken forthwith if the time and place at which it is to be taken are announced at the meeting at which it is demanded. In any other case at least seven clear days' notice shall be given specifying the time and place at which the poll is to be taken.

It is possible to amend this regulation by providing that notice is not required in respect of any poll, whether the time and place is announced immediately or not. The point has, however, little practical significance.

Regulation 53

> A resolution in writing executed by or on behalf of each member who would have been entitled to vote upon it if it had been proposed at a general meeting at which he was present shall be as effectual as if it had been passed at a general meeting duly convened and held and may consist of several instruments in the like form each executed by or on behalf of one or more members.

The articles of a listed company or one with a large number of shareholders will generally omit reg 53 as it will not be practical for a resolution to be signed by all the members entitled to vote on it.

Votes of members

Regulation 54

> Subject to any rights or restrictions attached to any shares, on a show of hands every member who (being an individual) is present in person or (being a corporation) is present by a duly authorised representative, not being himself a member entitled to vote, shall have one vote and on a poll every member shall have one vote for every share of which he is the holder.

This gives voting rights on a poll to all members but it would be clearer if this were restricted to members present, either personally or by proxy, at the meeting. The wording to achieve this is:

2.30   Members present or represented entitled to vote

> Regulation 54 of Table A is amended by replacing 'on a poll every member shall have one vote' with 'on a poll every member who is present in person, by representative or by proxy shall have one vote'.

The reference in the amendment to a member who is present by representative deals with corporate members who exercise their power to appoint representatives under CA 1985, s 375.

Regulation 55

> In the case of joint holders the vote of the senior who tenders a vote, whether in person or by proxy, shall be accepted to the exclusion of the votes of the other joint holders and seniority shall be determined by the order in which the names stand in the register of members.

This is acceptable.

Regulation 56

> A member in respect of whom an order has been made by any court having jurisdiction (whether in the United Kingdom or elsewhere) in matters concerning mental disorder may vote, whether on a show of hands or on a poll, by his receiver, curator bonis or other person authorised in that behalf by that court, and any such receiver, curator bonis or other person may, on a poll, vote by proxy. Evidence to the satisfaction of the directors of the authority of the person claiming to exercise the right to vote shall be deposited at the office, or at such other place as is specified in accordance with the articles for the deposit of instruments of proxy, not less than forty-eight hours before the time appointed for holding the meeting or adjourned meeting at which the right to vote is exercised and in default the right to vote shall not be exercisable.

Although the wording is a little old-fashioned, in that it is unnecessary to refer to the somewhat special categories of 'receiver' and 'curator bonis' as well as the comprehensively general description of the person authorised by the court 'in that behalf', an amendment is not technically required.

Regulation 57

> No member shall vote at any general meeting or at any separate meeting of the holders of any class of shares in the company, either in person or by proxy, in respect of any share held by him unless all moneys presently payable by him in respect of that share have been paid.

The sanction imposed by reg 57 on a member who fails to pay a call is accompanied by the restriction of dividends rights under reg 104, which provides for dividends to be paid according to the amounts paid up. These penalties on a member who fails to pay calls may be extended so as to withdraw all privileges attributable to his shares whilst the default continues. In addition, the regulation may be amended to apply the sanctions if the member has paid the amount called but has failed to reimburse expenses incurred by the company and payable by the member. The following article covers both these points:

2.31   Restrictions on holder with outstanding calls

Regulation 57 of Table A is amended:
(a) by adding after 'in respect of any share held by him' the words 'or to exercise any privilege as holder of the share'; and
(b) by replacing 'all moneys presently payable by him in respect of that share' with 'all moneys presently payable by him in respect of calls on that share'.

Regulation 58

No objection shall be raised to the qualification of any voter except at the meeting or adjourned meeting at which the vote objected to is tendered, and every vote not disallowed at the meeting shall be valid. Any objection made in due time shall be referred to the chairman whose decision shall be final and conclusive.

This does not cover questions as to whether votes should or should not have been counted. The following article deals with this:

2.32   Objections as to the qualifications of voters and/or the counting of votes

Regulation 58 of Table A is amended by replacing the first two sentences with the following sentences:
'An objection to the qualification of a voter or to the counting of, or failure to count, a vote may be raised only at the meeting or adjourned meeting at which the vote is tendered. Unless an objection is made in due time, every vote counted and not disallowed at the meeting or adjourned meeting is valid and every vote disallowed or not counted is invalid.'.

Regulation 59

On a poll votes may be given either personally or by proxy. A member may appoint more than one proxy to attend on the same occasion.

Section 372 of CA 1985 gives a shareholder a right to appoint a proxy to attend and vote at meetings on his behalf. In the case of a private company, the member may not appoint more than one proxy to attend on the same occasion unless the articles otherwise provide. This is the reason for the insertion of the second sentence in reg 59 and, if so desired in the case of a private company, it may be omitted (see Appendix A, art 39).

Regulation 60

An instrument appointing a proxy shall be in writing, executed by or on behalf of the appointor and shall be in the following form (or in a form as near thereto as circumstances allow or in any other form which is usual or which the directors may approve)—

'   PLC/Limited

I/We   , of

being a

member/members of the above-named company, hereby appoint

of

, or failing him,

of   , as my/our proxy to vote in my/our name[s] and on my/our behalf at the annual/extraordinary general meeting of the company to be held on   19 , and at any adjournment thereof.

Signed on   19 .'

The lengthy wording of this regulation setting out a form of proxy instrument is normally disregarded and a more general provision inserted in its place. A suitable article is:

2.33   Validity of form of proxy

An instrument appointing a proxy shall be in writing, executed by or on behalf of the appointor, and shall be in any usual form or in a form approved by the directors. The appointment shall be valid for an adjournment of the meeting and the instrument shall be deemed to confer authority to vote on amendments to resolutions put to the meeting for which the authority is given or at an adjournment, unless in each case the instrument of proxy states otherwise.

Regulation 61

Where it is desired to afford members an opportunity of instructing the proxy how he shall act the instrument appointing a proxy shall be in the following form (or in a form as near thereto as circumstances allow or in any other form which is usual or which the directors may approve)—

'   PLC/Limited

I/We   , of

                                              , being a
member/members of the above-named company, hereby appoint

                                                        of

                              , or failing him,

of   , as my/our proxy to vote in my/our name[s] and on my/our behalf at the annual/extraordinary general meeting of the company to be held on   19 , and at any adjournment thereof.

This form is to be used in respect of the resolutions mentioned below as follows:

Resolution No 1 *for *against
Resolution No 2 *for *against.

* Strike out whichever is not desired.

Unless otherwise instructed, the proxy may vote as he thinks fit or abstain from voting.

Signed this   day of   19 .'

As with reg 60, it is generally considered unnecessary to set out at length the form of proxy to be used by shareholders. A suitable replacement for the regulation is:

2.34 General form of proxy with voting instructions

Where it is desired to afford members an opportunity to instruct the proxy how he shall act, the instrument appointing a proxy shall be in any form which enables the members to direct how their votes are to be exercised on each of the resolutions comprised in the business of the meeting for which it is to be used.

Regulation 62

The instrument appointing a proxy and any authority under which it is executed or a copy of such authority certified notarially or in some other way approved by the directors may—

(a) be deposited at the office or at such other place within the United Kingdom as is specified in the notice convening the meeting or in any instrument of proxy sent out by the company in relation to the meeting not less than forty-eight hours before the time for holding the meeting or adjourned meeting at which the person named in the instrument proposes to vote; or

(b) in the case of a poll taken more than forty-eight hours after it is demanded, be deposited as aforesaid after the poll has been demanded and not less than twenty-four hours before the time appointed for the taking of the poll; or

(c) where the poll is not taken forthwith but is taken not more than forty-eight hours after it was demanded, be delivered at the meeting at which the poll was demanded to the chairman or to the secretary or to any director;

and an instrument of proxy which is not deposited or delivered in a manner so permitted shall be invalid.

Section 372(5) of CA 1985 invalidates a provision of the articles in so far as it would have the effect of requiring the instrument appointing a proxy, or other document relating to the appointment, to be received more than 48 hours before the meeting. This regulation is therefore generally adopted without material change although the reference to the rather inconvenient procedure of notarial certification is often omitted.

Regulation 63

A vote given or poll demanded by proxy or by the duly authorised representative of a corporation shall be valid notwithstanding the previous determination of the authority of the person voting or demanding a poll unless notice of the determination was received by the company at the office or at such other place at which the instrument of proxy was duly deposited before the commencement of the meeting or adjourned meeting at which the vote is given or the poll demanded or (in the case of a poll taken otherwise than on the same day as the meeting or adjourned meeting) the time appointed for taking the poll.

This regulation, which deals with the question of whether the revocation of a proxy is effective if not notified, is satisfactory although, in the case of listed companies, it is usual to provide that the notice of determination must be lodged a specified number of hours before the start of the meeting (see Appendix E, art 78).

Number of directors

Regulation 64

> Unless otherwise determined by ordinary resolution, the number of directors (other than alternate directors) shall not be subject to any maximum but shall be not less than two.

The reference in this regulation to alternate directors arises because reg 69 deems alternate directors to be directors. The intention of reg 64 is that the number of directors appointed as such should be limited and the minimum requirement should not be capable of being satisfied by the appointment of a single director who in turn appoints an alternate.

Section 282 of CA 1985 requires every public company to have a minimum of two directors. There is no statutory maximum and there is not usually much point in changing reg 64 to impose a limit although in special circumstances, such as joint venture companies, there may be reasons to do so. With private companies the minimum is often deleted and this can be achieved by substituting the following article for reg 64:

2.35   Sole director

> The minimum number of directors is one and, unless otherwise determined by ordinary resolution, the number of directors is not subject to a maximum. A sole director may exercise all the powers and discretions given to the directors by these articles and the Act.

The second sentence is added by way of clarification and is not essential.

Alternate directors

Regulation 65

> Any director (other than an alternate director) may appoint any other director, or any other person approved by resolution of the

directors and willing to act, to be an alternate director and may remove from office an alternate director so appointed by him.

Directors do not have an inherent right to appoint alternates but, subject to suitable protections, it is useful for them to be able to do so. Whilst under reg 65 an alternate director who is not already a director must be approved by a resolution of the directors, two alternative approaches may be considered. The first would entitle a director to appoint any person he chooses as his alternate; the second would require that the appointment of a person who is not already a director must be unanimously approved by all the other directors.

The first of these is effected by replacing reg 65 in its entirety by the following article:

2.36   Director's right to appoint any person as alternate

A director (other than an alternate director) may appoint as his alternate any other person who is willing to act and may remove from office an alternate director appointed by him.

The second alternative is achieved with the following article:

2.37   Alternate director to be approved by directors

Regulation 65 of Table A is amended by replacing 'or any other person approved by resolution of the directors' with 'or any other person approved by all the directors, other than the appointor and alternate directors who are not also directors'.

Regulation 66

An alternate director shall be entitled to receive notice of all meetings of directors and of all meetings of committees of directors of which his appointor is a member, to attend and vote at any such meeting at which the director appointing him is not personally present, and generally to perform all the functions of his appointor as a director in his absence but shall not be entitled to receive any remuneration from the company for his services as an alternate director. But it shall not be necessary to give notice of such a meeting to an alternate director who is absent from the United Kingdom.

The voting rights of a director who is also an alternate are covered by reg 88. However, neither reg 88 nor reg 66 deals with the position of a person who is an alternate for more than one director. An addition to reg 66 to cover this comprehensively is the following:

2.38   Multiple votes of alternate

> Regulation 66 of Table A is amended by adding at the end the following sentence:
>> 'An alternate director who is also a director or who acts as alternate director for more than one director shall have one vote for every director represented by him in addition to his own vote if he is also a director.'.

If this change is made to reg 66, the last sentence of reg 88 will need to be deleted.

Table A does not expressly state that an alternate director cannot vote on a resolution if his appointor is not entitled to vote. The main circumstance where a director is disenfranchised is where he has an interest in the resolution and reg 94 indirectly meets the point by providing that an alternate is deemed to be interested if his appointor has an interest. Another example which can arise is where there is a resolution of the directors to remove one of their number from office and the director concerned is excluded from voting (see the discussion in this chapter on reg 81 of Table A). The following article can be adopted to make the position clear in all cases:

2.39   Restriction on alternates' voting rights

> Regulation 66 of Table A is amended by adding at the end the following sentence:
>> 'An alternate director, in his capacity as such, is not entitled to vote on a resolution on which his appointor is not entitled to vote.'.

The reference to the alternate's 'capacity as such' deals with the common case of the alternate being a director in his own right. The words make it clear that the alternate retains the vote he has by virtue of being a director but loses the additional vote to which he is entitled as alternate.

Instead of the alternate director having no right to remuneration for acting as an alternate, it is possible to provide that his appointor may share his own remuneration with the alternate. An article to that effect is:

2.40 Remuneration of alternate

Regulation 66 of Table A is amended by replacing 'but shall not be entitled to receive any remuneration from the company for his services as an alternate director' with the following sentence:

'An alternate director shall not be entitled to remuneration from the company for his services as an alternate director except that he may be paid by the company such part of the remuneration otherwise payable to his appointor as the appointor specifies by notice to the company.'.

The second sentence of reg 66, which provides that it is not necessary to give notice of meetings to an alternate who is absent from the United Kingdom, should be deleted if the articles amend reg 88 so as to entitle a director who is abroad to receive notice of meetings.

Regulation 67

An alternate director shall cease to be an alternate director if his appointor ceases to be a director, but, if a director retires by rotation or otherwise but is reappointed or deemed to have been reappointed at the meeting at which he retires, any appointment of an alternate director made by him which was in force immediately prior to his retirement shall continue after his reappointment.

If, as is usual with private companies, the provisions relating to the retirement of directors by rotation are deleted, the reference to rotation in this regulation should be removed. This is achieved by the following:

2.41 Effect of an appointor's retirement on an alternate

Regulation 67 of Table A is amended by deleting the words which follow 'if his appointor ceases to be a director'.

Regulation 67 is unsatisfactory as it does not deal with the possibility of two directors sharing the same alternate. On the face of the regulation, the alternate ceases to represent both his appointors if one of them is no longer a director. An improvement on the first part of reg 67 is to provide that the alternate ceases to be an alternate only in relation to the retiring director. For this purpose, the following wording is a suitable alternative to the first part of reg 67 or may replace it in its entirety if directors are not subject to rotation:

An alternate director ceases to be an alternate for his appointor when his appointor ceases to be a director.

Article 83 in Appendix E deals with the retirement of alternate directors in more detail.

Regulation 68

Any appointment or removal of an alternate director shall be by notice to the company signed by the director making or revoking the appointment or in any other manner approved by the directors.

The procedure for appointing and removing an alternate can be made clearer by amending this regulation as follows:

2.42 Appointment and removal of alternates

Regulation 68 of Table A is amended by adding after 'by notice to the company signed by the director making or revoking the appointment' the words 'and delivered to the office or tendered at a meeting of the directors'.

Regulation 69

Save as otherwise provided in the articles, an alternate director shall be deemed for all purposes to be a director and shall alone be responsible for his own acts and defaults and he shall not be deemed to be the agent of the director appointing him.

This deals with the status of an alternate director and is satisfactory. As the regulation deems an alternate to be a director unless the articles provide otherwise, it is always necessary to consider whether it is intended in any particular article that a reference to directors should also cover alternates. This point arises, for example, in relation to reg 65.

Powers of directors

Regulation 70

Subject to the provisions of the Act, the memorandum and the articles and to any directions given by special resolution, the business of the company shall be managed by the directors who may exercise all the powers of the company. No alteration of the memorandum or articles and no such direction shall invalidate any prior act of the directors which would have been valid if that alteration had not been made or that direction had not been given. The powers given by this regulation shall not be limited by any special power given to the directors by the articles and a meeting of directors at which a quorum is present may exercise all powers exercisable by the directors.

This regulation contains the standard statement by which management of the company is delegated by the shareholders to the directors. The powers given to the directors of managing the company are made subject in particular to directions given by the shareholders in the form of a special resolution. The directors are expressly not affected either by a retrospective invalidation or by special powers being given to them by the articles.

By making the directors' powers subject to directions given by special resolution, reg 70 deals with the problem identified in *Automatic Self-Cleansing Filter Syndicate Co Ltd v Cunninghame* [1906] 2 Ch 34 that the shareholders do not have inherent power to control or restrict the directors in the way they exercise the powers which have been delegated to them.

The last sentence of the regulation covers two separate points. The first is rather obscure and appears to be dealing with the position where the articles specifically spell out particular powers of the directors. It would seem that the purpose is to ensure that their general powers are not limited by so doing. It is, however, unusual now to state specific powers—except perhaps in certain joint venture companies—and this part of the sentence will normally be redundant. Nevertheless, as it does no harm it is commonly retained.

The second part of the last sentence, which confirms that the powers of the directors can be exercised by a meeting at which a quorum is present, is curiously positioned and would sit better as part of reg 88 which deals with the way in which the directors conduct their affairs or of reg 89, which fixes the quorum. The alteration is barely worth making but, if it is made, an appropriate amendment should be required in relation to reg 88 or 89.

The regulation is otherwise satisfactory for most companies and will need to be modified only in the case of companies where the powers of the directors are subject to special limitations as, for example, in Appendices C and D.

Regulation 71

> The directors may, by power of attorney or otherwise, appoint
> any person to be the agent of the company for such purposes
> and on such conditions as they determine, including authority
> for the agent to delegate all or any of his powers.

It is possible that the powers given to the directors by reg 70 to
manage the company are sufficient to enable them to appoint agents
despite the common law rule that an agent (including a director), unless
otherwise authorised by the terms of his appointment, is not entitled to
delegate his powers (*Re Leeds Banking Co, Howard's Case* (1866) LR
1 Ch App 561). The purpose of reg 71 is to clarify the position beyond
doubt. It is curious that the regulation, unlike reg 72, appears before,
rather than after, the heading referring to the delegation of the powers
of the directors but nothing turns on that. The power of delegation to
agents is often amplified in the case of public companies or companies
with a large number of shareholders by giving the directors power to
appoint local boards. See the discussion in Chapter 6 in relation to
Appendix E, art 104.

Delegation of directors' powers

Regulation 72

> The directors may delegate any of their powers to any
> committee consisting of one or more directors. They may also
> delegate to any managing director or any director holding any
> other executive office such of the powers as they consider
> desirable to be exercised by him. Any such delegation may be
> made subject to any conditions the directors may impose, and
> either collaterally with or to the exclusion of their own powers
> and may be revoked or altered. Subject to any such conditions,
> the proceedings of a committee with two or more members shall
> be governed by the articles regulating the proceedings of
> directors so far as they are capable of applying.

Under the common law, directors cannot appoint themselves to an
office of profit or delegate their powers, unless the company resolves
otherwise or the articles permit them to do so (*Boschoek Proprietary Co
v Fuke* [1906] 1 Ch 148). This regulation complements reg 71 and is
another aspect of the articles giving the directors an express right to
delegate powers (Chapter 6, p 180 deals with the recommendations of

the Cadbury and Greenbury Codes in relation to the establishment of committees). In this case the delegation is to committees of directors and to executive directors. It may be thought helpful to permit persons who are not directors of the company—such as senior executives—to be members of committees but it is usual in such case to require that the non-directors are in a minority. The following article achieves this:

2.43   Delegation by directors to committees

Regulation 72 of Table A is amended by replacing the first sentence with the following:
'The directors may delegate any of their powers to a committee consisting of such persons as they think fit provided that a majority of the members of the committee are directors.'.

As a result of the decision in *Guinness plc v Saunders* [1990] 2 AC 663, in which the House of Lords held that the power of a committee to fix the remuneration of its own members is effective only if specifically stated, this regulation will need to be extended as follows if a committee is to be given the right to fix the remuneration:

2.44   Unlimited power of directors to delegate to committees

Regulation 72 of Table A is amended by adding the following as the second sentence:
'The power to delegate extends to the power of the directors to fix the remuneration of, or confer other benefits on, the members of the committee (whether in relation to their membership of the committee or in respect of any other office in the company) and is not limited by certain of these articles, but not others, referring expressly to particular powers, authorities or discretions being exercised by the directors or a committee of the directors.'.

The last sentence of reg 72 relating to the proceedings of committees is important because, in the absence of provisions as to the quorum at committee meetings, the whole committee must meet for the conduct of its business (*Re Liverpool Household Stores Association Ltd* [1890] 59 LJ Ch 616).

Appointment and retirement of directors

Regulation 73

At the first annual general meeting all the directors shall retire from office, and at every subsequent annual general meeting one-third of the directors who are subject to retirement by rotation or, if the number is not three or a multiple of three, the number nearest to one-third shall retire from office; but, if there is only one director who is subject to retirement by rotation, he shall retire.

The provisions relating to the rotation of directors are generally omitted in relation to private companies and, as the rotation articles therefore usually appear only in full length public company articles, it is unusual to adopt the Table A regulations directly. The comments on this and the succeeding two regulations therefore proceed on the basis that these regulations are replaced in full (see Appendix E, art 86 *et seq*).

Regulation 73 refers to the first annual general meeting of the company whereas, for most public companies, the appropriate reference will be to the annual general meetings taking place after the adoption of the articles. Regulation 84 provides that a managing director or executive director is not subject to retirement by rotation. It is suggested that this provision is more conveniently included in the article which is equivalent to reg 73.

Regulation 74

Subject to the provisions of the Act, the directors to retire by rotation shall be those who have been longest in office since their last appointment or reappointment, but as between persons who became or were last reappointed directors on the same day those who retire shall (unless they otherwise agree among themselves) be determined by lot.

The reference in this regulation to the provisions of the Act relates in particular to CA 1985, s 303(4), which is discussed in the commentary on reg 78.

The procedure which is set out for determining the sequence of retirements is generally acceptable. To deal with the somewhat unlikely event of there being a change in the composition of the board in the period between the preparation of the notice of the meeting and its being held, the following article can be adopted:

2.45 Effect of board changes on rotation

The directors to retire at an annual general meeting shall be determined (both as to number and identity) by the composition of the board of directors at the commencement of business on the day which is fourteen days prior to the date of the notice convening the meeting. A director shall not be required, or relieved from the obligation, to retire because of a change in the board after that time but before the close of the meeting.

A small drafting point in reg 74 is the position of the word 'last'. It seems unnecessary to refer to a director's last 'appointment' as directors are normally appointed only on one occasion, although it is perfectly sensible to deal with the occasion of his last being 'reappointed'. It would be preferable, therefore, to move 'last' so that it appears before 'reappointed' (this is done in Appendix E, art 87).

Regulation 75

If the company, at the meeting at which a director retires by rotation, does not fill the vacancy the retiring director shall, if willing to act, be deemed to have been reappointed unless at the meeting it is resolved not to fill the vacancy or unless a resolution for the reappointment of the director is put to the meeting and lost.

This regulation avoids the position, which arose in *Grundt v Great Boulder Proprietary Gold Mines Ltd* ([1948] Ch 145), of a director who lost the vote for his re-election but was nevertheless automatically re-elected as there was no appointment to replace him. Regulation 75 qualifies the general proposition so that it does not apply either if it is expressly resolved not to fill the vacancy or if a resolution to elect that particular director was put to the meeting and lost.

Regulation 76

No person other than a director retiring by rotation shall be appointed or reappointed a director at any general meeting unless—

(a) he is recommended by the directors; or
(b) not less than fourteen nor more than thirty-five clear days before the date appointed for the meeting, notice executed by a member qualified to vote at the meeting has been given to the company of the intention to propose that person for appointment or reappointment stating the particulars which would, if he were so appointed or reappointed, be required to be included in the company's register of directors together with

notice executed by that person of his willingness to be
appointed or reappointed.

The period for giving notice of an intention to propose the
appointment of a director other than one approved by the board is altered
by the Listing Rules of the London Stock Exchange. As mentioned in
Chapter 6, the maximum period for the giving of the notice is increased
from the 35 days specified in reg 76 to 42 days. Apart from this, two
amendments which may be made by companies which provide for the
rotation of their directors are:

(a) the director who is proposed for election should not be entitled,
in his capacity of a member, to sign the notice referred to in
para (b); and

(b) the requirement to give particulars of the director who is
nominated can be deleted.

An article which deals with these points is as follows:

2.46 Procedure for appointing a new director

Regulation 76 of Table A is amended:

(a) by replacing 'thirty-five clear days' with 'forty-two clear days';

(b) by adding after 'notice executed by a member' the words '(not
being the person to be proposed)'; and

(c) by deleting 'stating the particulars which would, if he were so
appointed or reappointed, be required to be included in the
company's register of directors'.

In the case of companies which delete the regulations relating to
rotation, reg 76 should be amended as follows:

Regulation 76 of Table A is amended by replacing 'No person other than
a director retiring by rotation shall be appointed or reappointed' with 'No
person shall be appointed' and by deleting the phrases 'or reappointment'
and 'or reappointed' where they occur in the regulation.

Regulation 77

Not less than seven or more than twenty-eight clear days before
the date appointed for holding a general meeting notice shall be
given to all who are entitled to receive notice of the meeting of
any person (other than a director retiring by rotation at the
meeting) who is recommended by the directors for appointment
or reappointment as a director at the meeting or in respect of
whom notice has been duly given to the company of the

intention to propose him at the meeting for appointment or reappointment as a director. The notice shall give the particulars of that person which would, if he were so appointed or reappointed, be required to be included in the company's register of directors.

This requires the company to give to the shareholders the statutory particulars of a director who is standing for election at the meeting otherwise than as a result of retirement by rotation and the regulation is usually omitted.

Regulation 78

Subject as aforesaid, the company may by ordinary resolution appoint a person who is willing to act to be a director either to fill a vacancy or as an additional director and may also determine the rotation in which any additional directors are to retire.

This regulation, dealing with the power of shareholders to appoint additional directors, although rarely used in practice, in part simply recognises the common law right of the shareholders in general meetings to fill casual vacancies in the directors (*Munster v Cammell Co* (1882) 21 ChD 183), whether occurring at the meeting or subsequently (CA 1985, s 303(3)). The regulation also entitles shareholders to appoint additional directors and to determine the way the directors are to rotate. A curious feature is that the opening words—'Subject as aforesaid'—bear no clear reference to anything and can be omitted. The wording of the regulation is otherwise acceptable.

The equivalent regulation in Old Table A, reg 97, referred to the shareholders having the power to fill 'casual' vacancies in the board. A casual vacancy is one which occurs for any reason, such as death, disqualification or resignation, other than retirement by rotation. The appointment of a new director to fill a vacancy arising from rotation was covered separately (reg 92). Regulation 78 of Table A simply refers to vacancies generally and does not distinguish those which are casual. This approach is satisfactory.

Section 303(4) of CA 1985 provides that a person appointed a director to replace a director who is removed by the shareholders is treated, in determining the rotation of directors, as having been appointed when the director he replaces was appointed. It is helpful to set this out in the articles by amending reg 78 as follows:

2.47   Retirement of replacement director by rotation

Regulation 78 of Table A is amended by adding at the end the following sentence:

'A person appointed to replace a director removed from office by the company in general meeting shall be treated, for the purposes of determining the time at which he or another director is to retire, as if he had become a director on the day on which the person in whose place he is appointed was appointed or last appointed a director.'.

In the case of a company which generally adopts Table A but excludes the rotation of directors, the regulation should be amended as follows:

Regulation 78 of Table A is amended by deleting 'and may also determine the rotation in which any additional directors are to retire'.

Regulation 79

The directors may appoint a person who is willing to act to be a director, either to fill a vacancy or as an additional director, provided that the appointment does not cause the number of directors to exceed any number fixed by or in accordance with the articles as the maximum number of directors. A director so appointed shall hold office only until the next following annual general meeting and shall not be taken into account in determining the directors who are to retire by rotation at the meeting. If not reappointed at such annual general meeting, he shall vacate office at the conclusion thereof.

The power of the directors to appoint additional directors is that generally utilised in practice and reg 79 embodies the safeguard, which is also included in the Listing Rules of the London Stock Exchange (see Chapter 6), that directors appointed in this way must submit themselves to re-election at the next following annual general meeting. This is inappropriate for a company which excludes the rotation of directors and for such a company the regulation should be amended as follows:

Regulation 79 of Table A is amended by deleting the second and third sentences.

There is a curious difference between regs 79 and 80. The former provides that, if the newly appointed director is not reappointed at the next annual general meeting, he ceases to hold office at the conclusion of the meeting. Regulation 80, however, provides that the director ceases to hold office when he is replaced or, if not replaced, at the end of the meeting. The point is not one of great significance but consistency is desirable and, of the two approaches, the latter is to be preferred. If it is thought necessary to change reg 79, the following will be appropriate:

2.48   Retiring director to vacate office at end of AGM

> Regulation 79 of Table A is amended by replacing 'he shall vacate office at the conclusion thereof' with 'he shall retain office until the meeting appoints someone in his place or, if it does not do so, until the end of the meeting'.

Regulation 80

> Subject as aforesaid, a director who retires at an annual general meeting may, if willing to act, be reappointed. If he is not reappointed, he shall retain office until the meeting appoints someone in his place, or if it does not do so, until the end of the meeting.

This regulation begins, as does reg 78, with the obscure words 'Subject as aforesaid' which appear to serve no useful function. The first sentence covers some of the same ground as reg 75 and it might be better to transfer it to reg 75. The second sentence is acceptable although it might be preferable to add 'or deemed to be reappointed' after 'If he is not reappointed'. This covers the deemed reappointment which occurs when reg 75 applies. In practice, however, the second sentence is unlikely to have any significance as it will rarely matter whether a retiring director is treated as having retired during the course of the meeting rather than at the end of it.

Disqualification and removal of directors

Regulation 81

> The office of a director shall be vacated if—
>> (a) he ceases to be a director by virtue of any provision of the Act or he becomes prohibited by law from being a director; or
>> (b) he becomes bankrupt or makes any arrangement for composition with his creditors generally; or
>> (c) he is, or may be, suffering from mental disorder and either—

(i) he is admitted to hospital in pursuance of an application for admission for treatment under the Mental Health Act 1983 or, in Scotland, an application for admission under the Mental Health (Scotland) Act 1960, or

(ii) an order is made by a court having jurisdiction (whether in the United Kingdom or elsewhere) in matters concerning mental disorder for his detention or for the appointment of a receiver, curator bonis or other person to exercise powers with respect to his property or affairs; or

(d) he resigns his office by notice to the company; or

(e) he shall for more than six consecutive months have been absent without permission of the directors from meetings of directors held during that period and the directors resolve that his office be vacated.

The list of circumstances in which a person ceases to be a director is generally acceptable, although special provisions will often be required in the case of joint venture companies of the type discussed in Chapter 5. The detailed wording may, however, be improved, as set out in the following article:

2.49   Vacating a director's office

Regulation 81 of Table A is amended:

(a) by replacing paragraph (c) with:
'he becomes of unsound mind or a patient for any purpose of a statute relating to mental health and the directors resolve that his office is vacated; or';

(b) by replacing 'by notice to the company' in paragraph (d) with 'by notice delivered to the office or tendered at a meeting of the directors'; and

(c) by adding in paragraph (e) after 'from meetings of the directors held during that period' the words 'and his alternate director (if any) does not attend in his place'.

A variation of the amendment to paragraph (c) of reg 81 would be:

he becomes incapable by reason of illness or injury of acting as a director and the directors (excluding the director concerned and, in his capacity as such, any alternate director appointed by the director) resolve that his office is vacated;

The exclusion from voting of an alternate director who has been appointed by the director whose removal is under consideration is strictly unnecessary if the suggestion which is made in the commentary on reg 66 is adopted and the alternate is excluded from voting on any resolution on which his appointor may not vote. Accordingly, the words in brackets apart from 'excluding the director concerned' may be omitted.

An article which permits the removal of a director on rather wider grounds but which requires the approval of all the directors is the following:

2.50   Removal of a director for mental disorder or inconsistent activities

> in the opinion of all the other directors (excluding alternate directors who are not also directors in their own right) he either becomes incapable by reason of mental disorder of carrying out his duties as a director or engages in activities inconsistent with those duties;

Paragraph (e) of reg 81 may also be amended by changing the six month period to a different period or by replacing it with a reference to absence from a specific number of board meetings regardless of the period of time involved. Additionally, the unanimous decision of all the other directors (other than alternate directors) could again be necessary. Another possible version is:

2.51   Removal of a director for failure to attend meetings

> he fails to attend three successive board meetings despite a notice being given to him prior to the third meeting that the provisions of this paragraph might apply and all the other directors (excluding the director concerned and, in his capacity as such, any alternate director appointed by the director) resolve that his office should be vacated;

It is useful to be able to remove a director who is incapable of working effectively with his colleagues and articles often provide that a director can be removed by a unanimous decision of all the other directors. This would make unnecessary the amendments mentioned above whereby the unanimous decision of the other directors would be substituted for a decision of a majority of them. Similarly, as discussed in Chapter 4, it is usual in the case of articles of wholly-owned subsidiaries to give the parent company the right to remove a director at any time. This principle can be extended so that any shareholder holding more than half the share capital can do likewise, the rationale being that the holders of a majority of the voting rights have an inalienable statutory right to remove directors (CA 1985, s 303; see Appendix A, art 50).

Remuneration of directors

Regulation 82

The directors shall be entitled to such remuneration as the company may by ordinary resolution determine and, unless the resolution provides otherwise, the remuneration shall be deemed to accrue from day to day.

This article is required because directors are not entitled to remuneration as directors unless otherwise provided in the articles or by agreement (*Re George Newman & Co* [1895] 1 Ch 674). The directors' power of managing the business of the company does not extend to fixing their own remuneration (*Foster v Foster* [1916] 1 Ch 532). The wording of reg 82 does not, however, make it clear that it is referring only to the remuneration to which directors are entitled as such, and not to remuneration to which they are entitled for executive services which are covered by reg 84. The following would clarify this:

2.52   Determination of directors' remuneration

Regulation 82 of Table A is amended by adding after 'entitled to such remuneration' the words 'for their services as such'.

In the case of large or listed companies it is common to fix a maximum for the aggregate fees payable to directors and to authorise the payment of additional remuneration for the performance of special services (see Appendix E, art 98).

The entitlement of a director who retires before the passing of the resolution fixing remuneration can be covered by the following:

2.53   Remuneration of retiring director

Regulation 82 of Table A is amended by adding the following sentence: 'A director who has ceased to hold office when the resolution is passed shall, unless it otherwise provides, be entitled to be paid the appropriate proportion of the remuneration voted to the directors for the period during which he held office.'.

Directors' expenses

Regulation 83

> The directors may be paid all travelling, hotel, and other expenses properly incurred by them in connection with their attendance at meetings of directors or committees of directors or general meetings or separate meetings of the holders of any class of shares or of debentures of the company or otherwise in connection with the discharge of their duties.

In the absence of express provision to the contrary, the remuneration of directors covers travel and other expenses incurred by them in the performance of their duties (*Young v Naval, Military and Civil Service Co-operative Society of South Africa* [1905] 1 KB 687). Regulation 83 confines the reimbursement to expenses incurred in attending meetings and in the discharge of the directors' duties whilst reg 84 deals with the entitlement of directors to receive additional remuneration for services provided outside the scope of their normal duties. Accordingly reg 83 is acceptable without amendment.

Directors' appointments and interests

Regulation 84

> Subject to the provisions of the Act, the directors may appoint one or more of their number to the office of managing director or to any other executive office under the company and may enter into an agreement or arrangement with any director for his employment by the company or for the provision by him of any services outside the scope of the ordinary duties of a director. Any such appointment, agreement or arrangement may be made upon such terms as the directors determine and they may remunerate any such director for his services as they think fit. Any appointment of a director to an executive office shall terminate if he ceases to be a director but without prejudice to any claim to damages for breach of the contract of service between the director and the company. A managing director and a director holding any other executive office shall not be subject to retirement by rotation.

This is a complicated clause covering a variety of matters:
(1) The board may appoint directors to hold executive office.

(2) The board may agree terms for the employment of a director by the company.

(3) The board may agree terms for a director to provide services outside the ordinary scope of his duties as a director.

(4) In particular, the directors may fix the remuneration payable for these services.

(5) A director's executive position will determine automatically if he ceases to be a director, but he shall remain entitled to compensation for breach of contract.

(6) Executive directors are not subject to retirement by rotation.

All of these can be changed although it is unlikely that the first three will give difficulty, unless there are special restrictions imposed on the powers of the directors. In the case of listed companies, the remuneration powers will generally be exercisable subject to the recommendations of a remuneration committee in accordance with the Cadbury Code, although this will not normally be expressed in the articles (see Chapter 6, p 180).

The third sentence of the regulation (see para 5 above) will often operate unfairly, for example where an employee wants to concentrate on his executive activities without the distraction of board responsibilities. An appropriate amendment is:

2.54 Continuation of retiring director in executive office

> The third sentence of regulation 84 of Table A is amended by adding after 'Any appointment of a director to an executive office shall terminate' the following:
> '(unless:
>   (a) the terms of his appointment provide otherwise; or
>   (b) the directors resolve otherwise, the director concerned and any alternate appointed by him being excluded from voting)'.

The last sentence of reg 84 has no application if the directors are not subject to retirement by rotation and, in that case, the following article will be appropriate:

> Regulation 84 of Table A is amended by deleting the last sentence.

Regulation 85

> Subject to the provisions of the Act, and provided that he has disclosed to the directors the nature and extent of any material interest of his, a director notwithstanding his office—

(a) may be a party to, or otherwise interested in, any transaction or arrangement with the company or in which the company is otherwise interested;

(b) may be a director or other officer of, or employed by, or a party to any transaction or arrangement with, or otherwise interested in, any body corporate promoted by the company or in which the company is otherwise interested; and

(c) shall not, by reason of his office, be accountable to the company for any benefit which he derives from any such office or employment or from any such transaction or arrangement or from any interest in any such body corporate and no such transaction or arrangement shall be liable to be avoided on the ground of any such interest or benefit.

Section 317 of CA 1985 requires a director to disclose an interest which he has in a contract or proposed contract with the company. Even if a director complies with the disclosure obligation, he will in principle remain subject to the fundamental rule that, if a director contracts with the company or is interested in a contract to which the company is a party and has not fully disclosed the contract or interest to the shareholders in a general meeting or the shareholders have not sanctioned it, the company is entitled to any profit which results to the director and the contract may be voidable (*Imperial Mercantile Credit Association v Coleman* (1873) LR 6 HL 189).

The purpose of reg 85 is to override the rule but it is curious that there is no express confirmation of the duty to declare interests imposed by s 317 (compare Appendix E, art 112). The reference to the regulation being 'Subject to the provisions of the Act' would appear to be a somewhat obscure attempt to incorporate the effect of s 317 into the regulation and it also makes the right of the director to enter into contracts conditional on compliance. There is no necessity for this condition and, particularly in the case of private companies where the requirements of s 317 impose a rather pointless administrative rule with criminal sanctions attached, it would be realistic to delete it. This can be achieved by the following:

2.55 Removal of directors' obligation to declare interest before acquiring it

> Regulation 85 of Table A is amended by deleting 'and provided that he has disclosed to the directors the nature and extent of any material interest of his'.

If this alteration is not made, the condition that the disclosure is made 'to the directors' can be amended to permit the disclosure for this purpose to be made to a committee. However, a disclosure to a committee will not suffice for the purposes of s 317 itself (*Guinness plc v Saunders* [1990] 2 AC 663) and the alteration accordingly cannot be recommended.

The regulation is otherwise satisfactory unless there is a special reason for prohibiting directors from having benefits from dealings with the company even though a declaration of the interest has been made.

Regulation 86

> For the purposes of regulation 85—
>
> (a) a general notice given to the directors that a director is to be regarded as having an interest of the nature and extent specified in the notice in any transaction or arrangement in which a specified person or class of persons is interested shall be deemed to be a disclosure that the director has an interest in any such transaction of the nature and extent so specified; and
>
> (b) an interest of which a director has no knowledge and of which it is unreasonable to expect him to have knowledge shall not be treated as an interest of his.

Paragraph (a) of reg 86 substantially follows CA 1985, s 317(3)(*b*) in permitting a general notice in relation to specific persons to be effective. For no obvious reason, however, it does not repeat s 317(3)(*a*), which relates to the disclosure of an interest arising by reason of membership of a particular company or firm, and an amendment for this purpose would be as follows:

2.56 Notice relating to a director's membership of another company

> Regulation 86 of Table A is amended by relettering paragraph (b) as paragraph (c) and by adding the following after paragraph (a):
> '(b) a general notice to the directors that a director is a member of a specified company or firm and is to be regarded as interested in contracts which are made with the company or firm after the date of the notice shall be deemed to be a sufficient disclosure of his interest in relation to the contracts; and'.

Paragraph (b), which excludes interests of which the director is, on reasonable grounds, unaware, goes beyond s 317 and does not affect the statutory duty of disclosure but merely relates to whether the director may benefit from the transaction.

If reg 85 is amended, as discussed above, so that the director's ability to contract with the company is not conditional on his having made a s 317 disclosure, reg 86 will have no application and should be omitted.

Directors' gratuities and pensions

Regulation 87

The directors may provide benefits, whether by the payment of gratuities or pensions or by insurance or otherwise, for any director who has held but no longer holds any executive office or employment with the company or with any body corporate which is or has been a subsidiary of the company or a predecessor in business of the company or of any such subsidiary, and for any member of his family (including a spouse and a former spouse) or any person who is or was dependent on him, and may (as well before as after he ceases to hold such office or employment) contribute to any fund and pay premiums for the purchase or provision of any such benefit.

The purpose of this regulation is to overcome the application of the fundamental proposition that a director cannot benefit from his office unless this is authorised by the shareholders through the articles or an appropriate resolution.

Proceedings of directors

Regulation 88

Subject to the provisions of the articles, the directors may regulate their proceedings as they think fit. A director may, and the secretary at the request of a director shall, call a meeting of the directors. It shall not be necessary to give notice of a meeting to a director who is absent from the United Kingdom. Questions arising at a meeting shall be decided by a majority of votes. In the case of an equality of votes, the chairman shall have a second or casting vote. A director who is also an alternate director shall be entitled in the absence of his appointor to a separate vote on behalf of his appointor in addition to his own vote.

This is another regulation which covers a rather mixed bag of items:

(1) The directors regulate their own proceedings.
(2) A director may call a meeting of the directors.
(3) The secretary shall call a meeting if required to do so by a director.
(4) A director absent from the United Kingdom is not entitled to notice of a meeting.
(5) Decisions are by majority vote.
(6) In the case of an equality of votes, the chairman has a casting vote.
(7) A director who is also representing an absent director as alternate has an extra vote.

The whole of the regulation is consistent with the important principle that, in contrast to the position with shareholders' meetings which are subject to considerable statutory intervention, the directors are given almost total freedom as to how they conduct their affairs. There is no specific formality that has to be followed and no set period of notice (*Browne v La Trinidad* (1887) 37 ChD 1). This is reinforced by reg 111 which specifies that the notice convening a meeting of the directors does not have to be in writing.

It is not unusual for a director to be given a right to receive notice of board meetings even whilst absent from the United Kingdom provided that he supplies an address to which notices are to be sent. An article which inserts in reg 88 the part of reg 111 which, as mentioned above, makes it unnecessary to give written notice of directors' meetings and which also deals with directors absent from the United Kingdom is the following:

2.57 Notice to director who is abroad

Regulation 88 of Table A is amended by replacing 'It shall not be necessary to give notice of a meeting to a director who is absent from the United Kingdom.' with:

'A director who is or is intending to be absent from the United Kingdom may request the secretary to give him notice of meetings at an address provided by him for that purpose. Notices of meetings of the directors shall be sent to him at that address but, if he does not provide an address, it shall not be necessary to give notice of meetings to him while he is absent from the United Kingdom. The notice calling a meeting of the directors need not be in writing.'.

If this amendment is adopted, corresponding changes should be made to reg 66, insofar as it provides that an alternate director who is absent from the United Kingdom is not entitled to notice of meetings, and to reg 111.

The casting vote of the chairman is commonly omitted in the case of joint venture companies (see Chapter 5, p 143).

If reg 66 is amended to clarify the voting rights of a person who is an alternate for more than one director, reg 88 will need to be altered by excluding the last sentence.

Regulation 89

> The quorum for the transaction of the business of the directors may be fixed by the directors and unless so fixed at any other number shall be two. A person who holds office only as an alternate director shall, if his appointor is not present, be counted in the quorum.

As this regulation enables the directors to fix the quorum, the wording can be left unchanged even if a different quorum is appropriate. However, where it is clear that a change is required, it is better to amend the regulation rather than leave it to the directors to deal with. If, under reg 64, there is no minimum number of directors, provision should be made for a single director to constitute a quorum. A suitable amendment to reg 89 would be as follows:

2.58 Sole director may be quorum

> Regulation 89 of Table A is amended by adding after 'unless so fixed at any other number shall be two' the words 'except when there is a sole director in which event he shall constitute a quorum'.

The regulation does not deal with the case where a director, who is an alternate for another director, is the only person present. If he is to be treated as two persons and thereby constitute a quorum, an appropriate amendment to reg 89 is:

2.59 Counting alternate directors for quorum

> Regulation 89 of Table A is amended by adding at the end the following sentence:
>> 'An alternate director who is also a director is treated as two directors at a meeting at which his appointor is not present.'.

If there is an objection to the possibility of one director being the quorum, the additional sentence should be reworded as follows:

2.60 Alternate director cannot alone constitute quorum

An alternate director who is also a director is treated as two directors at a meeting at which his appointor is not present but at least one other director must be present to constitute a quorum.

Regulation 90

The continuing directors or a sole continuing director may act notwithstanding any vacancies in their number, but, if the number of directors is less than the number fixed as the quorum, the continuing directors or director may act only for the purpose of filling vacancies or of calling a general meeting.

Unless the articles otherwise provide, the continuing directors cannot act if their number falls below the minimum specified in the articles (*Re Scottish Petroleum Co* (1883) 23 ChD 413). Regulation 90 overrides this and, although generally acceptable, it is essentially redundant if the minimum number of directors, and the quorum at board meetings when there is a single director, is one.

Regulation 91

The directors may appoint one of their number to be the chairman of the board of directors and may at any time remove him from that office. Unless he is unwilling to do so, the director so appointed shall preside at every meeting of directors at which he is present. But if there is no director holding that office, or if the director holding it is unwilling to preside or is not present within five minutes after the time appointed for the meeting, the directors present may appoint one of their number to be chairman of the meeting.

Although this regulation is satisfactory for a company where no special arrangements are made to protect the interests of one or more categories of shareholders, it is often amended in the case of joint venture companies (see Chapter 5, p 162). The powers of the chairman should not be underestimated, particularly by reason of his casting vote at general meetings and board meetings. Even in the case of companies which do not provide specific protection for minority shareholders, therefore, it may be desirable to be more specific as to how the chairman is to be appointed. One possible approach is to require that he is appointed by an ordinary resolution. An article to this effect is as follows:

2.61   Appointment of chairman by ordinary resolution

Regulation 91 of Table A is amended by replacing 'The directors may appoint one of their number to be the chairman of the board of directors' with 'The company may appoint and remove the chairman of the board of directors by ordinary resolution. If and so long as the position of chairman is vacant, the directors may appoint one of their number to be the chairman'.

Regulation 92

All acts done by a meeting of directors, or of a committee of directors, or by a person acting as a director shall, notwithstanding that it be afterwards discovered that there was a defect in the appointment of any director or that any of them were disqualified from holding office, or had vacated office, or were not entitled to vote, be as valid as if every such person had been duly appointed and was qualified and had continued to be a director and had been entitled to vote.

This regulation validates acts of a board even if there is a formal defect in the appointment of its members or the voting procedure. It should be noted that this regulation does not relieve the individual directors from a potential misfeasance action if they do not act *bona fide* in the belief that they have the necessary powers (*Dawson v African Consolidated Land and Trading Co* [1898] 1 Ch 6).

Regulation 93

A resolution in writing signed by all the directors entitled to receive notice of a meeting of directors or of a committee of directors shall be as valid and effectual as if it had been passed at a meeting of directors or (as the case may be) a committee of directors duly convened and held and may consist of several documents in the like form each signed by one or more directors; but a resolution signed by an alternate director need not also be signed by his appointor and, if it is signed by a director who has appointed an alternate director, it need not be signed by the alternate director in that capacity.

The ability to use signed written resolutions can be invaluable in an emergency and this regulation is acceptable for that purpose.

Regulation 94

Save as otherwise provided by the articles, a director shall not vote at a meeting of directors or of a committee of directors on any resolution concerning a matter in which he has, directly or indirectly, an interest or duty which is material and which conflicts or may conflict with the interests of the company unless his interest or duty arises only because the case falls within one or more of the following paragraphs—

(a) the resolution relates to the giving to him of a guarantee, security, or indemnity in respect of money lent to, or an obligation incurred by him for the benefit of, the company or any of its subsidiaries;

(b) the resolution relates to the giving to a third party of a guarantee, security, or indemnity in respect of an obligation of the company or any of its subsidiaries for which the director had assumed responsibility in whole or part and whether alone or jointly with others under a guarantee or indemnity or by the giving of security;

(c) his interest arises by virtue of his subscribing or agreeing to subscribe for any shares, debentures or other securities of the company or any of its subsidiaries, or by virtue of his being, or intending to become, a participant in the underwriting or sub-underwriting of an offer of any such shares, debentures, or other securities by the company or any of its subsidiaries for subscription, purchase or exchange;

(d) the resolution relates in any way to a retirement benefits scheme which has been approved, or is conditional on approval, by the Board of Inland Revenue for taxation purposes.

For the purposes of this regulation, an interest of a person who is, for any purpose of the Act (excluding any statutory modification thereof not in force when this regulation becomes binding on the company), connected with a director shall be treated as an interest of the director and, in relation to an alternate director, an interest of his appointor shall be treated as an interest of the alternate director without prejudice to any interest which the alternate director has otherwise.

This is an important restriction on the powers of directors which is invariably incorporated in the articles of listed companies, with the necessary modifications to comply with the Listing Rules of the London Stock Exchange (see Chapter 6, p 173). It may also be suitable for other companies with a large number of shareholders or where there is particular need to ensure that the directors are seen to be objective in the way they vote. In the case of the normal private company, however, it is usual to delete all these restrictions and to replace regs 94 to 97 with the following:

2.62   Director entitled to vote notwithstanding interest

A director may vote at a meeting of the directors or of a committee on a resolution which concerns or relates to a matter in which he has, directly or indirectly, an interest. He shall also be taken into account in determining whether there is a quorum present at the meeting.

The purpose of this regulation must be contrasted with that of reg 85, which frees the directors from the common law prohibition against having an interest in contracts to which the company is a party. Regulation 94 deals with the entitlement of directors to vote on such contracts and, as with reg 85, the director remains obliged to declare his interest in accordance with CA 1985, s 317. Although it is not necessary to do so, articles sometimes confirm this obligation and, for this purpose, the following addition can be made to the above article:

2.63   Obligation of director to declare interest

The director shall nevertheless be obliged to comply with the provisions of section 317 of the Act in relation to the disclosure of interests in contracts.

It will generally be the objective, if reg 94 is retained, to make the exceptions which it lists wider rather than narrower. There are several amendments which can be made and the wording contained in the Listing Rules of the London Stock Exchange forms a sound basis. The wording is set out in full in Chapter 6 and is discussed in the commentary on Appendix E, art 122. Some points for consideration are the following:

(1) Subsidiary undertakings include bodies which are effectively controlled by the company whilst falling outside the confines of the definition of a 'subsidiary'. The company can have an interest in such a body which would result in the director losing his voting right. It is consistent with the objectives of the exceptions embodied in these paragraphs that directors should be allowed to vote on transactions involving subsidiary undertakings despite the company's interest and the references to subsidiaries are changed accordingly.

(2) Paragraph (a) of the regulation is extended to cover persons other than the director because a director is deemed, by the final paragraph of reg 94, to have the interest that a person connected with him has.

(3) A new paragraph is inserted, which relates to a contract or arrangement with another company in which the director is interested only as an officer of the company or as the holder of securities of the company. This is a repeat of a provision which appeared in Old Table A but has been omitted from the current Table A. Although the width of the clause has been judicially criticised (*Prudential Assurance Co Ltd v Newman Industries* [1981] Ch 257)—which may be the reason that it no longer appears in Table A—it is nevertheless a useful addition.

(4) Paragraph (d) of the regulation is replaced by a broader exception where the resolution concerns an arrangement for the benefit of employees generally and does not give the director any special advantage.

(5) A reference is included to taking out insurance for the benefit of directors. This is discussed further in relation to reg 118.

An article making these amendments is the following:

2.64 Additional rights for directors to vote

Regulation 94 of Table A is amended:
(a) by replacing each reference to 'subsidiaries' with 'subsidiary undertakings';
(b) by replacing 'in respect of money lent to, or an obligation incurred by him for the benefit of, the company' in paragraph (a) with 'in respect of money lent by him or by another person to, or an obligation incurred by him or another person for the benefit of, the company'; and
(c) by replacing paragraph (d) with:
    '(d) the resolution relates to a contract or arrangement with another company in which he is interested only as an officer of the company or as the holder of shares or other securities;
    (e) the resolution relates to a contract or arrangement for the benefit of employees of the company or a subsidiary undertaking which does not award him a privilege or benefit not generally awarded to the employees to whom the contract or arrangement relates; or
    (f) the resolution concerns insurance which the company proposes to maintain or purchase for the benefit of directors or for the benefit of persons including directors.'.

In addition, reg 94 is unduly onerous in two respects: First, it does not pay regard to the state of knowledge of the director or his alternate. It would be reasonable to add a saving provision corresponding to para (b) in reg 86, as follows:

2.65   Disregarding the interest of a director who was unaware of it

The last paragraph of regulation 94 of Table A is amended:
  (a) by replacing 'For the purpose of this regulation, an interest of a person' with:
      'For the purpose of this regulation:
      (i) an interest of a person';
      and
  (b) by adding at the end of the paragraph:
      'and
      (ii) an interest of which a director or alternate director has no knowledge and of which it is unreasonable to expect him to have knowledge shall not be treated as an interest of his.'.

It is not strictly necessary to refer to alternate directors in this amendment as reg 69 treats an alternate director as if he were a director. The reference is included because the last paragraph of reg 94 makes express reference to alternates and an omission to do likewise in the proposed amendment could perhaps be regarded as significant.

The regulation applies not only to circumstances where the director has a material interest in the subject matter of the resolution but also if he has a material duty. This addition is unnecessary and can be deleted as follows:

2.66   Conflicting duties leave director's voting rights unaffected

Regulation 94 of Table A is amended by deleting the words 'or duty' in the phrases 'an interest or duty which is material' and 'his interest or duty arises'.

The final paragraphs of the regulation adopts the definition in CA 1985, s 346, as amended by any subsequent modification. The definition includes the person's spouse and children, trustees of a trust for their benefit and companies with which he is 'associated', being companies in which he and persons connected with him hold at least one-fifth of the equity or voting capital. This extension is made to achieve consistency because reg 1 provides that statutory definitions are adopted as in force when the regulation become binding on the company without regard to subsequent amendments. If the suggestion is followed which is made in the commentary on reg 1, that amendments to definitions made after the articles come into effect are adopted, a consequential amendment will be needed in relation to reg 94:

2.67   Effect of statutory changes in determining director's interest

The last paragraph of regulation 94 of Table A is amended by deleting '(excluding any statutory modification thereof not in force when this regulation becomes binding on the company)'.

Regulation 95

A director shall not be counted in the quorum present at a meeting in relation to a resolution on which he is not entitled to vote.

This regulation is inconsistent with the general proposition, embodied in reg 88, that the directors are free to determine how their meetings should be regulated. There is no objection in principle to a director who is interested in the subject matter of a resolution being counted in the quorum, as he has to declare the interest under CA 1985, s 317, although he may be excluded from being a party under the rules discussed in relation to reg 85 and he may be barred from voting under reg 94. It would therefore be reasonable to exclude reg 95 entirely or, alternatively, to amend it as follows:

2.68   Directors may agree to interested directors being included in quorum

Regulation 95 of Table A is amended by adding at the end 'unless the directors otherwise determine either generally or in relation to a particular resolution, but in the latter case the director affected and, in his capacity as such, any alternate director appointed by him shall not be entitled to vote on the determination'.

A possible additional problem arises with reg 95 and its interaction with reg 89. If a meeting of directors has the minimum number of directors present to make it quorate, the meeting would suddenly become inquorate. The possibility can be removed as follows:

2.69   Resolution to be disregarded if it makes meeting inquorate

Regulation 95 of Table A is amended by adding the following as the second sentence:
'If this would result in there not being a quorum, the meeting shall proceed as if the resolution had not been part of its business.'.

Regulation 96

The company may by ordinary resolution suspend or relax to any extent, either generally or in respect of any particular matter, any provision of the articles prohibiting a director from voting at a meeting of directors or of a committee of directors.

The power given to general meetings by reg 96 to relax the requirements of reg 94 will not be relevant if reg 94 is excluded but it will otherwise be theoretically desirable even though rarely likely to be used in practice. The voting restrictions imposed by reg 94 will normally be adopted only by companies which are unlikely to request a waiver from shareholders. If a change is required this will in practice be implemented by amending the articles to remove or modify any part of the regulation which has proved to be unsatisfactory in its operation. The wording of reg 96 is, however, acceptable although it could be improved by giving the shareholders power to ratify breaches, as follows:

2.70   Shareholders' power to ratify breaches of director's voting restrictions

> Regulation 96 of Table A is amended by adding at the end 'and ratify anything done in breach of a provision'.

Regulation 97

> Where proposals are under consideration concerning the appointment of two or more directors to offices or employments with the company or any body corporate in which the company is interested the proposals may be divided and considered in relation to each director separately and (provided he is not for another reason precluded from voting) each of the directors concerned shall be entitled to vote and be counted in the quorum in respect of each resolution except that concerning his own appointment.

Section 292 of CA 1985 provides that, in the case of a public company, a motion at a general meeting for the appointment of two or more directors may not be made by a single resolution unless the meeting has agreed this without any dissent. Regulation 97 echoes this by providing that a resolution at a board meeting to appoint two or more directors can be split into separate resolutions for each director with only the director concerned being prohibited from voting on the resolution relating to his own appointment. The scope of the regulation is rather limited in that it applies only if the resolution relates to the appointment of directors to offices or employments. It is convenient to extend the operation to other matters relating to their employment, as follows:

2.71   Separating resolutions relating to several directors

> Regulation 97 of Table A is amended by replacing 'concerning the appointment of two or more directors' with 'concerning the appointment,

the variation of the terms of appointment or the termination of the appointment of two or more directors'.

If, by adoption of the amendment to reg 66 which is suggested in the commentary, an alternate director may not vote on a resolution on which his appointor cannot vote, there is no need to alter reg 97 to cover that point. If, however, reg 66 has not been amended or if it is felt desirable to cover the point expressly in reg 97, the following article can be added:

> Regulation 97 of Table A is amended by replacing 'except that concerning his own appointment' with 'except that a director, and (in his capacity as such) any alternate director appointed by him, shall not be entitled to vote or be counted in the quorum in relation to the resolution concerning his own appointment'.

The regulation as a whole will be unnecessary if the restrictions imposed by reg 94 on directors voting on contracts in which they are interested are deleted. If reg 94 is retained but, as suggested in the commentary, reg 95 is excluded, reg 97 will need to be amended as follows:

> Regulation 97 of Table A is amended by deleting 'and be counted in the quorum'.

Regulation 98

> If a question arises at a meeting of directors or of a committee of directors as to the right of a director to vote, the question may, before the conclusion of the meeting, be referred to the chairman of the meeting and his ruling in relation to any director other than himself shall be final and conclusive.

This regulation is inadequate in that it does not provide for the resolution of a question relating to the chairman's voting rights. A suitable article to replace reg 98 is as follows:

2.72 Determination of chairman's right to vote

> If a question arises at a meeting of directors or of a committee as to the right of a director to vote which is not resolved by his voluntarily agreeing to abstain from voting, the question (except where the director concerned is the chairman of the meeting) may be referred to the chairman of the meeting for his ruling before the meeting concludes. If the question concerns the chairman, it shall be decided by a resolution of the directors, for which purpose the chairman shall be counted in the quorum but he shall not be entitled to vote. The chairman's ruling or the resolution of

the directors shall be conclusive unless the nature or extent of the interest of the director or the chairman which is relevant for making the ruling or considering the resolution (so far as it is known to him) has not been fairly disclosed to the meeting.

Although reg 98 is not solely dealing with cases of directors' interests, as a director may not be entitled to vote for other reasons (for example, because the subject matter is his removal from office), this is the main purpose of the regulation and it may therefore be excluded if the restrictions on the voting rights of directors with an interest are omitted.

Secretary

Regulation 99

> Subject to the provisions of the Act, the secretary shall be appointed by the directors for such term, at such remuneration and upon such conditions as they may think fit, and any secretary so appointed may be removed by them.

It is unusual for the secretary to have a formal contract of appointment but, if he does, reg 99 should not affect any right to compensation that he might have. This can be dealt with by amending the regulation as follows:

2.73 Secretary's right to compensation on removal

> Regulation 99 of Table A is amended by adding at the end 'but without prejudice to any right of compensation to which he is entitled'.

Minutes

Regulation 100

> The directors shall cause minutes to be made in books kept for the purpose—
> > (a) of all appointments of officers made by the directors; and
> > (b) of all proceedings at meetings of the company, of the holders of any class of shares in the company, and of the directors, and of committees of directors, including the names of the directors present at each such meeting.

Section 382 of CA 1985 requires minutes to be kept of all proceedings of general meetings, at meetings of its directors and at meetings of its managers. Although reg 100 makes no reference to managers—probably because it is now most unusual for a company to have managers who are not directors or deemed directors—in other respects it goes somewhat further than s 382. It requires records to be kept of all appointments of officers made by the directors and of proceedings at class and committee meetings. The names of the directors present at each meeting also have to be recorded. The requirement in Old Table A that every director present at a board or committee meeting must sign his name in a book is not repeated. Although the term 'officers' is defined in CA 1985, s 744 as including managers, it is not at all clear where the dividing line exists between senior employees and officers. In practice, the appointment of senior employees will in any event normally be recorded in board minutes but there is no reason to impose on the directors a greater duty in relation to the keeping of minutes than s 382 requires. Regulation 100 can be amended as follows.

2.74 Restriction on obligation to keep minutes

Regulation 100 of Table A is amended by replacing paragraphs (a) and (b) with 'of all proceedings of general meetings and at meetings of the directors'.

The seal

Regulation 101

The seal shall only be used by the authority of the directors or of a committee of directors authorised by the directors. The directors may determine who shall sign any instrument to which the seal is affixed and unless otherwise so determined it shall be signed by a director and by the secretary or by a second director.

Section 350 of CA 1985 no longer requires a company to have a common seal as, since the enactment of s 36A, any document can be executed by the signature of two directors or a director and the secretary where previously the seal had to be affixed. The prominence given to the seal in Table A is accordingly anachronistic and reg 101 can be omitted in the case of smaller companies. Alternatively, an amendment to the regulation which recognises the new position would be as follows:

2.75   Execution of deeds without sealing

Regulation 101 of Table A is amended:
- (a) by replacing 'The seal shall only be used' with 'If the company has a seal, it shall be used only'; and
- (b) by adding at the end the following sentence:
  'A document signed by a director and the secretary or by two directors and expressed to be executed by the company has the same effect as if executed under the seal.'.

Dividends

Regulation 102

Subject to the provisions of the Act, the company may by ordinary resolution declare dividends in accordance with the respective rights of the members, but no dividend shall exceed the amount recommended by the directors.

There is no statutory rule as to where the power to declare dividends lies. The directors accordingly have a general power to declare dividends without any sanction unless the articles provide otherwise (*Re Jowitt* [1922] 2 Ch 442). It is therefore not necessary to follow reg 102 in requiring the approval of an ordinary resolution or, conversely, to limit the powers of the shareholders so that they cannot declare a dividend greater than that recommended by the directors. Nevertheless, the regulation represents normal practice and, unless the special circumstances of the company require particular control to be exercised in relation to the declaration of dividends, it is usual to adopt the regulation without amendment.

Regulation 103

Subject to the provisions of the Act, the directors may pay interim dividends if it appears to them that they are justified by the profits of the company available for distribution. If the share capital is divided into different classes, the directors may pay interim dividends on shares which confer deferred or non-preferred rights with regard to dividend as well as on shares which confer preferential rights with regard to dividend, but no interim dividend shall be paid on shares having deferred or non-preferred rights if, at the time of payment, any preferential dividend is in arrear. The directors may also pay at intervals settled by them any dividend payable at a fixed rate if it appears to them that the profits available for distribution justify the payment. Provided the directors act in good faith they shall not incur any liability to the holders of shares conferring preferred rights for any loss they may suffer by the lawful payment of an interim dividend on any shares having deferred or non-preferred rights.

This regulation is mostly concerned with the position where directors pay interim dividends on shares having special rights, either deferred or preferred. For most companies this will be irrelevant but the regulation deals in a satisfactory manner with its subject matter—particularly in the way that it has a separate sentence for each point made—and can be left unchanged.

Regulation 104

Except as otherwise provided by the rights attached to shares, all dividends shall be declared and paid according to the amounts paid up on the shares on which the dividend is paid. All dividends shall be apportioned and paid proportionately to the amounts paid up on the shares during any portion or portions of the period in respect of which the dividend is paid; but, if any share is issued on terms providing that it shall rank for dividend as from a particular date, that share shall rank for dividend accordingly.

If, as is usual, the shares of the company are all fully paid, this regulation will be redundant. It is satisfactory if there are partly paid shares and may be left unchanged even if there are not. The regulation confers the authority to pay dividends in proportion to the amounts paid up on shares in accordance with CA 1985, s 119(c). In the absence of such a provision, it is arguable that dividends must be paid on shares without regard to the amounts paid up on them (*Oakbank Oil Co v Crum* (1882) 8 App Cas 65).

Regulation 105

A general meeting declaring a dividend may, upon the recommendation of the directors, direct that it shall be satisfied wholly or partly by the distribution of assets and, where any difficulty arises in regard to the distribution, the directors may settle the same and in particular may issue fractional certificates and fix the value for distribution of any assets and may determine that cash shall be paid to any member upon the footing of the value so fixed in order to adjust the rights of members and may vest any assets in trustees.

In the absence of express authority, dividends must be paid in cash (*Hoole v Great Western Railway Co* (1867) 3 Ch App 262). This regulation provides that authority and covers in considerable detail the procedures to be adopted. The use of this facility is rare, particularly in small companies, and taxation problems will often arise. The regulation is, however, satisfactory in its drafting and need not be amended.

Regulation 106

Any dividend or other moneys payable in respect of a share may be paid by cheque sent by post to the registered address of the person entitled or, if two or more persons are the holders of the share or are jointly entitled to it by reason of the death or bankruptcy of the holder, to the registered address of that one of those persons who is first named in the register of members or to such person and to such address as the person or persons entitled may in writing direct. Every cheque shall be made payable to the order of the person or persons entitled or to such other person as the person or persons entitled may in writing direct and payment of the cheque shall be a good discharge to the company. Any joint holder or other person jointly entitled to a share as aforesaid may give receipts for any dividend or other moneys payable in respect of the share.

Although the regulation seems to imply that, if the company follows the specified procedure for paying dividends, it will not be liable for any loss which the shareholder incurs because the procedure is defective, it is often amended to express the freedom from liability. The following article does this:

2.76   Company's liability for dividends delayed in the post

Regulation 106 of Table A is amended:
(a) by adding after 'sent by post' the words 'at the risk of the person to whom it is sent'; and
(b) by adding at the end the following sentence:
'The company has no responsibility for sums delayed in the post or in the course of transfer or where it has complied with directions given in accordance with this article.'.

In the case of listed companies, it is usual to make more detailed provisions for the means by which dividends can be paid (see Appendix E, art 140).

Regulation 107

> No dividend or other moneys payable in respect of a share shall
> bear interest against the company unless otherwise provided by
> the rights attached to the share.

This is satisfactory but, to avoid a dispute on the point, the regulation
can be amended to make it clear that the company has the right to the
benefit of the funds representing unclaimed dividends, as follows:

2.77 Investment of unclaimed dividends

> Regulation 107 of Table A is amended by adding at the end the following
> sentence:
> 'Unclaimed dividends may be invested or otherwise made use of for
> the benefit of the company until claimed.'.

Regulation 108

> Any dividend which has remained unclaimed for twelve years
> from the date when it became due for payment shall, if the
> directors so resolve, be forfeited and cease to remain owing by
> the company.

In the case of private companies the 12 year period is unrealistically
long and could reasonably be shortened to, say, three years by the
following article:

2.78 Reduced period for forfeiture of unclaimed dividends

> Regulation 108 of Table A is amended by replacing 'twelve years' with
> 'three years'.

Accounts

Regulation 109

> No member shall (as such) have any right of inspecting any
> accounting records or other book or document of the company
> except as conferred by statute or authorised by the directors or
> by ordinary resolution of the company.

Shareholders have no statutory right to inspect the company's books
and this regulation confirms that. It may, however, be appropriate to give
members the right to inspect the books in the case of wholly-owned
subsidiaries and joint venture companies (see Chapters 4 and 5). Section
222(1) of CA 1985 requires that the books of account are at all times to

be open for inspection by the officers and, although barely necessary, this could be confirmed by the following article:

2.79 Officers' right to inspect accounting records

Regulation 109 of Table A is amended by adding at the end 'but they shall at all times be open for inspection by the company's officers'.

Capitalisation of profits

Regulation 110

The directors may with the authority of an ordinary resolution of the company—

(a) subject as hereinafter provided, resolve to capitalise any undivided profits of the company not required for paying any preferential dividend (whether or not they are available for distribution) or any sum standing to the credit of the company's share premium account or capital redemption reserve;

(b) appropriate the sum resolved to be capitalised to the members who would have been entitled to it if it were distributed by way of dividend and in the same proportions and apply such sum on their behalf either in or towards paying up the amounts, if any, for the time being unpaid on any shares held by them respectively, or in paying up in full unissued shares or debentures of the company of a nominal amount equal to that sum, and allot the shares or debentures credited as fully paid to those members, or as they may direct, in those proportions, or partly in one way and partly in the other: but the share premium account, the capital redemption reserve, and any profits which are not available for distribution may, for the purposes of this regulation, only be applied in paying up unissued shares to be allotted to members credited as fully paid;

(c) make such provision by the issue of fractional certificates or by payment in cash or otherwise as they determine in the case of shares or debentures becoming distributable under this regulation in fractions; and

(d) authorise any person to enter on behalf of all the members concerned into an agreement with the

company providing for the allotment to them
respectively, credited as fully paid, of any shares or
debentures to which they are entitled upon such
capitalisation, any agreement made under such
authority being binding on all such members.

A capitalisation issue (also known as a bonus issue) involves the issue
to shareholders of new shares, credited as fully paid, in proportion to
their existing shareholdings. The proportionate interests of the
shareholders in the company remain unchanged and there are generally
two reasons which might motivate a capitalisation issue. The first is to
strengthen the capital base of the company by reducing the free reserves
that might otherwise be distributed to shareholders. The second arises
in relation to listed or traded shares where it is felt desirable to increase
the number of shares which are available for the market or to reduce the
market price for each share to a level which makes the shares
individually more attractive to purchasers. An issue may also be
required for technical reasons, for example to increase the share capital
of a private company which is about to be floated to the £50,000
minimum required for public companies (CA 1985, s 118).

The purpose of this regulation is to give the directors the power,
subject to receiving the authority of an ordinary resolution, to apply
undistributed profits or reserves either in paying up partly paid shares
or in paying up new shares in full. The Table A in the Companies Act
1929 had a notorious gap in that there was no equivalent of reg 110.
With companies formed under that Act, it is still necessary, unless the
deficiency has been rectified by the adoption of new articles, to pass a
special resolution to effect a capitalisation issue.

This regulation is very poorly drafted in that it consists of one long
sentence covering the following points:

(1) The directors must be authorised by an ordinary resolution to
exercise the power of making a capitalisation issue.

(2) They may capitalise either 'undivided profits', so far as not
required for the payment of preferential dividends, share
premium account or capital redemption reserve fund.

(3) The capitalisation is effected by appropriating the amount
involved to the shareholders in the proportions in which they
would be entitled to share it if it were paid out as dividend.

(4) Subject to the following paragraph, the capitalised amount can
be used in paying up amounts unpaid on partly paid shares or in

paying up in full new shares or debentures This is in accordance with CA 1985, ss 130 and 170 respectively which provide that the share premium account and capital redemption reserve can be applied in paying up unissued shares if they are allotted to members as fully paid bonus shares.

(5) Undistributable profits, share premium account and capital redemption reserve can be applied only in paying up, in full, shares which are unissued.

(6) Where fractions arise—because the new shares are not equal in number to or a whole number multiple of the existing shares—the directors may deal with them by issuing fractional certificates or making cash payments.

(7) An agreement may be signed on behalf of the members dealing with the matters arising on the issue.

The reference to 'undivided profits' is curious and seems to relate to profits which the directors have decided to distribute to shareholders. There appears to be no significant difference from 'undistributed profits' and that phrase, being more generally used, is to be preferred.

Apart from the cumbersome way in which it is drafted, the only amendment that may be required arises from the restriction of the reserves that can be capitalised to share premium account and capital redemption reserve. This can be widened by the following article:

2.80   Power to capitalise any reserves

Regulation 110 of Table A is amended by replacing 'capital redemption reserve' in paragraphs (a) and (b) with 'capital redemption reserve or other reserve or fund'.

As mentioned in para (7) of the summary above, the regulation refers to an agreement to be signed relating to the allotment. It is not the modern practice to have agreements in connection with bonus issues and para (d) of the regulation, which deals with this, can be omitted although it is normally left unchanged.

Notices

Regulation 111

Any notice to be given to or by any person pursuant to the articles shall be in writing except that a notice calling a meeting of the directors need not be in writing.

The effect of this regulation is to make it unnecessary to state, in those places throughout the articles where a reference is made to the giving of notice, that the notice should be written.

As explained in relation to reg 1, 'writing' includes a wide range of media and would probably extend to facsimile transmission. This can be stated expressly by the following amendment to reg 111:

2.81 'Written' notices to include faxes

Regulation 111 of Table A is amended by adding at the end the following sentence:
'A notice sent by facsimile transmission is deemed to be in writing.'.

The reference to notice in relation to meetings of the directors is inconveniently placed and is often deleted here and inserted in the equivalent of reg 88. In that case, reg 111 should be altered as follows:

Regulation 111 of Table A is amended by deleting 'except that a notice calling a meeting of the directors need not be in writing'.

Regulation 112

The company may give any notice to a member either personally or by sending it by post in a prepaid envelope addressed to the member at his registered address or by leaving it at that address. In the case of joint holders of a share, all notices shall be given to the joint holder whose name stands first in the register of members in respect of the joint holding and notice so given shall be sufficient notice to all the joint holders. A member whose registered address is not within the United Kingdom and who gives to the company an address within the United Kingdom at which notices may be given to him shall be entitled to have notices given to him at that address, but otherwise no such member shall be entitled to receive any notice from the company.

Although it is normal practice, as provided by reg 112, for notice in the case of joint holders to be given only to the first named, it may be desirable in special cases to give the company the right to choose any of the joint holders as the one entitled to receive notices. Another point in relation to joint holders is that, while the regulation deals clearly with the position where a sole shareholder is resident outside the United Kingdom, it is not apparent what happens where there is a joint holding and all but the first named of the joint holders have addresses in the United Kingdom. An article to cover both these points is as follows:

2.82   Notices to joint shareholders

Regulation 112 of Table A is amended by replacing the second and third sentences with:

'In the case of joint holders of a share, notices given to any one of them shall be sufficient notice to all of them. If the registered address of a member is, or the registered addresses of joint holders are, outside the United Kingdom, he or they may give the company an address within the United Kingdom at which notices may be given and notices shall be sent to him or them at that address. The member or joint holders shall not otherwise be entitled to receive notices from the company.'.

Regulation 113

A member present, either in person or by proxy, at any meeting of the company or of the holders of any class of shares in the company shall be deemed to have received notice of the meeting and, where requisite, of the purposes for which it was called.

The purpose of this regulation, whilst clear on the face of it, is rather obscure. It seems sensible to suggest that a member can hardly complain justifiably about non-receipt of a notice if he turns up at the meeting convened by it. But reg 39 provides that the meeting is not invalidated by the non-receipt of the notice and the only other significance of reg 113 would appear to be to remove any right of action which the shareholder might have on the ground of misfeasance or discrimination. It is unlikely that the regulation would provide the directors with protection if they deliberately withheld the notice from a particular shareholder but, whilst the regulation provides little, if any, benefit, there is no harm in adopting it.

Regulation 114

Every person who becomes entitled to a share shall be bound by any notice in respect of that share which, before his name is entered in the register of members, has been duly given to a person from whom he derives his title.

This regulation relates to persons becoming entitled to shares in any way and is not limited to entitlement arising by transmission on the death or bankruptcy of the registered holder. It would include, for example, a purchaser whose transfer has not been registered when the notice of the meeting is sent out.

Regulation 115

Proof that an envelope containing a notice was properly addressed, prepaid and posted shall be conclusive evidence that the notice was given. A notice shall be deemed to be given at the expiration of 48 hours after the envelope containing it was posted.

It is now not unusual to distinguish between first class and second class post in relation to the giving of notice. In many private companies, the distinction will be without practical significance as it is unlikely that the precise moment at which a notice is effective will be critical. The change, if desired, can be made as follows:

2.83 Time when notice deemed to be given

Regulation 115 of Table A is amended by replacing 'at the expiration of 48 hours after the envelope containing it was posted' with 'at the expiration of 24 hours after the envelope containing it was posted if sent by first class post and at the expiration of 48 hours if sent by second class post'.

A useful addition to the regulation deals with notices which are given by delivery or sent by facsimile transmission, as follows:

2.84 Notices delivered or sent by fax

Regulation 115 of Table A is amended by adding the following sentences: 'A notice which is served by being left at the registered address of the addressee shall be deemed to have been given when it was left there. A notice given by facsimile transmission shall be deemed to have been given when the message was sent.'.

A minor point on the drafting of reg 115 relates to the tense used in the second sentence—'deemed to be given' would be improved by being replaced with 'deemed to have been given'. Alternatively, 'was posted' could be replaced by 'is posted'. The wording of the amendment proposed above follows that of reg 115 for the sake of consistency and it is a matter of taste as to whether grammatical simplicity defers to consistency. Appendix A, art 71 takes the alternative approach.

Regulation 116

> A notice may be given by the company to the persons entitled to a share in consequence of the death or bankruptcy of a member by sending or delivering it, in any manner authorised by the articles for the giving of notice to a member, addressed to them by name, or by the title of representatives of the deceased, or trustee of the bankrupt or by any like description at the address, if any, within the United Kingdom supplied for that purpose by the persons claiming to be so entitled. Until such an address has been supplied, a notice may be given in any manner in which it might have been given if the death or bankruptcy had not occurred.

This heavy handed regulation is almost redundant as reg 31 puts the persons entitled by transmission in the same position, except in relation to attendance and voting at meetings, as the holder whose death or bankruptcy is involved. Nevertheless, the provision does no harm and can be adopted without change.

Winding up

Regulation 117

> If the company is wound-up, the liquidator may, with the sanction of an extraordinary resolution of the company and any other sanction required by the Act, divide among the members in specie the whole or any part of the assets of the company and may, for that purpose, value any assets and determine how the division shall be carried out as between the members or different classes of members. The liquidator may, with the like sanction, vest the whole or any part of the assets in trustees upon such trusts for the benefit of the members as he with the like sanction determines, but no member shall be compelled to accept any assets upon which there is a liability.

The reference to the Act is correct in pure drafting terms as the definition in reg 1 extends the term to cover re-enactments. The current legislation is contained in the Insolvency Act 1986, which in this area re-enacts the provisions which were contained in CA 1985, but it might be thought helpful to replace the reference to the Act with a reference to the Insolvency Act. It is, however, not worth amending the regulation merely to do this.

A liquidator has the power, with the sanction of an extraordinary resolution, to make arrangements with contributories and to compromise questions relating to the assets of the company (Insolvency Act 1986, s 165). Regulation 117 confirms this power but is so drafted that the sanction that the liquidator requires relates to the making of the distribution and to the vesting of assets in trustees but not to the power to differentiate as between different members or classes of members. In cases where there is concern that the liquidator might exercise the power unfairly, the regulation can be amended as follows:

2.85 Authority for liquidator to value assets

Regulation 117 of Table A is amended by replacing 'may, for that purpose, value any assets and determine how the division shall be carried out' with 'may, for that purpose and with the like sanction, value any assets and determine how the division shall be carried out'.

Indemnity

Regulation 118

Subject to the provisions of the Act but without prejudice to any indemnity to which a director may otherwise be entitled, every director or other officer or auditor of the company shall be indemnified out of the assets of the company against any liability incurred by him in defending any proceedings, whether civil or criminal, in which judgment is given in his favour or in which he is acquitted or in connection with any application in which relief is granted to him by the court from liability for negligence, default, breach of duty or breach of trust in relation to the affairs of the company.

The indemnity provided by reg 118 is in accordance with CA 1985, s 310, which invalidates a provision purporting to indemnify an officer against liability where he is at fault. Subsection (3)(*b*) allows an indemnity if the officer obtains judgment in his favour, if he is acquitted or if the court grants him relief. The section does not prohibit a wider indemnity provided that it does not cover circumstances where the officer is at fault. It is therefore possible to extend the regulation by covering any liability arising from the performance of his duties where he is not at fault. It is also helpful to make it clear that there is an entitlement to an indemnity if the proceedings are withdrawn or settled in his favour. The following would deal with these points:

2.86   Extension of indemnity for officers

Regulation 118 of Table A is amended:

(a) by adding after 'shall be indemnified out of the assets of the company' the words 'against losses and liabilities which he incurs, otherwise than as a result of his own negligence or default, in connection with the performance of his duties as such and'; and

(b) by adding after 'in which judgment is given in his favour' the words 'or where the proceedings are withdrawn or settled on terms which do not include a finding or admission of a material breach of duty by him'.

Following the amendment to s 310(3) made by CA 1989, it is now clear that a company can insure against liability and it is the practice generally to extend reg 118 as follows:

2.87   Officers' liability insurance

Regulation 118 of Table A is amended by adding at the end the following sentence:

'Subject to the provisions of the Act, the directors may purchase and maintain insurance at the expense of the company for the benefit of the directors or other officers or the auditors against liability which attaches to them or loss or expenditure which they incur in relation to anything done or omitted or alleged to have been done or omitted as directors, officers or auditors.'.

3

Articles of Association of a Private Company

Introduction

In the introduction to the discussion of Table A in Chapter 1 it is pointed out that a significant number of the regulations in Table A repeat statutory provisions which apply in any event and either cannot be validly amended at all by the company's articles or may be amended only to a limited extent. It is accordingly essential that, where Table A is varied, a check is made to ensure that nothing in the Companies Acts invalidates the change.

It is curious that Table A omits a number of statutory obligations which could usefully be included in the articles by way of reminder to those responsible for the company's administration. These include the following:

(1) A private company cannot offer shares or debentures to the public (CA 1985, s 81) and Appendix A, art 3 confirms this.

(2) Under CA 1985, s 366 a company must in every year hold an annual general meeting and not more than 12 months may elapse between the date of one annual general meeting and the next. This obligation may be excluded in the case of a private company by an elective resolution under s 366A but, in the absence of a resolution, it is helpful to have a reminder in the articles as to the statutory rule. This is covered by Appendix A, art 23.

(3) Section 372(3) of CA 1985 requires that, in every notice calling a meeting of the company, there shall appear with reasonable prominence a statement that a member entitled to attend and vote is entitled to appoint a proxy or, where that is

allowed, one or more proxies to attend and vote instead of him, and that a proxy need not also be a member. Section 372(2)(*b*) provides that a member of a private company is not entitled to appoint more than one proxy to attend on the same occasion unless the articles otherwise provide—which they would not usually do. Article 25 in Appendix A repeats the requirements of s 372(3).

(4) Under CA 1985, s 317, a director who is interested in a contract or proposed contract must declare the nature of his interest. Regulation 85 of Table A acknowledges the need for the declaration and, by making the regulation 'subject to the provisions of the Act', there may be an indirect adoption of the duties imposed by s 317. This is, however, far from clear and it is helpful for the statutory requirements to be spelled out in more detail, as is normally done with long form articles (see Appendix E, arts 110 to 112).

(5) A sole director cannot also be the secretary of the company (CA 1985, s 283(2)). This is confirmed by Appendix A, art 61.

Transfer of shares and pre-emption rights

In the case of the normal private companies, the most important regulation in the articles of association is that dealing with the ability of shareholders to transfer their shares. It is generally a matter of considerable concern that shareholders who are continuing as members of a private company should have some opportunity to intervene if a member wishes to dispose of his shares. Regulation 24 of Table A gives the directors the authority to reject transfers of partly-paid shares if they do not approve of the transferee. In short form articles for a private company it is common practice to extend this right of refusal to all shares of the company. An appropriate article for this purpose would be the following:

3.1 Director's right to reject any transfer of shares

The directors may, in their absolute discretion and without giving any reason for doing so, refuse to register the transfer of a share, whether or not it is fully paid.

For many private companies, it is, however, unsatisfactory, particularly from the point of view of minority shareholders, for the directors to be given an unfettered discretion to refuse proposed transfers. In such cases the articles normally contain extensive pre-emption provisions. Whilst these tend to adopt a fairly standard pattern, they differ enormously in their detail. Broadly, they will require a shareholder wishing to dispose of shares to offer them first to his fellow shareholders. They will be given the chance to acquire the shares in proportion to their existing holdings. If the shareholders do not want to buy all the shares on offer, those remaining can then be transferred to an outsider. A short form of pre-emption clause which indicates the principles involved is set out below:

3.2   Short form pre-emption clause

A member who wishes to transfer shares otherwise than to another member shall give notice to the directors containing particulars of the shares in question. The directors, as agents of the member, shall offer the shares to the other members at a price agreed between the offering member and the directors or, failing agreement, at a price determined by the auditors as their fair value. If, within 28 days of the price being agreed or determined, the directors are unable to find members willing to purchase all the shares, the offering member may dispose of the shares which remain unsold in any manner he thinks fit. The directors shall register a transfer of the shares which is lodged for registration within 14 days of the expiry of the 28 day period and their right to refuse to register the transfer under regulation 24 of Table A shall not apply.

The importance of pre-emption clauses is widely underestimated and there is a regrettable tendency for drafters of articles to adopt a standard form of wording automatically, without considering its suitability to the specific company. An extensive form of pre-emption clause appears as Appendix A, art 18. In reviewing its wording, the following points should be considered.

(1) Should a shareholder be allowed to dispose of part only of his holding?
The argument against permitting this is that a shareholder who wishes to dispose of some shares is likely to be less committed to the company than one who has no intention of selling. This could result in conflicts between him and the other shareholders as to how the company is operated. The point is, however, likely to be academic with most private

companies as, the smaller the shareholding, the more difficult it will be to sell it. Accordingly, a shareholder will rarely be interested in retaining a reduced holding and will generally want to sell all his shares if he wishes to sell any.

If a shareholder may sell part of his holding, follow art 18. If he must sell all his shares when he wants to sell any, replace para (i) of art 18(a) with the following:

3.3   Offeror required to sell all his shares

> A member who wishes to transfer shares or an interest in shares (a 'Vendor') shall give to the directors a notice (a 'Transfer Notice') offering to dispose of all the shares held by him (the 'Offered Shares') and stating the number of the Offered Shares which, or an interest in which, he wishes to transfer (the 'Specified Shares'), the third party (the 'Proposed Transferee') to whom he wishes to transfer the Specified Shares or interest if the Offered Shares are not purchased by the members in accordance with this article and the price per share (the 'Offer Price') at which he intends to transfer the Specified Shares or interest to the Proposed Transferee.

Consequential amendments will be required to the rest of art 18(a) to distinguish between the Offered Shares and the Specified Shares, references to the latter being generally replaced by the former.

(2) Should the vendor be required to name a third party to whom he would propose to transfer the shares if his co-shareholders do not take them up?

The offerees will generally have a considerable legitimate interest in knowing where the sale shares will end up if they are unwilling or unable to buy them themselves. From the point of view of the vendor, however, it may not be realistic to expect his prospective third party purchaser to commit to buy the shares so far as they are not acquired by the existing shareholders and for the commitment to remain in place for the weeks— or even months if a fair price has to be determined—that it takes for pre-emption rights to be exhausted. Although it is common practice to require the vendor to nominate a specific third party purchaser, this can work harshly unless the pre-emption process is structured so that it can be carried out within a short period. An alternative approach is to allow the vendor not to designate a proposed purchaser but to give the directors a reasonable discretion to refuse to accept a transfer to a person who is not a member if he has not been previously designated as the proposed transferee. This approach is discussed further at question 12 below.

If the third party must be named, follow article 18. If not, para (i) of art 18(a) should read as follows:

3.4 Transferer not required to name proposed transferee

A member who wishes to transfer shares or an interest in shares (a 'Vendor') shall give to the directors a notice (a 'Transfer Notice') specifying the number of shares (the 'Specified Shares') which, or an interest in which, he wishes to transfer. The Transfer Notice may name a third party (the 'Proposed Transfcree') to whom he wishes to transfer the Specified Shares or interest if the Specified Shares are not purchased by members in accordance with this article and the price per share (the 'Offer Price') at which he intends to transfer the Specified Shares or interest to the Proposed Transferee.

(3) Should the vendor be required to state the price which he wants for his shares?

This is a common requirement, the effect of which is to inhibit the vendor from specifying an unduly high offer price in case he finds himself without any acceptances from the other members whilst being allowed to sell to a third party only at the inflated price. Nevertheless, there is no good reason why the vendor should not have a choice as to whether he states a price or leaves it to be determined by the directors or the auditors.

If the price must be stated, follow art 18. If a price need not be stated, the possibilities are that:

(i) the directors are obliged automatically to instruct the auditors to determine the fair price;
(ii) the directors are given the task of trying to agree a price with the vendor and only if they are unable to do so will the fair price be determined;
(iii) the negotiations as to the price are left to the vendor and the members who are willing to purchase.

Whichever of the above is adopted, para (i) of art 18(a) will need to be amended to the following:

3.5 Transferor not required to specify offer price

A member who wishes to transfer shares or an interest in shares (a 'Vendor') shall give to the directors a notice (a 'Transfer Notice') specifying the number of shares (the 'Specified Shares') which, or an interest in which, he wishes to transfer. The Transfer Notice may name a third party (the 'Proposed Transferee') to whom he wishes to transfer the Specified Shares or interest if the Specified Shares are not purchased by members in accordance with this article and may state the price per Share (the 'Offer Price') at which he wishes to transfer the Specified Shares or interest.

If the directors are obliged to instruct the auditors to determine the fair price, a new para (ii) will need to be inserted in art 18(a):

3.6   Directors to obtain determination of fair price

The directors shall, within seven days of receipt of the Transfer Notice, instruct the auditors to determine the fair price of each of the Specified Shares (the 'Fair Price').

Allowing the vendor a choice as to whether or not to specify an offer price results a considerable number of complications which are discussed further in Chapter 5 in relation to Appendix C, art 8.

If the directors must try to agree a price with the vendor before having the fair price determined, the wording of the new paragraph will instead be:

3.7   Directors to seek to agree fair price

The directors shall, within 14 days of receipt of the Transfer Notice, seek to agree with the Vendor a fair price (the 'Offer Price') for each of the Specified Shares. If they are unable to reach agreement within the period of 14 days, they shall, within seven days of the end of the period, instruct the auditors to determine the fair price (the 'Fair Price').

Finally, if the vendor and the members who are willing to purchase are required to negotiate a price, all references to the Offer Price and the Fair Price can be omitted. A new para (iii) should be inserted in art 18(a) as follows:

3.8   Offeror and offerees to negotiate price

The Vendor and each offeree who wishes to purchase any of the Specified Shares shall enter into negotiations with a view to agreeing a price for each of the Specified Shares. If an offeree is unable to agree a price within 14 days of the offer being made to him, he shall be deemed to have declined the offer. If agreement is reached, the offeree may accept the offer in respect of all or part of his allocation and may apply for excess shares at the same price. The acceptance and application will be effective only if notified to the directors within the period of 14 days.

Article 18(a) will require additional amendment to provide that, if the vendor and the other shareholders cannot reach agreement on the price, the vendor is entitled to sell the shares to a third party but subject to the right of the directors on reasonable grounds to reject the transfer. A suitable paragraph to include in the article is the following:

3.9   Offeror's right to sell to approved third party

If all the offerees of the Specified Shares decline, or (in accordance with paragraph [(iii)]) are deemed to have declined the offer, the Vendor shall be entitled to sell the Specified Shares to a third party but subject to the right of the directors, on reasonable grounds which they must disclose to the Vendor on request, to refuse to register the transfer.

(4) If the vendor must state an offer price, should there nevertheless be a right for the offerees to require a determination of a fair price for the shares?

The advantage of omitting the procedure for determining a fair price is that the pre-emption process is quicker, simpler and cheaper to implement. It would be necessary to provide the standard safeguard that, if existing members are not prepared to buy the shares at the offer price, the vendor may sell to a third party as long as the sale is not for a smaller consideration. It is, however, the normal practice to give the offerees a right to require a determination of the fair price. This is partly to avoid the vendor circumventing the pre-emption procedure by specifying an unduly high price and then selling to a third party where the price apparently paid by the third party is not a true reflection of the bargain with the vendor, perhaps because of collateral deals between them. It is also generally felt to be reasonable that the continuing shareholders should have the right to retain ownership of the company without being forced to pay an unreasonable price.

If the offerees can require a valuation, follow art 18. If they cannot require the fair price to be determined, the third sentence of para (ii) of art 18(a) should be replaced with the following:

3.10   Accepting offerees to accept offer price

Each offeree shall be asked to state whether he wishes to accept the offer and, if so, the number of shares (whether more or less than his allocation) he wishes to purchase. The offer shall provide that, if the offeree does not accept the offer in respect of any of the shares allocated, he shall be deemed to have declined it.

Further amendments will be required to remove the various references to the fair price.

(5) What should be the procedure for determining the fair price of the shares?

The determination of a fair price is one of the most complicated elements in implementing the normal pre-emption provisions. It is common practice to disregard the difficulties and simply leave the matter to the auditors with a broad statement such as that the determination is to be 'on the basis of a going concern' or 'on the basis of the net value of the assets of the company and its subsidiaries'. In practice this seems to work well enough but the shareholders may prefer to provide more detailed guidelines to be followed by the auditors.

If a simple formula is to be adopted, follow art 18. If a more specific formulation is required, the main choice will be between asset value and a multiple of earnings.

Asset value is the simplest formula provided that it is based on book values as shown in the latest audited accounts. If, however, there are significant assets whose market value is likely to be materially different from the book value, then arrangements should be made for their valuation on a current basis with an appropriate deduction being made for any tax which would be incurred on disposal at that value. As the cost and time involved in obtaining professional valuations are likely to be considerable, it would be reasonable to provide that a valuation cannot be required if there has been a revaluation of all or most of the fixed assets within the past, say, three years. It will be also be necessary to decide who should in fairness be responsible for the costs but, as the valuation is likely to be of interest to the company itself, it would generally be acceptable for the cost to be borne by the company. Unless the cost would be such as to reduce the net assets of the company to a material extent, it is suggested that paying for the valuation would not constitute financial assistance within CA 1985, s 151 as the payment would not appear to fall within any of the heads of s 152(1)(*a*). Suitable wording would be the following:

3.11   Fair price based on asset value

The Fair Price shall be determined in accordance with the net asset value of the company

(1) based on its latest available audited accounts; and

(2) adjusted to take account of acquisitions and disposals after the end of the period to which the accounts relate; but (unless there has been a valuation of all or substantially all of the fixed assets of the company and its subsidiaries within the preceding three years) the auditors may, and at the request of the Vendor or an offeree shall, at the cost of the company obtain valuations of the fixed assets of the company and its subsidiaries. The valuations shall be substituted for the values in the relevant accounts and the auditors shall make such adjustments as they consider appropriate to take account of any taxation cost or benefit which would arise if the assets were sold for their valuations. The auditors, in determining the Fair Price, shall be acting as independent experts and not as arbitrators and their determination shall, in the absence of manifest error, be conclusive.

An alternative valuation procedure which may be more suitable for a company whose main value is as a trading entity is on the basis of a multiple of its net earnings. The auditors will be assisted in making their valuation if an indication can be given of the basis for determining the multiple, such as the average multiple for listed companies in the same sector of business as shown in the *Financial Times*. The multiple for a private company, whose shares are not readily traded, will be less than that for a listed company and a discount should be applied to reflect this. A problem in applying a multiple to the company's earnings arises if the latest accounts of the company are not very recent. The auditors can be instructed to have regard to the company's management accounts but these vary greatly in their quality. A suitable article which adopts a fairly broad brush approach is the following:

3.12   Fair price based on earnings

The Fair Price shall be determined by applying an appropriate multiple to the adjusted net profits of the company. For this purpose, the adjusted net profits are the net profits, after taxation, of the company and its subsidiary undertakings as shown in the latest available audited accounts adjusted:
  (a) to take account of events occurring after the end of the period to which the accounts relate;
  (b) to reflect the information available in the latest available management accounts of the company and its subsidiary undertakings; and
  (c) otherwise as the auditors consider desirable for determining the Fair Price.
The appropriate multiple shall be [one-half] of the average of the price-earnings ratios of the shares of listed companies in the sector, as shown in the Financial Times, which the auditors consider to be closest to the

businesses of the company and its subsidiary undertakings. The auditors, in determining the Fair Price, shall be acting as independent experts and not as arbitrators and their determination shall, in the absence of manifest error, be conclusive.

(6) If the shares concerned constitute a minority holding, should the valuation apply an appropriate discount and, if they are a majority holding, should there be a premium for the control conferred by the shares?

A minority holding in a private company is generally valued at less than a proportionate part of the value of the company as a whole. This is because the minority shareholder has few worthwhile rights and his only expectation of benefiting from his holding is the receipt of such dividends as the majority choose to approve. Conversely, a majority holding may carry a premium because of the advantages conferred by control. It is normal in fair value clauses to require that the discount attributable to minority holdings, but not the premium carried by a majority, should be disregarded.

If there is to be neither a discount nor a premium, follow art 18. If there is to be an adjustment to reflect the disadvantage of a minority holding or the benefit of a majority, the following should replace the third sentence of para (vi) of art 18(a):

3.13   Valuation to reflect whether offered shares are majority or minority holding

If the Specified Shares are less than one-half of the issued shares, the auditors shall reduce the Fair Price to such extent as they consider appropriate to reflect the fact that they constitute a minority holding and, if the Specified Shares are more than one-half of the issued shares, the auditors shall increase the Fair Price by such amount as they consider appropriate to reflect the control they confer.

(7) Who should pay for the auditors' valuation?

If the vendor, having named an offer price, is nevertheless required to agree to the fair price being determined, it is usual to provide that he should not be responsible for any of the costs of the valuation unless the offer price was excessive. For this purpose, an offer price which exceeded the fair price by, for example, more than five or ten per cent could be deemed to be excessive. It would also arguably be fair for the vendor to pay all the costs if he has profited by the fair price being significantly (say fifteen or twenty per cent) more than the offer price.

If the vendor exercised a right not to specify an offer price in the transfer notice, it is reasonable that he should bear the cost of the valuation.

If, on the other hand, the vendor exercises a right to withdraw the transfer notice if the fair price turns out to be too low to be acceptable, it is not obvious where the cost of the valuation should fall. It might be said that the vendor should not have started the whole process if he was not reasonably willing to accept a valuation but this additional burden on a potential vendor makes the already onerous pre-emption procedure prospectively unworkable.

It should be noted that, in contrast to the case where the valuation concerns assets of the company, there would seem to be no justification for the company bearing the costs of the share valuation.

If the vendor is to share the costs of the valuation with the offerees unless the valuation is close to the offer price, follow art 18. If the vendor is required to pay all the costs of the valuation if he benefits from an increased price, the following sentence should be inserted after the first sentence of para (vii) of art 18(a):

3.14 Offeror to bear valuation costs

If the Fair Price exceeds the Offer Price by more than [fifteen] per cent and the Vendor sells all the Specified Shares for the Fair Price, the fees and expenses of the auditors shall be paid in full by the Vendor.

If the vendor is to pay the costs where he has exercised a right not to specify an offer price, the following clause should replace para (vii) of art 18(a):

3.15 Sharing the costs of valuation

If the Fair Price has been determined because offerees accepted the offer but did not accept the Offer Price, the fees and expenses of the auditors shall be paid by those offerees in proportion to the numbers of the Specified Shares (including excess applications) in respect of which they accepted the offer. If the Transfer Notice did not specify an Offer Price, the fees and expenses shall be paid by the Vendor.

(8) Should the vendor be entitled to withdraw the transfer notice when he learns of the valuation?
It is reasonable, and is generally the practice, not to force the vendor to accept the fair price in advance of its being quantified. If, however, the difference between the fair price and the offer price is marginal, it might be considered appropriate that the vendor should not have a right of

withdrawal but that, having suffered a small reduction in the purchase price, he should not also be required to pay for the valuation. The argument for requiring the vendor to proceed at the lower price is that it is not in the interests of the other shareholders to have a reluctant fellow member and the vendor cannot reasonably complain if he receives fair value for his holding. The percentage reduction which permits a withdrawal of the offer should be the same as that which triggers an obligation to contribute to the cost of determining the fair price of the shares.

If the vendor has a right to withdraw if the fair price differs more than marginally from the offer price, follow art 18. If there is no right of withdrawal, para (viii) of art 18(a) should be omitted.

(9) Should offerees who were willing to accept the offer price be bound by the valuation?

If some of the offerees are willing to pay the offer price but others insist on the fair price being determined, it is reasonable to provide that the offerees who are satisfied with the offer price should not be obliged to pay the fair price if it turns out to be higher, unless, perhaps, the difference between the two prices is minimal. The converse of this would be that they should not be entitled to benefit if the fair price is less than the offer price. A reasonable alternative is to provide that all sales that take place must be at the fair price but that an offeree, like the vendor, should have a right not to proceed once the fair price has been determined.

If the offerees must accept the fair price if they proceed, follow art 18. If an offeree who accepts the offer price must proceed at that price unless the vendor exercises a right of withdrawal, art 18(a) should be amended by inserting a new para (iv) as follows:

3.16   Offeree bound by accepted offer price

If an offeree accepts the Offer Price for all or part of his allocation, he shall be required to purchase all the shares for which he has accepted the offer at the Offer Price unless the Vendor withdraws the offer in accordance with the following provisions of this article.

(10) Should an offeree who required a determination of the fair price be entitled to withdraw his acceptance when the price has been quantified?

Although it would seem reasonable that an offeree should be entitled to defer a decision as to whether he wants to buy shares until the price has been quantified, the ability to withdraw causes additional expense and delay to arise without any certainty of a satisfactory outcome. If the vendor has taken a chance of getting the price wrong by stating a price at which he will sell, an offeree who wants a valuation should equally be prepared to stand by the result.

There are, however, two cases in which it might be considered reasonable to allow the withdrawal of his acceptance by an offeree who has required a determination of the fair price. The first of these is where the vendor has exercised a right to elect not to specify an offer price. The second is if the fair price exceeds the offer price by a significant margin. In this context it would be reasonable to apply a larger percentage than that which enables a offeree who accepted the offer price to withdraw his acceptance.

If an offeree who requires a determination of the fair price is bound to buy at that price, follow art 18. If the offeree has a right to withdraw only if the fair price is significantly more than the offer price, para (ix) of art 18(a) should be replaced with the following:

3.17 Accepting offeree's right to withdraw acceptance where offer price stated

If the Fair Price is substantially more than the Offer Price, an accepting offeree may within seven days of being given notice of the Fair Price withdraw his acceptance. The shares apportioned to him shall, so far as possible, be allocated amongst the offerees who have accepted the offer as if they were unclaimed shares to which paragraph (iii) applied. If he does not withdraw his acceptance, he shall be required to purchase the shares apportioned to him at the Fair Price. For this purpose, the Fair Price is substantially more than the Offer Price if, where the accepting offeree is an Assenting Offeree, it exceeds the Offer Price by more than five per cent or, where the accepting offeree is a Dissenting Offeree, it exceeds the Offer Price by more than fifteen per cent.

If the offeree is entitled to withdraw his acceptance in cases where the vendor has not specified an offer price, an appropriate article (which assumes a provision along the lines of the alternative wording proposed in relation to para 3(b) above) is the following:

3.18 Accepting offeree's right to withdraw acceptance where there is no offer price

If the Vendor did not specify an Offer Price, an offeree who accepted his allocation, either in whole or in part, may withdraw his acceptance within seven days of his being given notice of the Fair Price.

(11) Should an offeree be entitled to purchase a part only of his allocation?

Unless there is a very small number of shareholders, there seems to be no reason to force an offeree to choose between accepting the whole of his allocation or rejecting the offer. If the company has only a few members, a partial purchase could affect the balance of voting rights and, in that case, it may be appropriate to prohibit partial acceptances. The counter-argument is that the offerees could together make the vendor sell part of his holding and thereby leave him with an unsaleable rump which the offerees would hope to pick up cheaply at a later date. This point is largely dealt with by giving the vendor the right to withdraw his offer if full acceptances are not received.

If the offerees can accept in respect of part of their allocations, follow art 18. If partial acceptances are not permitted, the references to excess allocations in art 18(a) will not be applicable and the closing words of para (ii) should be modified to read as follows:

3.19   Partial acceptances by offerees not permitted

> ... and the offeree shall provide that, if the offer is not accepted by him in respect of all of the shares allocated, he shall be deemed to have declined it.

(12) To whom can the vendor sell shares not taken up by his fellow shareholders?

The position will depend on whether the vendor is obliged to name a third party purchaser and the price that purchaser will pay. This imposes a severe restriction on the ability of a member to sell his shares and it is only reasonable that he should be permitted to sell his shares to the nominated third party at the offer price if the other shareholders do not themselves wish to buy. If, however, the vendor has an option as to whether he names a third party, it would be reasonable to give the directors a right to reject a transfer to an outside purchaser if the pre-emption rights are not exercised.

If the Vendor has a right of sale, which is not subject to the directors' approval, only if he has named the outside purchaser, follow art 18. If the Vendor exercises a right not to nominate a proposed purchaser and the directors may in that event refuse a transfer to a third party, para (xiii) of art 18(a) should be replaced with the following:

3.20   Directors' right to reject third party transferee

If the directors do not find purchasers for all the Specified Shares under the above provisions and the Vendor has not exercised his right to withdraw the Transfer Notice, the Vendor shall be entitled to sell the Specified Shares, or so many of them as have not been purchased, for a cash price per share which is not less than the Offer Price or, if there was none, which is not less than the Fair Price. The directors may, before registering the transfer, require the production of evidence to enable them to satisfy themselves reasonably that the consideration shown on the instrument of transfer is a cash price and that no circumstances exist in relation to the sale which make that consideration misleading. If the Transfer Notice specified a Proposed Transferee, the sale may be made to him without the approval of the directors. The directors may otherwise, on reasonable grounds which they must disclose to the Vendor on request, refuse to register the transfer.

If the vendor can sell the shares to any third party, the second and fourth sentences of para (xii) of art 18(a) should be omitted.

(13) Are there any transfers, such as to close relatives or, in the case of a corporate shareholder, to another member of the shareholder's group, which can be made freely without the pre-emption procedure being invoked?

In a company where the relationships between the shareholders are critical, it might be acceptable to prohibit free transfers to members of the family and associates. A difficulty with an article which permits such transfers is that it can be used as a device for introducing outside shareholders. Thus, for example, a right to transfer shares to the trustees of a family trust could be exploited by making the chosen third party both a trustee and a beneficiary of what is on the face of it, but not in reality, a trust for the member's family. It is, nevertheless, common practice to permit such transfers and to include, particularly in the case of transfers within a group of companies, protection against a subsequent change in the relationship which caused the transfer to be initially acceptable (see Appendix A, art 18(6)).

If transfers are permitted to relatives and associates, follow art 18. If there are no permitted transfers which escape the pre-emption obligation, omit para (b) of art 18.

There are a number of standard provisions in full pre-emption clauses which will (or should) invariably be included:

(1) The offerees should be given the right to apply for shares in excess of their allocations. If not all the offerees wish to take up the shares allocated to them, excess applications should be satisfied pro rata.

(2) The directors should endeavour to find acceptances at the offer price for the offered shares by satisfying excess applications from members who are willing to pay the offer price.

(3) The vendor should be entitled to withdraw his offer if acceptances are received for some only of the offered shares. The saleability of shares of a private company is limited in any case and, the smaller the holding, the less chance there is of finding a buyer.

(4) If there are clearly not going to be acceptances in respect of all the offered shares, either at the offer price or the fair price, the vendor should be given the opportunity to withdraw his offer before the cost of valuing the shares is incurred.

(5) If the pre-emption procedure does not find buyers for any of the offered shares or if buyers are found for some of them and the vendor chooses to sell the remainder to outsiders, the price at which he sells to non-members should not be less than the offer price stated by him. If he did not indicate an offer price, the minimum price of the sale to the outsider should be the fair price. If he stated an offer price but, in accordance with the pre-emption procedure, a fair price was also determined, the offer price should be the benchmark and a sale to an outsider should be permitted at that price even if it is less than the fair price.

(6) If the vendor is free to sell to a third party, there should be a time limit within which the sale should be completed.

(7) The directors should be entitled to require evidence to be produced that the price paid by the third party purchaser is genuine and that there is no arrangement for an effective reduction by means of some collateral arrangement between the vendor and the third party.

(8) Equally, if certain transfers are permitted without the pre-emption procedure being implemented, the directors should be entitled to require the production of reasonable evidence to satisfy themselves that the necessary relationship exists between the transferor and the proposed transferee.

Commentary on articles in Appendix A

The following commentary relates to the articles contained in Appendix A. In drafting those articles, the opportunity has been taken to bring together and adopt all the recommended changes which are discussed in the commentary on Table A in Chapter 2. As will be indicated below, it will rarely be the case that all those amendments are appropriate to any particular company and it will usually be the case that a substantial number of the regulations in Appendix A can be omitted. Those articles which will rarely be required are marked with an asterisk.

The commentary proceeds on the basis that the company in question does not fall within any of the special categories covered in the following chapters.

Table A

Article 1: With short form articles it is customary to adopt Table A subject to specified exclusions and this approach has been adopted in Appendix A. It is of assistance to persons who need to refer to such articles to annex a copy of Table A to each print of the articles. The regulations which are excluded are the following:

Regulation 26: it is generally not desirable to give the company express power to suspend the registration of transfers as, once the pre-emption procedure has been followed, there is no reason to delay registration further. The statutory power (CA 1985, s 358) to close the register of members cannot, however, be removed.

Regulation 41: it is usual to have a different article in relation to inquorate meetings (eg art 27).

Regulation 44: there is no important reason for omitting this regulation, which deals with the right that directors have to attend meetings, but see the comment on art 31.

Regulations 60 and 61: the provisions relating to the forms of proxies are unnecessarily complicated but there is no fundamental objection to them (see art 40).

Regulation 64: this deals with the number of directors and art 41, which replaces it, is slightly to be preferred.

Regulation 65: the ability to appoint alternate directors is important and consideration should be given as to whether regulation 65 adequately protects the interests of the shareholders (see the comments on arts 42 to 45).

Regulation 67: this deals with the termination of an alternate's appointment if his appointor ceases to be a director and should be disapplied if the regulations relating to the rotation of directors are excluded.

Regulations 73 to 80: it is unusual for the directors of private companies to be subject to the rotation procedure but it may be appropriate if there is an unusually large number of shareholders.

Regulation 86: the omission of this regulation follows from the amendment to reg 85 which is made by art 53.

Regulation 89: although there is no major objection to the way reg 89 deals with the quorum at meetings of the directors, an improved version is provided by art 56.

Regulations 94 to 98: the restrictions on directors' voting powers in relation to resolutions where they have an interest are rarely suitable for private companies. An exception may arise if the company has a large number of shareholders and there are directors who could have serious conflicts of interest.

Article 2: This may be safely omitted as it deals purely with drafting points.

Private company

Article 3: This article is added as a reminder of the restrictions imposed by CA 1985, s 81. The statutory position applies whether the articles confirm them or not and it is therefore not essential that art 3 is included.

Share capital

Article 4: A statement of the share capital, which will in any case be part of the memorandum of association, need not be included in the articles unless there are different classes of shares with rights which have to be set out. It is nevertheless common practice to include an article of this kind.

Article 5: This amendment to Table A will not be of significance for most private companies unless it is anticipated that issues of shares with differing rights will be made.

Article 6: Section 80 of CA 1985 provides that the directors may not exercise a power to allot shares unless authorised to do so by the company in general meeting or by its articles of association. An authority must limit the number of shares to which it applies and the period of time, being a maximum of five years, for which it is given. It is usual, in the case of private companies, to allow the directors the maximum permitted freedom to issue new shares.

Article 7: It is also the normal practice with private companies which do not require specific protection for minority shareholders to exclude the obligation under CA 1985, s 89 to offer new shares on a pre-emptive basis. If, however, it is intended that there should be an obligation to issue new shares to members in proportion to their existing holdings, the following article should replace art 7:

3.21 New shares to be offered to members in proportion to existing holdings

Unless otherwise determined by an ordinary resolution, unissued shares shall be offered to the members in proportion, as nearly as possible, to their holdings of shares immediately before the issue. The offer shall be made by notice specifying the number of shares offered and a period, not being less than 14 days, within which the offer, if not accepted, will be deemed to have been declined. A member shall be entitled to accept the offer for all or any of the shares offered to him. After the expiration of the period of 14 days or, if earlier, on receipt of notices from all the members as to whether or not they accept the offer, the shares for which acceptances are not received shall be offered to the members who have accepted the offer in full in proportion to their then holdings of shares and the offer shall be open for the same period as the original offer. Shares which were offered but for which acceptances are not received may be disposed of by the directors to any person they choose but the disposal shall not be on terms more favourable to the acquirer than the terms offered to the members.

Article 8: This can be omitted unless the company is likely to issue warrants to bearer. As most private companies are concerned to know the identity of their members, it is very unusual for warrants to be issued.

Share certificates

Article 9: This makes a small technical amendment to reg 5 of Table A and, as with art 8, may generally be omitted.

Lien

Article 10: Regulation 8 of Table A gives the company a lien on partly-paid shares in respect of sums payable on the share. As mentioned in Chapter 2, p 18 in the commentary on the regulation, it is usual with private companies to extend the right to a lien so that it applies to all shares and in respect of all sums owed by the holder to the company. The article also extends the lien to all distributions in respect of the share.

Articles 11 and 12: Liens on shares are rarely met in practice even with private companies. This may be because it is in practice difficult to dispose of shares on which the lien is exercised and, as arts 11 and 12 deal with minor drafting points and not matters of principle, they may generally be omitted.

Calls on shares and forfeiture

Articles 13 to 17: These articles make a number of drafting improvements to Table A which are discussed in Chapter 2. It is, however, unusual for a private company to issue partly paid shares and the articles should be omitted unless there are grounds for believing that such an issue will be made. If that is the case, the articles contain helpful amendments.

Transfer of shares

Article 18: This is discussed in detail above.

Article 19: Although it is common practice to omit reg 24, either because the directors are given a total discretion as to whether to accept transfers or because the articles contain detailed pre-emption rights, the regulation does contain provisions which are convenient in those cases where the directors' discretion is not total. It is accordingly reasonable, but not essential, to retain the regulation amended as set out in para (a) of art 19. Paragraph (b) operates by way of a reminder and can be omitted.

Article 20: It is unreasonable for the directors to be able to delay their response to a transfer for more than a few days. Although the pre-emption provisions in art 18 impose definite time limits which the directors must observe, there are permitted transfers under para (b) of art 18 where no time constraints apply. Article 20 therefore provides a useful protection for shareholders but, according to the circumstances of each company, it may be appropriate to extend or shorten the suggested period of 14 days.

Articles 21 and 22: These are unlikely to be of practical significance in the case of a private company and may be omitted.

Annual general meetings

Article 23: As mentioned above, this provides a reminder of the obligation to hold annual general meetings unless an elective resolution has been passed.

Notices of general meetings

Article 24: It is pointed out in Chapter 2 that reg 38 of Table A imposes a number of administrative procedures which normally serve no useful purpose. Article 24 removes them.

Article 25: The statutory obligation (CA 1985, s 372(3), to notify shareholders of their right to appoint proxies is not repeated in Table A but is a helpful addition to the articles.

Proceedings at general meetings

Article 26: This article is useful if there is a fear that a meeting which begins by being quorate may be rendered inquorate, before it has completed its business, by shareholders walking out. This is unlikely to be a matter of real concern unless there are only a few shareholders and, in such a case, the articles contained in Appendix D, which provide detailed protection for minority shareholders, may be more suitable than those in Appendix A.

Article 27: This is an improved version of reg 41 of Table A which is discussed in Chapter 2. As, however, it is relevant only if there is a risk of there being inquorate general meetings—which is unlikely to be a problem with small companies—it can generally be omitted. If this is done, art 1 will need to be amended so that reg 41 is not one of the regulations of Table A that is excluded.

Article 28: This is a useful provision for companies in which the chairman plays an important role. An example would be where the company is owned equally by two families and an independent chairman is appointed to hold the balance where there is disagreement.

Article 29: This makes a minor wording change to reg 43 and is included in Appendix A only for the sake of completeness. Nothing will be lost by omitting it.

Article 30: This article repeats the provisions of CA 1985, s 375 and provides a reminder of the statutory position where there are, or may be, corporate members. If such members are unlikely, the article can be omitted.

Article 31: Unless there is a large number of members of the company and the proceedings at meetings are conducted on a formal basis, this article can be omitted. It is more appropriate for public companies and, in particular, those whose shares are traded. If art 31 is not adopted, reg 44 of Table A should not be excluded by art 1.

Article 32: It should be possible for a single member to demand a poll and the amendment to reg 46 of Table A is worthwhile.

Articles 33 to 35: These make a number of minor changes to Table A and are unnecessary for the normal private company.

Votes of members

Article 36: This provides a clarification of Table A, as discussed in Chapter 2.

Article 37: Unless there are partly paid shares in existence or anticipated, the article may be omitted. It otherwise should be included as it provides appropriate additions to the sanction imposed on a member who is in default in respect of calls.

Article 38: This article can be omitted unless the affairs of the company are likely to be conducted in a very formal manner.

Article 39: It is unnecessary in the case of private companies to give shareholders the power to appoint more than one proxy each to represent them at meetings. Article 39 should therefore generally be included.

Article 40: It is a matter of personal taste whether regs 60 and 61 of Table A are replaced or retained. Although art 40 is more suitable for most companies, the differences are in the details and are unlikely to matter in practice.

Number of directors

Article 41: This provides a good alternative to reg 64 of Table A.

Alternate directors

Articles 42 to 45: Most small companies would not expect to take advantage of the ability to appoint alternates and, despite their limitations, the provisions of regs 65 to 69 of Table A could be left unchanged as a harmless irrelevance. Different considerations may apply in the case of wholly-owned subsidiaries (discussed in Chapter 4) and joint venture companies (Chapter 5).

Where, however, the circumstances are such that directors want to have the right to appoint alternates to attend meetings at which they are unable to be present, these articles should be included. In particular, the second amendment to reg 66, which confirms the restrictions on the voting rights of alternate directors, is desirable in view of the deletion of reg 94 of Table A.

As mentioned in the commentary on reg 65 of Table A in Chapter 2, it needs to be considered whether a director should have a free right to choose any alternate (as provided by art 42) or whether some approval should be required from the other directors. If a majority approval is sufficient, reg 65 can be adopted without change. If all the other directors must approve, reg 65 should not be one of the regulations of Table A excluded by art 1 but it should be amended by art 42 as follows:

3.22   Alternate director to be approved by all directors

Regulation 65 is amended by replacing 'or any other person approved by resolution of the directors' with 'or any other person approved by all the directors, other than the appointor and alternate directors who are not also directors'.

If the restrictions on directors' voting rights imposed by reg 94 of Table A are retained, there should be added to the amendment made by para (b) of art 43 the following sentence:

3.23   Restriction of voting rights of alternate director

An alternate director, in his capacity as such, is not entitled to vote on a resolution on which his appointor is not entitled to vote.

It will also be necessary to replace 'sentence' at the start of para (b) with 'sentences'.

Delegation of directors' powers

Article 46: Committees of the board are essential for the operation of large companies but will rarely be required in the normal private company. Article 46 can therefore be excluded unless there is an intention to make use of committees.

Appointment and retirement of directors

Article 47: The rotation of directors is most unusual in any but listed companies. Accordingly, this article will almost invariably be appropriate but, if there is to be rotation, regard should be had to the comments in Chapter 2 on regs 73 to 80 of Table A and to arts 86 to 92 in Appendix E.

Article 48: The purpose of this article is to restore those parts of regs 78 and 79 of Table A which remain relevant despite the exclusion of the regulations relating to rotation.

Article 49: This statement is not required as directors do not have to hold qualification shares unless there is an express provision in the articles to the contrary (CA 1985, s 291). It may therefore be omitted.

Disqualification and removal of directors

Article 50: A range of amendments may be considered in relation to reg 81 of Table A and those set out in art 50 are generally appropriate. One significant alternative which should be considered separately for each company is whether the directors should be given the right, either by majority vote or by unanimous agreement, to remove a director of whom they do not approve. The argument against this approach is that it is really for the shareholders to decide who should be members of the board and a director who is unpopular with his colleagues may well be serving the interests of the company by making a nuisance of himself. The alternative approach takes the view that the directors need to work together as a team and that the involvement of someone who is seen as obstructive is detrimental to a small company.

If the articles provide that a director can be removed by a resolution of the other directors, para (e) of reg 81, either in the Table A form or as replaced by art 50, can be omitted and the following substituted for para (a) of art 50:

3.24 Removal of a director by board resolution

  (a) by replacing paragraph (c) with the following:
  '(c) he is required to resign by a resolution of the directors (the director concerned and, in his capacity as such, any alternate appointed by him being excluded from voting);'.

As mentioned in Chapter 2 in the commentary on reg 81 of Table A, the express exclusion from the vote of an alternate appointed by the director is not strictly necessary if reg 66 is amended to provide a general exclusion (see, for example, the second sentence of para (b) of art 43) but it is included here because it provides a clear reminder of the position.

Article 51: Section 293 of CA 1985 provides for an age limit for directors of 70 in public companies and those private companies which are subsidiaries of public companies. The requirement is subject to the provisions of the articles (s 293(7)) and, for private companies which are affected by s 293, art 51 is generally appropriate. For any other private company it may be omitted, but it is useful to include it in a standard form in case it is overlooked in those circumstances where it is important.

Remuneration of directors

Article 52: This may be omitted except for those rare private companies where there is the possibility of dispute as to the remuneration rights of executive and non-executive directors.

Directors' appointments and interests

Article 53: This article provides an improvement to reg 84 of Table A where there are executive directors whose membership of the board is not an important feature of their employment. The last sentence of reg 84 is deleted by art 47 as it is applicable only if the directors are subject to retirement by rotation.

Article 54: This retains the basic concept of reg 85 of Table A that a director may not, except in respect of transactions of the kind specified in the regulation, be a party to a transaction with the company. This is generally an important protection although, even in the absence of the regulation, it is clear that the fiduciary obligations of directors prevent them from profiting from such transactions. Nevertheless, the smaller private company may not need to impose a restriction through the articles and, in that case, the following article could replace art 54:

3.25   Director may be party to transaction in which company interested

> A director may be a party to, or otherwise interested in, any transaction or arrangement with the company or in which the company is otherwise interested.

If art 54 is not replaced, reg 86 of Table A should not be disapplied but should be amended as follows:

3.26   Director's notice as to membership of another company

> Regulation 86 is amended by relettering paragraph (b) as paragraph (c) and by adding the following after paragraph (a):
> '(b) a general notice to the directors that a director is a member of a specified company or firm and is to be regarded as interested in contracts which are made with the company or firm after the date of the notice shall be deemed to be a sufficient disclosure of his interest in relation to the contracts; and'.

Proceedings of directors

Article 55: It may be thought desirable that a director who is for a time outside the United Kingdom should not be required, as he is under reg 88 of Table A, to provide an address for giving notice of board meetings while he is abroad. An alternative arrangement is to allow the notice to be given to the usual address for receiving notices, unless a specific address is provided for the period of absence, and to leave it to the director to make arrangements for the notices to be forwarded to him. For this purpose a suitable form for para (a) of art 55 is:

3.27   Notice to director who is abroad

> Regulation 88 is amended by replacing 'It shall not be necessary to give notice of a meeting to a director who is absent from the United Kingdom' with:

'A director who is or is intending to be absent from the United Kingdom may request the secretary to give him notice of meetings at an address provided by him for that purpose. Notices of meetings of the directors shall be sent to him at that address but, if he does not provide an address for that period, notices of meetings shall be sent to him at the usual place to which they are sent. The notice calling a meeting of the directors need not be in writing.'.

Paragraph (b) of art 55 is required because the point is covered by para (b) of art 43. If art 43(b) is omitted, the last sentence of reg 88 should be retained.

Article 56: This provides that a director who is also an alternate may be counted as an extra person for each director he represents but that at least one other director must be present for the meeting to be quorate. In the smaller company, it may be acceptable for one director to constitute a quorum by virtue of his dual capacity. If this is intended, the second and third sentences of art 56 should be replaced with:

3.28   Counting alternate director for quorum

An alternate director, if his appointor is not present, is counted in the quorum and, if he is also a director, he is treated as two directors.

Article 57: It is unlikely that, in the absence of an express provision, a telephone discussion would be treated as a meeting. It is not clear how far the articles may go in providing otherwise but principle would suggest that the conversation must fulfil the characteristic of a physical meeting so that all participants can take part in the discussion. This requires that all the directors can hear each other speak and it is unlikely that it would be sufficient if one director merely relayed his views by telephone to another director who then recounted them to the other participants. Although the ability to have telephone meetings is in principle attractive, its real use is likely to be limited to those cases where it is not possible to assemble a quorum at a single location.

Article 58: It is only in the case of companies where there are different groups of shareholders who have their own representatives on the board that the powers of the chairman are likely to be important. For most private companies, the identity of the chairman will either be obvious or immaterial and in such cases this article may be omitted.

Article 59: For most private companies the protection given by disenfranchising directors in relation to resolutions on transactions in which they have an interest will not be required and art 59 will be appropriate.

Secretary

Article 60: As the secretary of a private company is unlikely to be a person occupying that position in an executive capacity, this article may be omitted.

Article 61: This provides a reminder of the statutory prohibition (CA 1985, s 283) against a single person acting both as sole director and secretary.

Minutes

Article 62: As explained in Chapter 2 in the commentary on reg 100 of Table A, CA 1985, s 382 goes further than is necessary in practice in specifying what minutes should be kept. The amendment effected by art 62 accords with what happens in practice.

The seal

Article 63: The purpose of this article is to reflect the current law (CA 1985, s 350) in relation to the obligation to have a common seal which has changed since Table A was introduced. The article is not technically required and may be omitted.

Dividends

Articles 64 to 66: Private companies are unlikely to pay numerous dividends and, unless the company has a large number of shareholders or is conducted on a particularly formal basis, these articles are not required.

Accounts

Article 67: This article merely states the law (CA 1985, s 222) and may be omitted.

Capitalisation of profits

Article 68: This is a drafting amendment which can safely be ignored.

Notices

Article 69: The first amendment to reg 111 is a consequence of the deleted words being effectively included in art 55.

Articles 70 and 71: These make administrative improvements to Table A and may be omitted.

Winding up

Article 72: In general, it will not be necessary to make this change to Table A as the procedures to be adopted on a winding up will rarely be of great concern to the shareholders establishing a private company.

Indemnity

Article 73: As a reminder of the arrangements which may be made in relation to directors, this article is worth including.

4

Articles of Association of Wholly-Owned Subsidiaries

Introduction

The articles of wholly-owned subsidiaries should satisfy a number of special features:

(1) The formalities, particularly in relation to those affecting the members, should be kept to a minimum. This is an acceptable principle as there are no minority interests which need protection but the directors remain subject to their normal fiduciary duties.

(2) The parent company will need to be able to appoint and remove directors without complications.

(3) The powers and discretions of the directors should be restricted in relation to those aspects which affect only the shareholders. An example is the power of directors to issue new shares which could result in a dilution of the parent company's ownership.

(4) The powers of the directors to appoint additional directors, and perhaps their right to nominate alternate directors, should be controlled.

The most extreme form of protection is to provide that the directors simply cannot carry out acts which are not part of their inherent power to manage the affairs of the company. The problem with this way of protecting the parent company is that whenever the parent company is in agreement that a prohibited act may be carried out, the articles will need to be formally amended to allow this.

A more moderate approach, which has the advantage of flexibility without putting the position of the parent company materially at risk, is to specify that the directors, before exercising the powers in question, must first obtain the approval of the parent company. If this approval has to be given formally, for example by means of written notice deposited at the registered office, there is danger that the procedure will be overlooked and the transaction will then be improper so far as the directors are concerned (third parties will generally be protected by CA 1985, s 35A). Conversely, if an informal approval will suffice, there is room for misunderstanding between the directors and the parent company as to whether consent has been given in a particular case.

Perhaps the most widely adopted technique is to rely on the probity and good sense of the directors and to impose no special restrictions on them. In such a case, it is important that the parent company has the ability to appoint directors whenever it wishes and—more importantly—can remove them without the delays involved in the procedures under CA 1985, s 303.

The articles in Appendix B adopt a restrictive approach and the commentary indicates the importance of the protection offered in each case and the variations that may be considered. Although the articles are drafted on the basis that the sole owner is a company, the same principles apply if the owner is an individual and the amendments which are appropriate if that is the case are covered in the commentary.

Single member companies

The long standing rule, which was contained in CA 1985, s 24, was that a company must have at least two members. This requirement is a tiresome formality in the case of a company which has a single owner and has been rendered pointless by the standard practice of the second shareholder being a bare nominee of the owner in respect of a small number of shares.

As a result of the passing of the Companies (Single Member Private Limited Companies) Regulations 1992 (SI No 1699) it is now possible for a private company to have a single member. Unfortunately, the details of the legislation, which has been implemented by making a number of amendments to CA 1985, are unhappily conceived. Certain formalities have to be observed which, if they are overlooked, can involve an offence:

(1) If the membership of a private company falls to one, an entry to that effect must be made in its register of members and another entry made if the membership increases (CA 1985, s 352A).

(2) If the sole member is also a director, a contract between him and the company which arises otherwise than in the ordinary course of business a phrase which can give rise to endless litigation must be recorded in writing or in the minutes of the first board meeting which follows the making of the contract (CA 1985, s 322B). Although this formality is most likely to be relevant if the sole shareholder is an individual, it could theoretically apply also to a wholly-owned subsidiary. This is because a 'director' is a person occupying the position of a director by whatever name called (CA 1985, s 741(1)) and a parent company which becomes too closely involved with its subsidiaries could be caught by the definition. In practice this is unlikely and a more real possibility is that the parent company is a 'shadow director', being a person in accordance with whose directions or instructions the directors are accustomed to act (s 741(2)). Section 322B does not apply, however, where the shareholder is a parent company which would be treated as a shadow director by reason 'only' that the directors are accustomed to act in accordance with its directions or instructions (s 741(3)). The use of the word 'only' is curious as it suggests that there can be other factors which make the parent company into a shadow director but, as the definition in s 741(2) is comprehensive, there are no other factors which are possible. In practice therefore it may be taken that the requirements of s 322B can be disregarded in relation to wholly-owned subsidiaries.

(3) If the sole member of a single member company takes a decision which may be taken in general meeting and has effect as if agreed in general meeting, he must either effect the decision by written resolution or provide the company with a written record of it (CA 1985, s 382B). It is not helpful for the section to refer to a decision which 'may' be taken in general meeting and it will not always be easy to determine whether a particular decision is caught. An example might be the payment of an interim dividend which could have been paid as a result of a shareholder resolution.

Because of these technical matters, the use of single member companies is less widespread than it might otherwise have been and many groups are continuing with the old practice of having one share held by a nominee (which might well be another member of the group) who signs a declaration of trust and a blank share transfer form. The articles in Appendix B nevertheless deal with the possibility that there is only one member.

Commentary on articles

The following comments apply to the articles set out in Appendix B. They should be read in conjunction with the relevant parts of Chapter 2.

Table A

Article 1: The definition of 'Parent Company' refers to the ownership (being the legal ownership determined from the register of members) of not less than ninety per cent of the issued shares in case there are two shareholders, one of which is a nominee for the parent. If advantage is taken of the ability to have a single shareholder, the definition may be replaced by:

4.1 Definition of 'parent company'

> 'Parent Company' means a company which is the registered holder of all the issued shares.

If the owner of the company is an individual, the phrase 'Parent Company' can be replaced by 'Owner'.

Article 2: Regulations 8 to 22 of Table A are excluded because the parent company will wish to avoid the possibility of its losing shares either as a result of the exercise of a lien on its shares or by the shares being forfeited. In the unlikely event of it being intended that shares should be issued partly paid, regs 12 to 17 could be retained as they relate merely to the making of calls.

The reason for omitting regs 24 to 26 is that the parent company cannot accept the possibility of a decision which it makes to transfer shares being frustrated by a refusal of the directors to approve the transfer.

Regulation 64 is omitted because the restriction on the number of directors is more satisfactorily covered by art 10.

Regulations 65 to 69 deal with the appointment of alternate directors. The parent company is very dependent on the quality of the directors it appoints and there is no reason why it should allow them to hand over their powers to appointees who might not be approved by the parent company. If directors have difficulty in attending meetings, the parent company should be capable of appointing additional directors so that problems do not arise.

As with most private companies, the provisions of regs 73 to 80, which relate to the rotation of directors, should be excluded.

Regulation 86 is omitted because it is made redundant by the amendment which art 29 makes to reg 85. Regulation 89, which relates to the quorum at meetings of the directors, is replaced by art 21.

It is the normal practice with private companies to exclude reg 94, which concerns the voting rights of directors when they have an interest in the subject matter of the resolution.

Share capital

Article 3: This may be omitted although it is customarily included.

Transfer of shares

Article 4: It would probably be sufficient to delete reg 24 of Table A if, as is suggested above, the parent company wishes to remove the directors' discretion to refuse transfers. It is nevertheless helpful to include art 4 so that the position is made quite clear.

General meetings

Article 5: It is unlikely that a parent company would ever need to requisition a meeting of the shareholders as it is able to appoint directors who will do this on its behalf. In principle, however, the directors should be obliged to respond to the requisition immediately rather than at the somewhat leisurely pace specified by Table A.

Notices of general meetings

Article 6: This makes two standard amendments to reg 38 (see Chapter 2, p 34).

Proceedings at general meetings

Article 7: This has the dual effect of providing that a representative of the parent company is both necessary and sufficient to constitute a quorum at general meetings. If there is only one member of the company, this article is not required as reg 40 of Table A is overridden (CA 1985, s 370A). It is, nevertheless, helpful to state the position expressly. If the articles are drafted on the basis that the sole shareholder may be an individual, who is defined as the 'Owner', art 7 should be replaced by:

> The Owner, if there is one, or his proxy or (if the Owner is a corporation) its representative constitutes a quorum at general meetings.

Article 8: As mentioned above, CA 1985, s 382B requires that a decision which a sole shareholder takes and which could have been taken in general meeting is recorded by written resolution or by a written record given to the company. The circumstances in which the section applies are not at all clear but the obligation is repeated in the articles by way of reminder.

Number of directors

Article 9: This is a standard replacement for reg 64 of Table A (see Chapter 2, p 51).

Alternate directors

Article 10: For the reasons discussed above, it is considered unnecessary for the directors of a wholly-owned subsidiary to have the right to appoint alternate directors. Article 10 makes this clear although a negative statement is not strictly required as directors do not have an intrinsic power to appoint alternates. The article also makes consequential changes to Table A. If the ability to appoint alternates is retained, the parent company should have a right of veto over the appointees. A suitable article for this purpose is the following:

4.2 Approval of parent company required in relation to alternate director

> Subject to his obtaining the prior approval of the Parent Company (if there is one), a director, other than an alternate director, may appoint any person to be an alternate director and may terminate the appointment. An alternate director ceases to be an alternate for his appointor when his appointor ceases to be a director.

Appointment and retirement of directors

Article 11: This confirms the effect of excluding regs 73 to 80 of Table A.

Article 12: One of the most important protections that can be provided for the parent company is a simple and immediate procedure enabling it to appoint directors. Less important is to exclude the power of the directors to appoint additional directors which is given by reg 79 of Table A. If that right is to be retained, reg 79 should not be restored—as it deals also with the effects of the rotation of directors—but art 12 should be amended by deleting '(if there is no Parent Company)'.

Article 13: This is included by way of reminder but, as a share qualification is required only if the articles expressly so provide, it may be omitted.

Disqualification and removal of directors

Article 14: The important amendment to reg 81 of Table A is that which enables the parent company to remove a director by giving notice to the company. The other amendment to reg 81, which is contained in para (a), clarifies the resignation procedure but may be omitted.

Article 15: Section 293 of CA 1985 provides an age limit for directors which may be overridden by the articles. The section does not apply to private companies unless they are subsidiaries of public companies. Accordingly, art 15 is not required if the parent company is not a public company but it is easier to treat this as a standard article so that it is not overlooked when it does matter.

Directors' appointments and interests

Article 16: The parent company will wish to retain the right to veto the appointment of executive directors. It would be perfectly possible for the parent company to rely on the directors to obtain approval before making an appointment without making a specific provision in the articles but art 16 reduces the chance of a misunderstanding. There is, however, a disadvantage to art 16 in that the obligation—as opposed to the commercial need—to obtain parent company approval may be overlooked. It is a matter for decision in relation to each company as to whether it is better on balance to include or omit art 16.

Article 17: Regulation 85 of Table A permits a director to enjoy a benefit from transactions in which he is interested provided that he has disclosed his interest. The amendment effected by art 17 is to substitute for that requirement an obligation to obtain the approval of the parent company. It should be noted that this does not—and, indeed, cannot—relieve the director from his statutory obligation to disclose his interest under CA 1985, s 317.

Directors' gratuities and pensions

Article 18: The effect of art 18 is to make it necessary for the directors to obtain the approval of the parent company before providing pension benefits and the like for directors. In the case of most groups of companies, executive directors will be members of the group pension scheme and the need for parent company approval is likely to be minimal. The article does prevent the directors setting up a special scheme for themselves and is therefore on balance worth including in the articles.

Proceedings of directors

Article 19: The wording of this article is slightly preferable to that of reg 89 of Table A which it replaces. If the power to appoint alternate directors is retained, the following sentences may be added to the article:

4.3 Alternate director counted in quorum

> An alternate director, if his appointor is not present, is counted in the quorum. If he is also a director, he is treated as two directors.

Article 20: This is the standard addition to all articles where it is intended to allow board meetings to be held by telephone (see also the comments in Chapter 3 on Appendix A, art 57).

Article 21: Although the chairman's powers are not of great significance in the case of wholly-owned subsidiary companies, the parent company necessarily has to repose a considerable degree of trust in the directors and might reasonably look upon the chairman as being a person to set, and ensure compliance with, the appropriate standards. For this reason, the parent company is given the ability by art 21 to ensure that the chairman is approved by it.

Article 22: This article provides the standard exclusion of the voting restrictions imposed by reg 94 of Table A in relation to directors who have an interest in the subject matter of a resolution.

Minutes

Article 23: As explained in the commentary on reg 100 of Table A in Chapter 2, the obligation to keep records which is imposed by that regulation is wider than is required by statute (CA 1985, s 382) and is probably often not observed in practice. Article 23 makes a practical change which accords with the statutory duty.

Dividends

Article 24: The payment of final dividends requires shareholder approval (Table A, reg 102) and the objective of art 24 is to subject interim dividends to the same control. The directors would otherwise have the ability to avoid the need to obtain parent company approval by declaring interim rather than final dividends and, although the parent company would receive the dividends, it is contrary to principle for the distinction to exist.

Accounts

Article 25: Although members do not normally have the right to inspect the company's books, there is no reason to prevent a parent company from having a right of inspection and art 25 makes an alteration to permit this.

Notices

Article 26: As mentioned above, it is desirable that the affairs of a wholly-owned subsidiary can be conducted with the minimum degree of formality. A useful administrative facility is to be able to give notices by fax and this is dealt with by art 26.

Indemnity

Article 27: This is a standard amendment to reg 118 of Table A and is discussed in Chapter 2.

5

Joint Venture Companies

Introduction

Joint ventures can take many forms but, when considering the contents of their articles, they fall into two broad categories. The first of these is the deadlock company which provides for an equality of power as between the various parties. The second type allows one party to have a dominant position but builds in substantial protection for the minority participant.

Deadlock companies

General

A true deadlock company is one where there is a number of shareholders who, whilst perhaps having different interests in the income or capital, enjoy equal degrees of control. Although there are generally only two participants, there may in certain cases be a greater number but the deadlock concept becomes unduly cumbersome if there are more than three or four groups with equal rights of control and veto.

A distinction may be drawn between those deadlock companies where each participant has the same degree of control as the others and those where the participants include one or more groups of investors. In the latter case, it may well be necessary to include in the articles procedures for deciding how the investors who make up a single group determine as between themselves the way in which they are to exercise the rights given to them as a group. This is discussed further in relation to the articles set out in Appendix C.

137

It is usual in the case of deadlock joint ventures for the parties to enter into a joint venture agreement and it is often a matter of individual preference to decide what provisions should appear in the agreement and which should be exclusively, or perhaps additionally, contained in the articles. The advantage of the agreement is that it is a private document and is therefore a suitable means of dealing with confidential matters. It is also easier to amend an agreement than it is to alter articles of association—although this may be thought to be a disadvantage. Articles have the benefit of binding the members for the time being and they also provide a mechanism for restricting the freedom of the directors, who will not normally be parties to and bound by the joint venture agreement.

Principles underlying deadlock articles

The broad principles adopted by deadlock articles are as follows:
(1) The shares will be divided into different classes—one for each group of shareholders.
(2) These shares will commonly be designated as 'A' shares or 'B' shares, etc. If the shares confer equal rights to dividends and capital, they will be expressed to rank *pari passu* except in the respects specifically set out in the articles. If the shareholders have different economic entitlements, they can hold different numbers of shares in each class; although the shares rank *pari passu* for dividends and capital distributions, the shareholders' participations will be proportionate to the numbers of shares in the respective classes. This formulation is adopted in Appendix C. Alternatively, the different economic interests can be achieved by having equal numbers of shares of the various classes and by providing that they confer different dividend and capital rights.
(3) At general meetings, the quorum will be at least one member holding shares of each class. If there are only two classes of shareholders, one vote will be conferred by each class of shares, regardless of how many shares there are in the class. A more complicated arrangement is required if there are more than two classes of shareholders as otherwise members in different classes could combine together to outvote the other participants. One way of dealing with this is to provide that on a vote each member voting in favour of the resolution has a number of votes equal to the number of members voting against the resolution,

and vice versa. The chairman of the meeting, in each case, will not have a casting vote. Any resolution of the shareholders will thus require unanimous approval.

(4) Each class of shares will confer the right to appoint and remove one or more directors. These directors are usually categorised with the same letter as the class of shares by which they are appointed so that, for example, the 'A' shares will entitle the holders to appoint one or more 'A' directors.

(5) The provisions applicable to shareholders' meetings will be mirrored in relation to meetings of the directors and of committees of the directors. The quorum will be a director of each category, each of them will need to vote in favour of a resolution if it is to be passed and the chairman will not have a casting vote. This will have the essential result that any action of the board will need the support of all parties and, conversely, that any party will have a veto over action by the company and will be able to bring about a deadlock. Resolving the problem which arises if there is a deadlock is an area where the shareholders' agreement and certain of the provisions of the articles can make a significant contribution.

From the above summary it will be seen that a deadlock structure operates by the negative power of each participant, either directly as a shareholder or through its nominated directors, to veto or prevent action and not by giving the parties the ability to compel any action. It may be possible through the shareholders' agreement to impose some positive obligations on the participants—such as a duty to act in good faith when vetoing actions which are in accordance with the agreed objectives of the venture or by requiring a participant who prevents action to spell out the reason for doing so. It is, however, difficult to achieve any positive duties through the articles.

Matters requiring shareholder approval

Whilst the special terms described above will generally provide sufficient assurance that no decision can be made by the board without the approval of each shareholder, it nevertheless has to be borne in mind that directors, even though nominated by particular shareholders, must conduct themselves in accordance with their fiduciary duties. They cannot simply vote in accordance with the interests of the party they represent but must have regard to the interests of the company as a whole (*Percival v Wright*

[1902] 2 Ch 421), failing which they may be liable in negligence or for breach of duty (*Scottish Co-operative Wholesale Society Ltd v Meyer and Another* [1959] AC 324). Furthermore, directors may not pass confidential information to their appointors.

If this is a matter of concern, the articles should specify those matters of particular significance which cannot be implemented without the approval of a special resolution. Shareholders, unlike directors, are entitled to be wholly selfish in deciding how to vote and need have no regard to the interests of the company or of the other shareholders. Examples of the matters which might be the subject of this kind of arrangement are:

    (a) making substantial disposals of the company's assets;

    (b) engaging or dismissing senior employees;

    (c) incurring significant capital expenditure;

    (d) carrying out transactions with associates of shareholders.

An alternative way to give this additional protection is to provide that the passing of a resolution to carry out any of the specified transactions constitutes a variation of the class rights of each of the classes of shares and accordingly requires approval at separate class meetings. Wording which achieves this alternative is as follows:

5.1 Transactions varying class rights

> The rights attached to the A Shares and to the B Shares are deemed to be varied by any of the following:
> [matters such as those listed above would then be set out].

Terminating the venture

One of the most difficult areas in relation to a deadlock venture is what to do when a deadlock arises which cannot be resolved. If the effect is that board meetings cannot be held as they are always inquorate or decisions are always vetoed, it is open to any member to apply to the court for a winding-up order under the Insolvency Act 1986, s 122. The court is likely to order a winding-up under s 122(1)(g) on the ground that it is just and equitable to do so if the shareholders fall into equally divided groups such that the business of the company can no longer be effectively carried on (*Re Yenidje Tobacco Co Ltd* [1916] 2 Ch 426).

The sanction of a forced liquidation of the company is generally so severe and the effects are likely to be so disadvantageous to all the members that there will be considerable pressure on the parties to reach a compromise. It is therefore often suggested that there is no need for the documentation to cover what should happen when there is a deadlock.

Nevertheless, in preparing a joint venture agreement and the articles of a joint venture company, an attempt should generally be made to provide an alternative mechanism for dealing with a deadlock that reaches the stage of being apparently permanent. This could, for example, be evidenced by three or four successive board meetings being abandoned because they are inquorate or by a specific resolution being the subject of a deadlock vote at a number of board meetings.

A favourite mechanism for dealing with a deadlock is an arrangement along the lines of Appendix C, art 11, which is often called the 'Texas option' (also 'Russian roulette' or 'Mexican shoot out'). This works without undue complication only if there are two shareholders. Although variations exist, the basic concept is that either shareholder may at any time (perhaps after the expiry of an initial period) serve a notice on the other shareholder specifying a price for the shares. The recipient of the notice then has a choice: it must either purchase the first shareholder's shares for the specified price or sell its own shares for that price. The theory is that the party initiating the disposal procedure has to be very cautious in specifying the price of the shares as it does not know at that stage whether it will end up being a buyer or a seller. There are, however, circumstances which can render the underlying theory unsound. In particular, it will not work fairly if one of the shareholders has greater financial resource than the other. In such a case, the stronger shareholder will run little risk in specifying a low price as it is much more likely to pick up a bargain than to find itself a forced seller at an unattractive price. In other cases, the value of the shares may differ considerably for the two shareholders and a shareholder who has a particularly strong interest in retaining its shareholding may find itself almost in a position of being blackmailed. Finally, one of the shareholders may, as a result of closer involvement in the running of the company, have confidential information which is relevant in valuing the shares but is not available to the other shareholder.

Another variation, which does not meet the difficulties described above but which may go some way to prevent the purchaser having to pay a price totally unrelated to value, is to require each shareholder to specify a price. The shares are then independently valued and the party whose nominated price is the closer to the valuation has the right either to buy the other shares or to sell its own shares at the price it specified (see comments on art 11).

It is probable that in practice the full rigour of these clauses rarely comes into operation and the parties will somehow negotiate a settlement. The negotiating process is, however, likely to be assisted if the articles of the joint venture company or the shareholders' agreement provide an exit mechanism which is rather more realistic than the possibility of a compulsory liquidation.

Commentary on deadlock articles

Appendix C contains a form of deadlock articles which assumes that there are two groups of shareholders, each comprising a number of participants. The principles underlying the articles, which are discussed below, enable the form to be readily adapted where there are more than two shareholder groups. Many of the articles are also discussed in Chapters 2 and 3 and these should be referred to for further details.

Article 1
Although it is possible to adopt long form articles and to disapply Table A in its entirety, it is more usual to amend Table A to deal with the appropriate variations. The articles set out in Appendix C exclude a number of Table A regulations as follows:

Regulation 17: this gives the directors power, on the issue of shares, to arrange for calls to differ as to the amount called or to vary the time for payment as between different shareholders. Where the articles provide for a strict deadlock at board level it is not essential that this power should be excluded, as it will not be capable of being exercised without the approval of all the directors, but to do so makes the position completely clear.

Regulation 24: Table A gives the directors a power to reject a transfer of partly-paid shares in favour of a transferee of whom they do not approve. This discretion is, however, both too wide in relation to partly-paid shares and too narrow for other shares for many companies and, as discussed in Chapter 3, is often replaced by comprehensive pre-emption rights. In the case of a deadlock company, it is invariably desirable to have a full pre-emption clause and the details are discussed below in relation to arts 8, 9 and 10.

Regulation 26: this entitles the directors to suspend the registration of transfers for periods of up to 30 days. Although the deadlock provisions will ensure that this right is not exercised unless there is unanimity amongst the different classes of directors, the regulation is excluded on the basis that closing the register will never be of practical importance.

Regulation 39: the effect of this regulation is that the accidental omission to give notice of a meeting to a member or the non-receipt of the notice does not invalidate the meeting. Whilst it may be appropriate to exclude this regulation in the case of minority protection articles, it is less necessary, although not unreasonable, to do so in the case of a deadlock company. The absence of a member, arising, for example, because it does not know the meeting is being held, will render it inquorate unless there are other members of the same class who do attend. The regulation will, however, have real significance if the shareholders' agreement or the articles impose a sanction on a member who causes a meeting to be inquorate by failing to attend.

Regulation 40: this provides that the quorum at general meetings is two and must be replaced by a specific quorum article such as art 17.

Regulation 41: another provision relating to the quorum at meetings, which will be replaced by a more appropriate article along the lines of art 18.

Regulation 50: the chairman's casting vote will not apply. This can be achieved either by excluding reg 50 (often accompanied by an express statement that the chairman does not have a casting vote) or, less usually, by amending the regulation by inserting 'not' before the words 'be entitled to a casting vote'.

Regulation 54: the standard voting rights of one vote per share will be replaced by special class rights.

Regulation 64: this provides that, unless otherwise determined by ordinary resolution, the minimum number of directors should be two and there should be no maximum. Although this is generally satisfactory, it is customary to have a somewhat different provision for the reasons discussed below in relation to art 22.

Regulation 65: this deals with the appointment of alternate directors. Because of the need to specify carefully how the members of the board are appointed, so as to maintain a full deadlock, it is usual to replace this regulation with one which is more precisely applicable.

Regulations 73 to 80: all the regulations of Table A dealing with the rotation of directors will be omitted. It will rarely be appropriate in this kind of company to have a system in place which requires the automatic rotation of the directors.

Regulation 81(e): reg 81, which deals with special cases in which directors vacate their office, is generally acceptable, apart perhaps from para (e) which permits the removal from office of a director who fails to attend board meetings for six consecutive months. The power of removal can be exercised only by a resolution of the directors and, as the voting rights mean that a resolution cannot be passed unless both groups of directors are in favour, in practice it cannot be used to upset the board balance. Nevertheless, it is contrary in principle to the way in which membership of the board should be determined and its removal avoids any doubt as to the position.

Regulation 86: the exclusion of this regulation follows from the amendment to reg 85 in relation to the obligation of the directors to give notice of their interests.

Regulations 88 to 91: this group of regulations deals with the proceedings of directors, including quorum requirements, voting rights and the chairman's casting vote. They are replaced by the specific provisions of art 34 onwards.

Regulation 94: for a discussion of this see Chapter 2 p 77. It is usual to replace the regulation in almost all private company articles and not especially in relation to deadlock companies.

Regulation 95: the provisions of Table A relating to the position of directors who have an interest in the subject matter of a resolution and the numbers required to make a quorum are inappropriate and are replaced by detailed provisions such as art 36 in Appendix C.

Regulation 96: this mainly relates to restrictions on the rights of directors to vote on resolutions in which they have an interest and, because of the exclusion of reg 94, is in that respect redundant. It could, however, also apply to any other circumstances whereby the directors may be prevented from voting, such as in relation to Deadlock Business. It is inappropriate for these special arrangements to be capable of being suspended by ordinary resolution even though the deadlock voting structure effectively requires that there has to be unanimity if a resolution of the shareholders is to be passed.

Regulation 97: this is another provision dealing with the voting rights of directors and is inappropriate to companies where the restrictions of reg 94 are omitted.

Regulation 98: in most private companies, and in relation to deadlock companies in particular, it is not intended that the chairman should have the power to determine whether directors can vote on a particular resolution.

In addition, it is quite common to find other regulations being omitted or varied in joint venture articles:

Regulation 2: this provides that shares may be issued with such rights as the company by ordinary resolution determines. It is sometimes amended so that a special resolution is required to attribute particular rights to shares. In a true deadlock company this is unnecessary as it will be as impossible to pass an ordinary resolution without the approval of both groups of shareholders as it is to pass a special resolution. The amendment is more appropriate for articles providing protection for minority shareholders and this is considered further in the part of this chapter dealing with such articles.

Regulation 9: this permits the directors to determine the procedure for selling shares on which the company has a lien. In the case of a deadlock company it will not be possible for one group to impose any particular procedure on the other but it may be appropriate to restrict the freedom of the directors in cases where full minority rights are included. In particular, the regulation could be amended by requiring the pre-emption provisions to be observed; suitable wording would be as follows:

5.2 Procedure for selling lien shares

Regulation 9 is amended by deleting 'in such manner as the directors determine' and by adding at the end the following sentence:
'A sale shall be effected by the directors giving a Transfer Notice in respect of the shares without specifying an Offer Price.'.

Regulation 20: as with reg 9, the ability of the directors to sell forfeited shares can be restricted by applying the pre-emption provisions. A suitable article for this purpose, which will replace reg 20 in its entirety, is the following:

5.3 Procedure for selling forfeited shares

Subject to the provisions of the Act, a forfeited share may be sold or re-allotted. A sale shall be effected by the directors giving a Transfer Notice in respect of the share without specifying an Offer Price. The share may be re-allotted in accordance with the provisions of article 6(c).

Regulation 30: this permits a person becoming entitled to shares as a result of the death or bankruptcy of a member to elect either to be registered as the holder of the shares or to transfer the shares to another person. In either case, it is treated as if he was proposing to transfer the shares and any restrictions in relation to share transfers come into operation. The following amendments to this may be appropriate:

(1) a time limit could be imposed within which the person entitled to the shares must make his election. Failure to make a choice within that time could be treated as an election to transfer to a third party so that the pre-emption provisions in the articles then come into play. An appropriate article for this purpose is the following:

5.4   Time limit for election to be registered following transmission

Regulation 30 is amended by adding at the end the following sentence:
'If the person entitled to the share does not make an election, the directors may give him notice requiring him to make the election and, if he fails to do so within 90 days, he shall be deemed to have given a Transfer Notice to the company in respect of the share and not to have specified an Offer Price.'.

(2) an election to be registered as the holder of the shares could be exempted from the transfer rules which would apply only if the election was to transfer to a new shareholder.
(3) an election to transfer to a 'Permitted Transferee' (such as a relative of the original holder) could be permitted without the pre-emption procedure being involved. An article covering paras (2) and (3) is the following:

5.5   Election by successor in relation to registration of transmission shares

Regulation 30 is amended by replacing the last sentence with the following:
'If the person entitled elects to be registered as the holder of the share or elects that a person who would have been a Permitted Transferee of the deceased or bankrupt member is registered as the transferee, the directors shall comply with the election and make the appropriate entries in the register of members. In any other case, article 8 shall apply to the notice or instrument of transfer as if it were an instrument

of transfer executed by the member and his death or bankruptcy had not occurred.'.

Regulation 32: this is similar to reg 2 and permits changes in the share capital to be effected by ordinary resolution. As with reg 2, the requirement is sometimes amended to a special resolution but this change is more relevant for minority protection articles than for deadlock companies.

Regulation 59: this permits a member to appoint more than one proxy to attend a meeting. It is an unnecessary facility for private companies but it can do no harm in practice. It is a matter of taste whether to exclude the regulation but, if it is omitted, the first sentence, which states that on a poll votes may be given either personally or by proxy, should either be retained or should be duplicated (see Appendix A, art 39).

Article 2

Table A contains a number of useful definitions which are reviewed in Chapter 2 and includes the defined terms that are relevant in relation to the pre-emption provisions in art 8. The new definitions which appear in art 2 will be discussed in relation to the articles in which they appear. Two of the defined terms, however, have particular significance, namely Deadlock Business and Passive Member.

The need for these arises from a major difficulty which arises from the concept that, in a deadlock company, no action can be taken by the company without the agreement of both classes of shareholders. The effect of this is to enable one of the shareholders who is in default in respect of some obligation to prevent the company taking steps to enforce performance either by voting against any action or, more simply, by ensuring that the meeting considering what action to take is rendered inquorate.

The term Deadlock Business is used to describe actions which it is in the interests of the company to take even without the co-operation of the member who is adversely affected by the action, designated in art 2 as the Passive Member. The definition covers the following:

(1) Enforcing a lien on shares. This is particularly significant if the lien conferred by Table A in relation to outstanding sales is extended to all sums owing by the shareholder to the company. The Passive Member, who is prevented from vetoing the necessary action, is the holder of the shares on which the lien is

to be enforced. To avoid unfairness, the definition requires that there must be no discrimination in relation to the shares in respect of which the enforcement proceedings are carried out.

(2) Forfeiting a share on which calls remain unpaid. The same principles apply as in relation to liens. The declaration under reg 22 which is referred to in paragraph (b) of the definition is one made by a director and the secretary that the share has been forfeited. This declaration is conclusive evidence of the facts stated in it.

(3) Compliance with the article dealing with compulsory transfers following the occurrence of a 'relevant event'. A member should not be able to frustrate its operation by persuading its nominated directors to veto enforcement action.

(4) Although deadlock articles can effectively prevent board decisions being taken without the approval of all members, they cannot restrict the ostensible authority which an executive director has to bind the company. Furthermore, CA 1985, s 35A relieves a third party from being affected by restrictions placed by the articles on the powers of the directors. To try to ensure that directors do not override the deadlock concept by entering into unauthorised transactions, the articles in Appendix C impose two sanctions. The first is to give to the directors of the other class the ability to take action against the director for exceeding his authority; this is achieved by making the decision to take action one of those areas where only the directors of the other class can vote. The second sanction is to exclude the director from the benefit of the indemnity conferred by art 48.

(5) Taking action against a member, or third parties associated with it, in relation to transactions entered into between the company and the member or its associates. In an ideal joint venture, either care will be taken that there is no trading activity between the company and any of the joint venturers or, alternatively, the joint venture agreement will identify the areas where this type of activity is expected and set out a code for ensuring that the relationships are conducted at arm's length. One type of transaction which occurs very commonly is the financing of the company. The joint venture agreement will, in many cases, provide that further funds are to be provided by the participants in proportion to their initial

commitments. Failure by one party to meet its share would entitle the other participant to take enforcement action under the agreement. A more suitable remedy will, in many cases, be a direct claim by the company. This will require not only that the company is a party to the joint venture agreement—which is not unusual—but also that the party who is in default cannot take advantage of the deadlock structure to prevent the company making the claim.

(6) Implementing the pre-emption rights where all or a majority of the shares of one class are transferred to the holders of the other class. The transferor, who is deemed to be the Passive Member, may have little interest in ensuring that the formalities of the transfer are completed once it has handed over the share transfer form and received payment for its shares.

(7) Approving transfers by a member, who is deemed to be the Active Member, to relatives or members of the same group of companies who are Permitted Transferees. The Passive Member should not be able to frustrate the registration of the share transfers unless requests made to the transferor to provide evidence that the transferee meets the criteria of a Permitted Transferee remain outstanding.

The list of matters suggested for inclusion in Deadlock Business may not be suitable for every case and the definition will need to be examined critically to see if anything should be omitted or whether other items should be added.

Article 4

As indicated above, the share capital is divided into two classes of shares on the assumption that there are two groups of shareholders. If there were more, further classes could be created. The numbers of shares in each class will affect dividend rights and entitlements to capital distributions but not the rights which create equality of control for each class. Although art 4 treats the different classes as ranking *pari passu* except where specifically provided to the contrary, this need not be the case if, for example, it is intended to give one class priority in respect of dividend entitlement.

Article 5

A share warrant is a bearer document which entitles the holder to the shares represented by the warrant and the entitlement is transferred by delivery of the warrant to the transferee. CA 1985, s 188 permits a limited company, which is authorised by its articles, to issue warrants.

In the case of a joint venture company, it is generally important that the identity of the members is known and warrants will not normally be acceptable. Although it is not technically necessary to exclude power to issue warrants—as power will not exist unless expressly given—art 5 is included by way of reminder.

Article 6

This largely follows the standard article dealing with the power of the directors to issue new shares and reference should be made to the discussions in Chapters 2 and 6. The only special feature is at the end of para (c) which provides that the new shares to each member are to be designated as the same class as the shares already held by it.

Article 7

The wording of this article is the normal form for private companies and extends the company's lien to cover not only sums due on calls but also any indebtedness of the member to the company. If a lien arises, the member who holds the shares concerned will be able, in the absence of suitable provisions in the articles, to veto any action to enforce the lien. Accordingly, the term Deadlock Business which is defined in art 2 includes the taking of steps to enforce a lien. To ensure that the concept of Deadlock Business is not used to enforce a lien against one member when there are outstanding liens on other shares, the definition requires that the proposed action must also be taken on all other shares on which a lien exists.

An alternative way of dealing with the point is to add the following to art 7:

5.6   Resolution to enforce lien

> On a resolution to determine whether to exercise a lien on a share and on any matter concerning the exercise, the directors appointed by the holders of the shares of the same class as the shares on which the lien exists shall be deemed to have voted in the same way as the other directors, regardless of how they actually voted.

It should be noted that the point does not have practical significance if reg 9 of Table A is not excluded, since that gives rise to liens only in relation to outstanding calls and partly-paid shares are unusual in joint ventures. The importance of the lien arises because of the form of art 7 which entitles the company to a lien for all indebtedness of the member.

Article 8

The pre-emption rights are largely the same as those discussed in Chapter 3 and reference should be made to that chapter for detailed comments. The article does, however, cover in much greater detail the different results which can arise from the pre-emption procedure.

If, for example, two A shareholders, A1 and A2, each have 25 A shares and two B shareholders, B1 and B2, each have 25 B shares, some of the possibilities which can arise if A1 wishes to sell his shares are as follows. The other shareholders will each be offered nine shares (as a result of rounding upwards). If A1 names an offer price, A2 and B1 each offer to buy 15 shares at the offer price and B2 offers to buy five shares but does not accept the offer price, the allocation should be as follows. A1, being a member of the same class, is allocated in full; B1 receives the remaining ten shares; and B2, having rejected the offer price, receives none.

If, in the above example, B1 had also rejected the offer price, the directors would have been required to determine the fair price. On the assumption that there is no exercise of withdrawal rights following the determination, A1 will be allocated its 15 shares at the fair price and the remaining ten shares will be allocated to B1 and B2 in the proportions of 9:5 (being in proportion to the lesser of their original allocations and their applications). This will give rise to fractions which will be allocated by the drawing of lots.

These examples are not comprehensive and, in many cases (as, for example, where there is only one holder of shares of a class) it may not be necessary to cover all the variations dealt with in art 8.

The only other matters requiring special mention are the following:

Paragraph (a): it is in general reasonable to require a joint venturer who wishes to leave to offer all its shares for sale even if it would prefer to retain some of them. Accordingly the transfer notice is treated as an offer of all the vendor's shares. The vendor is given a choice as to whether to specify a third party purchaser and an offer price.

Paragraph (b): if the vendor chooses not to specify an offer price, the directors immediately obtain a valuation which is paid for by the vendor (para (j)).

Paragraph (c): the article proceeds on the basis that the shares are offered to all members in proportion to their existing shareholdings. An alternative, lengthier procedure, which may be appropriate if more than one person holds shares of each class, is to offer the shares first to the members holding shares of the same class as the offered shares. Any unsold shares would then be offered to the holders of the other class.

Paragraph (p): if shares of one class are acquired by the holder of shares of the other class, the shares are automatically re-designated, unless the result would be that all the issued shares would be of a single class.

Article 9

The concept underlying this article is that, if something occurs in relation to a member which makes the continuation of the joint venture unrealistic, the member who has not caused the problem should have an opportunity to buy the shares of the other member. The obvious circumstances relate to the insolvency of a member and there is not likely to be any disagreement that the solvent member should have the right to acquire the insolvent member's shares at a fair price. There may, however, be some disagreement as to the fairness of the provisions of para (b)(iii) of this article. The intention is to impose a sanction on a shareholder who frustrates the continuing business of the company by causing a number of successive shareholders' meetings to be inquorate or by allowing its nominated directors to prevent board meetings being held by failing to attend. The principle is also extended to a member who tries to circumvent the pre-emption rules although, as any such attempt is unlikely to be effective in practice, the sanction will hardly be required.

For the article to work properly, there must be a reasonably well defined moment which starts the pre-emption procedure. Paragraph (c) entitles the directors nominated by the holders of the shares of the other class to require the giving to them of information which will enable them to determine whether a relevant event has occurred.

Article 10

This is largely standard form and is discussed in Chapter 3. An additional circumstance in which transfers can be made freely is in para (vi) of art 10(a). This allows the transfers of shares amongst holders of the same class.

Paragraph (iv) permits transfers to an 'associated party' of a shareholder. This term is defined in art 2(a), as extended by art 2(b), but an alternative formulation is the definition contained in CA 1985, s 346.

This is widely drawn and includes the member's spouse and children and companies in which they hold at least 20 per cent of the issued equity or voting capital. If this definition is adopted, the appropriate wording to insert in the definition of 'Associated Party' in art 2(a) is in relation to a member, a person who, if he were a director, would be connected with him under s 346 of the Act,'.

As explained in Chapter 3 a problem can arise if a transfer is made to an associate of the transferor, thereby avoiding the pre-emption procedure, and the relationship between the transferor and the transferee, which enabled the transfer to be made, ceases to exist. Article 10 provides a very rigorous sanction which requires the transferee in that event to offer to sell its shares at their fair price under the pre-emption article. The obligation can in practice be overcome if the transferee re-transfers the shares to its transferor before the change in their relationship takes effect, thereby restoring the original shareholdings. An alternative way to deal with the point in this article is to require that the re-transfer is carried out but, in the final analysis, this is not significantly different as a sanction will be needed if the obligation is simply ignored.

Article 11

This article is intended to provide a possible means of resolving a deadlock in the manner described above in relation to the termination of joint ventures. The features of the article are as follows:

(1) The procedure can be initiated by any shareholder once a preliminary period has expired. The appropriateness of having a period, and if there is one its length, will depend upon the particular circumstances of each joint venture. The reason for having a period at all is to give the venture time to get off the ground before the parties have a right to bring it to an end.

(2) The party starting the process should at least hold a majority of the shares of one class and should be able, if required to do so, to sell or procure the sale of all the shares of the class.

(3) If the member initiating the process does not hold all the shares of one class, the members to whom the offer is made should have the right to elect either to take just the shares that the initiator holds or to require that all the shares of the class are made available for purchase.

(4) The arrangement does not work easily if there is more than one member of each class. The precedent contemplates that the recipients of the offer decide jointly how to act. If there is

a real possibility of the members of the class giving different responses to the offer made to them, the article will need to contain a provision for resolving the disagreement. One possible way would be to provide that, in the event of a disagreement, the offerees should be treated as agreeing to sell their shares unless the member wishing to buy the shares offered also buys the shares of its fellow class member. Suitable wording would be as follows:

If there is more than one Recipient Member and they do not agree whether to purchase shares from or to sell shares to the Majority Member, they shall be deemed to have agreed to sell their shares.

(5) To minimise repetition, the mechanical elements of art 8 are adopted by reference. It would, of course, be perfectly acceptable to set these out at length in this article.

As mentioned above, an alternative approach is to require both shareholders to state a price which is then compared with the fair value. An article dealing with this is the following:

5.7 Termination of joint venture with all shareholders specifying share price

(a) Any member may, after the expiration of a period of at least three years from the date of the adoption of these articles, give notice to the directors that it wishes the provisions of this article to be activated.
(b) The directors shall, within 14 days of the receipt of the notice, give notice to all the members requiring them, within a period of 28 days, to give notice to the company stating a price for each of the shares. A member who fails to comply with the notice shall be deemed to have stated a price which differed from the fair value to a greater extent than the price stated by the other members.
(c) The directors shall instruct the auditors to determine the value of all the shares on the basis of the value of the company and any subsidiaries as going concerns and to specify the fair value of each share, being an amount equal to the value of the company and its subsidiaries as determined by them divided by the number of shares in issue. In making their determination the auditors shall be acting as independent experts and not as arbitrators and the determination shall, in the absence of manifest error, be conclusive. The fees and expenses of the auditors shall be borne by the members in proportion to their holdings of shares.
(d) The member who has stated the price which is closest to the fair value shall be entitled, at its discretion, to require the other

shareholders either to sell their shares or to buy its shares at a price for each share equal to the price stated by it. The members shall be required to complete the sales and purchases within 28 days of the auditors completing their determination of the fair value and the provisions of article 8 shall apply for implementing the transactions as if the price stated were the Offer Price and the shares to be purchased were the Specified Shares.

Article 12
This repeats those parts of reg 24 which are not concerned with the discretion of the directors to refuse to register share transfers.

Article 13
The directors have a residual right to refuse transfers under art 12 and the purpose of this amendment is to ensure that notice of refusal is given promptly. The point is, however, largely theoretical as the shareholder will know from its nominated directors if a transfer has been rejected.

Article 14
Section 368 of CA 1985 entitles members holding not less than one-tenth of the voting share capital to requisition an extraordinary general meeting. If the directors do not convene the meeting within 21 days, the requisitionists may do so themselves. As a result of an amendment to s 368 made by CA 1989, the directors are deemed not to have convened the meeting if it is convened for a date more than 28 days after the date of the notice which convenes it.

Regulation 37 requires the directors to convene the meeting for a date which is not later than eight weeks after receipt of the requisition. Although in the case of a deadlock company it is most unlikely that a shareholder will need to resort to requisitioning a meeting or will benefit from doing so, it would nevertheless seem reasonable to reduce the period within which the meeting must be held.

Articles 15 and 16
These are routine provisions which are discussed in Chapter 2.

Article 17
This sets out one of the basic mechanisms for ensuring a deadlock structure in relation to the holding of shareholders' meetings by specifying that the quorum consists of one A Shareholder and one B

Shareholder. If there were other classes of shares, the quorum would require also the presence of a representative of each other class.

Article 18
Under reg 41 of Table A, if at the adjourned meeting a quorum is not present, the meeting is simply adjourned again and this can continue indefinitely. Article 18 provides instead that the adjourned meeting is dissolved if it is inquorate. An alternative approach, which is contrary in spirit to the deadlock concept, is for the members present at the adjourned meeting to constitute a quorum.

Article 19
This is a standard amendment to the Table A provision that at least two members are required to be able to demand a poll unless the poll is demanded by a single member who holds not less than one-tenth of the share capital. In practice the amendment will be of minimal importance as no shareholder is likely to hold less than ten per cent of the share capital and, if it does, it will find no advantage in demanding a poll.

The alteration made to para (b) to give the power to a single member renders the other methods of determining whether the power exists, which are contained in paras (c) and (d), superfluous.

Article 20
The usual approach in deadlock articles is to give all the representatives of each class one vote and this is adopted in art 20. An alternative technique for ensuring a deadlock structure at general meetings would be to provide that each A Shareholder present has a number of votes equal to the number of B Shareholders present and vice versa. A suitable article is the following:

5.8   Votes at general meetings

On a show of hands or on a poll, each of the A Shareholders present in person, by proxy or by corporate representative has a number of votes equal to the number of B Shareholders similarly present; and they each have a number of votes equal to the number of A Shareholders similarly present.

This approach may be more appropriate than the single vote for each class given by art 20 if there is more than one shareholder of each class but it has the disadvantage of permitting some members of one class to join with holders of the other class in defeating their fellow class members. Thus, for example, in a company where there are two A shareholders, with 40 A shares and 10 A shares respectively, and four B shareholders two of whom have 20 B shares each and two of whom have 5 B shares each, at a meeting at which all shareholders are present the A shareholders will each have four votes (making a total of eight votes) and each B shareholder will have two votes (again making eight votes). This works satisfactorily if the A shareholders all vote the same way and the B shareholders also vote together. If, however, the A shareholder with the smaller holding breaks rank and votes with the B shareholders and against his fellow A shareholder, the deadlock will be broken. This will be so even though the out-voted A shareholder has the largest shareholding.

A different, and generally preferable, way of providing for the possibility of disagreement among the holders of a class is that adopted in art 21.

If there are more than two classes of shares, none of the above would provide a full deadlock as a majority of the classes could join together to out-vote another class. As the essence of a deadlock structure is that any party should have the ability to veto decisions, the principle can be preserved where there are more than two classes by providing that the shareholders voting against a resolution shall each have a number of votes equal to the number of shareholders voting in favour of the resolution and conversely in relation to the votes of the members voting in favour. The following article would be suitable:

5.9 Preserving deadlock voting rights

On a show of hands or on a poll, each shareholder present in person, by proxy or by corporate representative who votes in favour of the resolution shall have a number of votes equal to the number of shareholders similarly present who vote against the resolution; and they shall each have a number of votes equal to the number of shareholders similarly present who vote in favour of the resolution.

Article 21

This provides for the resolution in private of a disagreement amongst the holders of one class as to how to deal with the holders of the other class.

Article 22
Table A provides for the minimum number of directors to be two unless otherwise determined by ordinary resolution. It would, in most cases, be acceptable for the Table A regulation to be left unchanged although, for the avoidance of any misunderstanding, reg 64 could be amended to require the passing of a special, rather than an ordinary, resolution to change the minimum. In view of the weighted voting rights created by the articles, this change would be purely cosmetic.

Article 23
It is usual to give each class of shareholders the right to appoint the same numbers of directors although this is not essential in view of the voting rights conferred by art 40. Four is an arbitrary number but it strikes a reasonable balance between giving each class a sufficient number of nominated directors to ensure that board meetings are unlikely to be inquorate by accident and avoiding an unduly large board.

Article 24
The main part of this article deals with the removal and replacement of nominated directors. If appropriate, it can be altered by requiring that the removal and replacement (or either of these) requires a special majority—such as agreement of holders of at least 75 per cent of the shares of the relevant class—to be effective. This could be achieved by replacing 'the holders of a majority of the share of the class whose holders appointed him' in art 24 with 'the holders of not less than 75 per cent of the shares of the class whose holders appointed him'.

Article 24 also provides a significant sanction in respect of a director who breaches the restrictions imposed on directors by art 39 by permitting his removal to be effected by the holders of the shares of the other class than that held by his appointors.

Article 25
It is usual to require notices, such as those appointing or removing directors, to be lodged at the registered office of the company. In many cases, however, the company's registered office is at the offices of the auditors and it will in such cases be more helpful for notices to be lodged at the company's head office. If a special majority is required under art 24 to effect the appointment or removal, a consequential change will be necessary in art 25.

Articles 26 and 27
These are normal provisions in the articles of private companies and reference should be made to the commentary in Chapter 3 at pp 122 and 123.

Article 28
Although it would be possible to give a director an unfettered discretion to appoint any alternates he chooses, it is preferable that the approval of his appointors should be required.

As in the case of the directors (Appendix C, art 41), notice of meetings must be given to an alternate director even if he is out of the United Kingdom and the last sentence of reg 66 of Table A is accordingly disapplied.

Articles 29 and 30
These cover standard points in respect of alternate directors and are discussed in Chapter 2.

Articles 31 and 32
These articles contain routine alterations to Table A in respect of directors' interests.

Articles 33 and 34
These repeat the first two sentences of reg 88.

Article 35
In a similar manner to the requirements for general meetings, the quorum at board meetings is an A Director and a B Director unless Deadlock Business is involved. If it were not for this exception, the directors nominated by shareholders who were in default in relation to an obligation to the company could prevent action being taken to enforce performance by staying away from the relevant board meeting. If there are more than two classes of shares, this article should provide that the quorum consists of at least one director nominated by each class.

Article 36
As with general meetings, a meeting of the directors, if not quorate within half an hour or if inquorate during the course of the meeting, is adjourned for a week. If then the quorum requirements are not satisfied, the meeting is cancelled. Although this enables one group of directors to bring the

company to a standstill by boycotting meetings, the alternative of providing that the directors present at an adjourned meeting shall constitute a quorum would result in a serious possibility of the deadlock structure being by-passed. This is generally not acceptable.

Article 37
The directors are authorised under reg 32 of Table A to delegate powers to committees. It is to be expected that the directors would be careful to ensure that the terms of any delegation are not such as to conflict with the deadlock arrangements. It is nevertheless a sensible precaution to enshrine in the articles a requirement that both (or all) classes must be represented on committees.

Article 38
An executive director has ostensible authority to bind the company and, because of CA 1985, s 35A, a third party is generally not affected if the directors as a whole exceed their powers. The provisions in the articles which prevent board decisions being taken without the approval of both classes of directors can thus be rendered practically useless unless some sanction is introduced which minimises the likelihood of a director ignoring the restrictions. For this purpose, the articles identify certain types of transactions as being of such significance that a director who implements them without obtaining board approval can be removed by the holders of the shares of the other class than those who nominated him. It would be possible to go further and provide that, if a director entered into a major transaction without board approval, the shareholders who appointed him would be treated as having given a transfer notice in respect of their shares under art 8. This can be achieved by adding a new para to art 9(b)(iii) as follows:

5.10 Director approving unauthorised transaction

(E) a director appointed by the member carrying out or authorising a Major Transaction without having first obtained approval at a meeting of the directors.

This sanction is, however, extremely onerous and, if it is included, the parties should, before the articles are adopted, be made aware of the implications to ensure that it is acceptable to them.

A further provision which is intended to encourage the directors to follow the terms of this article is the exclusion of a director who is in breach from a right of indemnity under art 49 if the company suffers loss as a result of his acts.

The matters listed in art 38 are by way of example. In any particular company the details need to be reviewed in the light of the proposed activities of the joint venture and the interests of the parties that require protection. The list should always be as precise as possible to minimise the possibility of an inadvertent infringement.

Article 39

This follows the principles applied by art 20 in relation to general meetings by giving equal votes to each group of directors both at board meetings and at committee meetings. The details are, however, slightly different from art 20. Whereas the voting rights given to shareholders at general meetings can be freely defined by the articles, it is probable that directors cannot be disenfranchised. This could be the effect if art 20 were followed because a director of one class who disagreed with the other directors of that class could theoretically find himself without a vote. To avoid any argument as to the validity of this approach, art 39 therefore provides that directors of each class have as many votes between them as the directors of the other class, regardless of the numbers present. It should, however, be pointed out that this introduces the risk that a resolution may be passed against the wishes of a majority of the directors of a class because of one of their colleagues siding with the other directors. If this is a matter of concern, it can be dealt with by adding the following to art 39:

5.11 Deadlock voting at board meetings

> In determining the voting rights of each director, an A Director who votes in the same manner as the B Directors, or majority of the B Directors, on a resolution in respect of which a majority of the A Directors have voted in a different manner shall be treated as if he were a B Director at the meeting, and vice versa in relation to a B Director voting in the same manner as the A Directors.

It should also be noted that the voting rights are different if the vote concerns Deadlock Business. As is explained in the discussion relating to art 3, the deadlock principle does not work sensibly in relation to certain matters where it is in the interests of one party to frustrate the taking of action which in principle the company should be entitled to take.

Article 40

The articles render the position of the chairman less important than in most companies by excluding the chairman's casting vote. Nevertheless, the chairman does have practical importance in that he is responsible for the conduct of shareholders' and directors' meetings. Article 41 provides for the chairman to rotate annually between the two classes but an alternative approach is to agree that an independent chairman should be appointed. The following article would provide for this:

5.12   Appointment of independent chairmen

> The chairman of the board of directors shall be a person appointed by special resolution and he may be removed at any time by notice to the company given by any member. The chairman shall be treated as neither an A Director nor a B Director. He shall preside at every meeting of the directors and of committees of the directors at which he is present but he shall not have a second or casting vote.

As the chairman would be entitled to vote in the normal way, art 39 would have to be amended by providing that, if any directors vote in a manner different to the way the chairman votes, the chairman should be treated as if he were a director of the same class as the directors who voted in the same way. By this means, his vote will be neutralised. An appropriate addition after the first sentence of art 40 is:

5.13   Chairman to ensure deadlock if disagreement at board meeting

> If the chairman exercises his vote on a resolution in a manner that is the same as that in which some, but not others, of the directors vote, he shall be treated, for the purpose of determining the numbers of votes to which the A Directors and the B Directors are entitled, as if he were a director of the same class as the directors who voted in the same manner as he did.

Article 41

Regulation 88 of Table A allows directors to decide how to regulate their proceedings and accordingly does not specify how much notice is required for their meetings. If it is felt that a fixed minimum period, as provided by art 41, is too inflexible, the article can be amended by providing that a shorter period will suffice if agreed by at least one (or more) of the directors of each class.

Unlike Table A, art 41 entitles director to give an address outside the UK to which notices of meetings should be sent.

Article 42

This requires an agenda to be provided for each board meeting and for the agenda to be comprehensive. At the cost of introducing some inflexibility, the article provides the shareholders with some protection against matters being raised unexpectedly at directors' meetings without the directors necessarily having had an opportunity to discuss them with their nominators.

Articles 43 to 45

These are standard provisions which are discussed in Chapter 2.

Article 46

In the case of a joint venture it is reasonable that the standard rule, that a member cannot inspect the books of the company, should be reversed (see the comments on reg 109 of Table A in Chapter 2, p 89).

Article 47

Table A disentitles a member who is outside the United Kingdom from receiving notices unless it provides an address for this purpose which is within the United Kingdom. In the case of a joint venture it is appropriate that all members should be entitled to receive notices at whatever address they choose to specify and reg 112 is amended to allow this.

Article 48

These are standard amendments to reg 118 which are discussed in Chapter 2. A director who fails to observe the obligation to obtain board approval before implementing a major transaction is, however, excluded from the right to the indemnity if the company suffers as a result.

Minority protection companies

General

Although many joint ventures are conducted through the vehicle of a deadlock company, the extremely restrictive arrangements are often modified in a number of respects. Ultimate control will often be given to one of the participants with the other investors having varying rights to veto certain specified actions. To achieve this effect, the articles will include provisions along the following lines:

(1) The shares will commonly be categorised individually but they will not usually confer equal voting rights.

(2) The minority shares may be given weighted voting rights, either to enable them to prevent the passing of a special resolution or in relation to resolutions dealing with matters of particular importance as listed in the articles. By this means, the minority shareholder will be able to veto acts of particular significance.

(3) As an alternative to weighted voting rights, the articles can provide that the implementation of specified transactions of major importance constitutes a variation of the class rights of the minority shares. In that case, the transactions must first be approved by a class meeting either in accordance with CA 1985, s 125 or as provided in the articles.

(4) The member in the minority position will normally have to be present at meetings of shareholders even though it cannot actually block a resolution in respect of which it does not have weighted voting rights. If it does not attend meetings, it will normally be provided that its absence from a re-convened meeting will not render the meeting inquorate.

(5) The minority shareholder will have the right to appoint a minority number of directors and the presence of at least one director nominated by it may be necessary to constitute a quorum at board and committee meetings in the first instance but, if a meeting has to be re-convened because it is inquorate, the directors then present will constitute a quorum.

(6) New shares will be classified in the same manner as the existing shares and the relative proportions of the different classes will be maintained.

The protection given to the minority shareholders will vary from case to case but in general they will have limited powers. Apart from the ability to prevent the carrying out of specified, and usually narrowly proscribed, acts by voting against the required special resolution, they will not have the right to prevent a determined majority shareholder from operating the company largely as it chooses.

Commentary on minority protection articles

The articles in Appendix D are very similar to those in Appendix C and reference should be made to the commentary in Chapter 5. The following points deal with differences between the two documents.

Article 1

Regulation 20 of Table A, which deals with the right of the directors to sell or re-allot forfeited shares, is excluded and replaced by art 10.

Regulation 39, which provides that the accidental omission to give notice of a meeting to a member, or the non-receipt of it, does not invalidate the meeting, is not excluded. The minority shareholder should not be able to frustrate the holding of a meeting by maintaining that the notice of the meeting was not received by it. An alternative approach would be to provide that failure to give it notice, but not the non-receipt of a notice that was sent, should invalidate the meeting and this can be achieved with the following wording:

> Regulation 39 of Table A is amended by deleting the words 'The accidental omission to give notice of a meeting to, or'.

One of the protections which the minority shareholder will seek is to prevent the majority shareholders awarding their directors excessive fees. Regulation 82, which enables the company by ordinary resolution to determine the remuneration of directors, is therefore excluded and the fixing of remuneration is one of the matters specified in art 41 as requiring the approval of a special resolution.

Dividends are a matter of considerable interest to minority shareholders. Whilst their main objective will be to ensure that there is a full distribution of profits insofar as the company's requirements do not necessitate the retention of funds, they will also want to protect against excessive distributions which deplete the company's resources. Regulation 102 requires that final dividends are subject to approval by an ordinary resolution. Article 41 makes all dividends subject to the approval of a special resolution and art 47 replaces reg 102 to reflect this.

Regulations 50 and 54, which deal with voting rights at general meetings, and reg 88 which covers the voting rights at board meetings are not excluded from applying to the articles in Appendix D as the special voting arrangements which replace them in Appendix C are not relevant. Finally, reg 91 is retained because it deals with the appointment of the chairman, which is not a critical matter in the case of companies which merely provide minority protection.

Article 4

It is assumed in these articles that the minority shares for which protection is provided are the B Shares.

Article 6
Regulation 2 of Table A permits the issue of shares with such rights as the company, by ordinary resolution, determines. The minority shareholder will wish to ensure that shares with preferential rights cannot be issued without its approval and art 6 does this by requiring that, instead, a special resolution is needed.

Article 7
Paragraph (c) of this article provides that a special resolution, rather than an ordinary resolution, is required if new shares are to be offered otherwise than to the shareholders in proportion to their existing holdings.

Article 9
The purpose of this amendment, which is discussed above in relation to deadlock companies, is to require the pre-emption procedure to be followed in relation to shares on which the company exercises a lien.

Article 10
This is similar to art 9 and ensures that the re-allotment or transfer of shares which have been forfeited is carried out in accordance with the pre-emptive principles applicable to the issue of new shares or the sale of existing shares.

Article 11
This closely follows art 8 in Appendix C except that partial transfers of shareholdings are permitted. This is because, where the minority shareholder has limited rights, there is no strong argument for prohibiting it from making a disposal whilst retaining some part of its shareholding. In addition, para (e) provides that the members holding shares of the same class as the offered shares have a preferential entitlement to take up more than their proportional allocation. This may be important if the minority shareholding is split amongst a number of members. The priority arrangement enables those minority members who wish to retain their position in the company to avoid dilution of their voting rights by acquiring the shares which another member of their class wishes to sell.

Article 12
A significant feature of art 12 results from the option which the transferee has as to whether or not to name a proposed transferee. If the

minority participant chooses not to name the transferee, it is reasonable that the protection given to the minority shareholder should lapse in relation to the shares which are sold. If, on the other hand, it does name a transferee and the majority shareholders nevertheless do not exercise their pre-emptive right to buy the shares, they can hardly object that the transferee is someone of whom they do not approve and to whom they do not wish to afford the same protections. The distinction is effected in art 12 by providing that, if the offeror has not named a third party purchaser, it can transfer freely any shares not purchased by the other shareholders but, on registering the transfer to the third party, the shares automatically become A shares. This means that the protections given to B shareholders do not operate but the transferred shares, being a minority holding, cannot cause difficulties for the majority shareholders as they will be able to out-vote the transferee on any question.

Articles 15 and 16

Regulation 30 of Table A permits a person entitled to shares as a result of the death or bankruptcy of a member to elect either to be registered as the holder of the shares or to transfer them to another person. There is, however, no time limit within which the election must be made and the purpose of this article is to enable the directors to require that a decision is made one way or the other. The sanction is that, if a decision is still not made, the person in question is treated as having elected to become the registered holder. A perfectly reasonable alternative is to deem the person to have served a transfer notice in respect of the shares if an election is not made within the time limit which is specified. To make this change, the last part of the revised wording as set out in art 15 should read:

> ... and, if he does not do so, he shall be deemed, at the end of the period of notice, to have served a Transfer Notice in respect of the share without specifying an Offer Price or a third party to whom he wishes to transfer the shares.

A different approach was adopted in Old Table A in which a proviso was included to reg 32 (being the regulation corresponding to reg 30 of Table A) which authorised the withholding of dividends and other moneys payable on the share if and so long as the person in question failed to comply with the notice requiring him to make an election. The wording for this purpose is:

... and, if and so long as he does not do so, the directors may withhold payment of dividends, bonuses and other moneys payable in respect of the share.

This last sanction is unlikely to be very compelling in the case of a private company unless dividends are normally paid.

Article 17

A concern that a minority shareholder will often have is that its stake in the company can be diluted by the company making a rights issue in which it does not want to participate. Although the directors should raise new capital by the issue of shares only if it is in the interests of the company to do so, there may be circumstances where the motivation for the issue is complex and the minority shareholder believes, but cannot prove, that in part the objective is to apply financial pressure to it. It is therefore an important protection to provide that an issue of shares can be made only if the minority shareholder agrees. Article 17 achieves this by amending reg 32 so as to require the passing of a special resolution, rather than an ordinary resolution, before the share capital can be increased.

Regulation 32 deals not only with increases in the company's share capital but also with a variety of other changes. These are unlikely to affect the position of the minority member but the alteration made to reg 32 by art 17 is extended to all the specified events.

Article 21

Although it is reasonable that the presence of the minority member should be required at general meetings in the first instance to make them quorate, it is not generally appropriate that it should be able to prevent shareholders' meetings ever being held simply by staying away. Article 21 therefore differs from the corresponding article in Appendix C by providing that the members present at an adjourned meeting constitute the quorum. In addition, to reduce the risk of the minority member losing its ability to veto a special resolution at an adjourned meeting because it is quorate despite its absence, a requirement has been added that not less than three days' notice of the adjournment must be given to the members. This will at least ensure that the minority member knows about the adjournment.

Article 22

Table A permits the adjournment of a general meeting at which a quorum is present but does not specify any minimum or maximum period for the adjournment and requires fresh notice to be given to the members only if the adjournment is for more than 14 days. Because the regulation applies where the original meeting is quorate, the minority shareholder will have been present at the meeting and will therefore be aware of the details of the adjourned meeting. It is nevertheless good practice to require that formal notice is given and it is likely to assist the minority shareholder in making representations in relation to the matter which caused the adjournment to impose a minimum period before the meeting can be resumed. It may also be helpful to provide—although this has not been done in art 22—that there should be a limit to the time during which the adjournment can continue. The wording for these purposes, is as follows:

5.14   Notice of adjournment of general meeting

Regulation 45 is amended by replacing the last two sentences with the following:

'The adjournment shall be for not less than fourteen nor more than twenty eight days. At least seven clear days' notice of the adjourned meeting shall be given, specifying the time and place of the adjourned meeting and the general nature of the business to be transacted.'.

Article 24

The main purpose of this article is to ensure that the B Shareholders, who are in the minority position, are together given enough votes to be able to block a special resolution. A further aspect relates to the voting rights if a resolution is proposed to remove the director nominated by the minority shareholders. The formula adopted follows that which was the subject of the decision in *Bushell v Faith* ([1970] AC 1099). In that case, a director–shareholder was voted off the board on a show of hands. He demanded a poll because the articles provided that, on a poll in relation to a resolution to remove a director, any share held by the director conferred the right to three votes for each share. On that basis the resolution was defeated and the court upheld the weighted voting rights even though the result was effectively to nullify the inherent power of shareholders to remove directors by ordinary resolution (CA 1985, s 303). It is possible, as a result of the pre-emption procedure in art 11, that all the issued shares are classified as A shares. In that event, the quorum is changed so that it is effectively any two shareholders.

Article 32

The deletion of the last sentence of reg 88 of Table A, which relates to the voting rights of directors who are also alternates, is made because the point is covered in more detail in the penultimate sentence of art 32. The change is, however, of limited significance if the directors of each class are given block voting rights.

Article 38

Article 27 gives the minority shareholder the right to appoint one director. These articles as a whole give the minority shareholder very little protection at board level as the nominated director cannot veto decisions but merely has the ability to make his voice heard in the debate. It is therefore not unusual for the minority shareholder to refrain from exercising the right of nomination so long as the business of the company is proceeding to plan. Article 38 recognises this by making the B Director part of the quorum only whilst a B Director in fact holds office.

Article 40

If a B Director holds office, he must be included in the membership of committees.

Article 41

As the minority shareholders will not usually be given the power to veto resolutions generally, it is common practice to specify major transactions which do require the minority support. There are two ways in which this can be achieved. The first, which is adopted by art 41, is to require the passing of a resolution in respect of which the minority shareholders are given sufficient votes to be able to prevent approval being given. The second approach is to provide that implementation of the specified acts constitutes a variation of the class rights of the minority shares and thus needs to be approved at a class meeting. This latter approach is particularly suitable where there are several minority shareholders as the class approval will need the support of the holders of at least 75 per cent of the minority shares. The necessary wording involves replacing the first sentence of art 41 with the following:

5.15   Transactions constituting a variation of minority class rights

The entry by the directors into a Major Transaction shall constitute a variation of the class rights of the B Shares.

The detailed provisions to be covered will differ from case to case and art 41 should be looked upon as merely providing some suggestions. In every case it will, however, be necessary to ensure that the transactions which are covered are clearly described and that the scope for disagreement as to whether any particular proposal needs approval is kept to a minimum.

Articles 42 and 43

These follow the deadlock articles in Appendix C by requiring certain formalities to be satisfied in relation to the convening of meetings of the board and committees. As these are relevant in relation to minority articles for the protection of the minority shareholder, the articles apply only if there is a B Director in office and are subject to waiver by him.

Articles 47 and 48

These amendments are consequential upon the requirement, contained in art 41, that all dividends must be approved by special resolution.

Article 49

A minority shareholder is likely to have a keen interest in the ability of the company to pay dividends. If distributable profits are capitalised and used to pay up bonus shares, they are no longer available for dividend purposes. Accordingly, art 49 changes reg 110 by requiring that a capitalisation issue must be authorised by a special resolution and not just by an ordinary resolution.

6

Articles of Association of Public Companies

Introduction

Public companies usually, and listed companies invariably, adopt long form articles to the entire exclusion of Table A. There are a number of reasons for this practice and unless otherwise indicated, article references herein are to Appendix E:

(1) The articles need an additional degree of formality and comprehensiveness because of the existence of a large body of shareholders who have no voice in the day-to-day management of the company. Examples relate to the arrangements for holding shareholder meetings where there is a possibility of disorderly conduct or excessively large numbers (art 57) and the power to disenfranchise shareholders who refuse to provide details as to the beneficial ownership of the shares they hold (art 41).

(2) Certain specific provisions are expected by the investing institutions, such as limitations on borrowing powers (art 103).

(3) The listing requirements of the London Stock Exchange require that a number of provisions must be incorporated in the articles and that certain powers, if adopted by the company, must be limited in specified ways which are detailed below.

(4) Many of the provisions which are found useful in relation to private companies—such as the ability to hold board meetings by telephone—will also be desirable for public companies (see Chapter 3, p 125).

It would be possible, although cumbersome, to achieve all these objectives by adopting Table A subject to detailed modifications, but in the case of companies with a large spread of shareholders it is much more convenient if the articles are a single document which can be referred to with ease when a problem arises. It is, nevertheless, normal practice to base long form articles on Table A, with the opportunity being taken to amend some of the perceived infelicities in the drafting of Table A which have been mentioned elsewhere in Chapter 2.

London Stock Exchange requirements

The London Stock Exchange Listing Rules (which are contained in what is known as the *Yellow Book*) set out in Appendix 1 to Chapter 13 a number of matters which must be provided for in the articles of listed companies. They are summarised below (the references to specific articles are to those in Appendix E which comply with the obligation in question).

(1) Where there is more than one class of share, the name of each class and how they rank for dividends and capital distributions must be stated.

(2) Equity shares which do not carry voting rights must include the words 'non-voting' in their designation. Equity shares with less than full voting rights must include the words 'restricted voting' or 'limited voting'.

(3) Listed preference shares must carry voting rights at the least when their dividends are more than six months in arrear and on a resolution for winding-up the company.

(4) Transfers and other documents or instructions relating to or affecting title to shares must be registered without payment of a fee. This corresponds to reg 27 of Table A (art 35).

(5) Fully paid shares must be free from liens (art 14) and from any restriction on transfer except for a restriction imposed by reason of a failure to comply with a notice given under CA 1985, s 212 (which is dealt with under (13) below). Partly paid shares which are listed may be subject to restrictions so long as they do not prevent dealings in the shares taking place on an open and proper basis (art 32). The requirements in relation to fully paid shares are satisfied by reg 24 of Table A.

(6)   In exceptional circumstances approved by the London Stock Exchange, power may be taken to disapprove transfers so long as exercise of the power does not disturb the market.

(7)   If the articles limit the number of shareholders on a joint account, the limit must not prevent the registration of up to four persons. This is consistent with para (c) of reg 24 of Table A (art 32).

(8)   The closing of the register of transfers must be discretionary. Section 358 of CA 1985 restricts to 30 days the period for which the register of members may be closed in any year and reg 26 of Table A satisfies both requirements (art 34).

(9)   A new certificate replacing one that has been worn out, lost or destroyed must be issued without charge (apart from exceptional out of pocket expenses) although an indemnity may be required. The restriction on expenses that may be charged is slightly narrower than that contained in reg 7 of Table A, which refers to 'expenses reasonably incurred by the company in investigating evidence' (art 13).

(10) A holder of securities other than bearer securities who has sold part of his holding is entitled to a certificate for the balance without charge. Regulation 6 of Table A is to similar effect (art 11).

(11) If power is taken to issue share warrants to bearer (that is, documents conferring on the holders of the documents title to the shares and which transfer title by delivery of the documents), a new warrant must not be issued to replace a lost one unless the company is satisfied beyond reasonable doubt that the original has been destroyed. Section 188 of CA 1985 provides that a company limited by shares may, if authorised by its articles, issue fully paid bearer warrants but no provision is made for this by Table A. It is comparatively rare for a listed company to issue bearer shares, perhaps in part because the warrants are stampable at the rate of $1\frac{1}{2}$ per cent of the market value of the shares they represent. It is nevertheless fairly common practice to take power to issue warrants and the articles will generally authorise the directors to lay down conditions for the issue and replacement of warrants, the giving of notices of shareholders' meetings, the procedures to be followed by a warrant holder who wishes to attend and vote and arrangements whereby a

warrant holder can become a registered holder of the shares represented by the warrants (art 11).

(12) A corporation may execute a form of proxy under the hand of a duly authorised officer. This is consistent with reg 60 of Table A, which refers to a proxy form being executed 'by or on behalf of the appointor'. Regulation 68 of Old Table A was more specific and provided that, if the appointor was a corporation, the proxy form should be either under seal or under the hand of an officer or attorney duly authorised. Appendix E, art 74 provides a more flexible approach and this is discussed further below.

(13) Section 212 of CA 1985 entitles a public company to require a person who the company has reason to believe has during the preceding three years had an interest in shares of the company to state whether or not the belief is correct and to give certain other information. If, as is generally the case with listed companies, the articles impose sanctions on a shareholder who defaults in complying with a s 212 notice:

(a) the sanctions may not take effect earlier than 14 days after service of the notice;

(b) for a shareholding of less than 0.25 per cent of the relevant class, the only sanction allowed is a prohibition against attending at meetings and voting; for larger holdings the articles may provide:

    (i) for the withholding of the payment of dividends (including shares issued in lieu of dividends); and

    (ii) for the placing of restrictions on transfers of the shares provided that they do not apply to a sale to a *bona fide* unconnected third party (such as a sale through the London Stock Exchange or an overseas exchange or by the acceptance of a takeover offer);

(c) sanctions must cease after a specified period of not more than seven days after the earlier of:

    (i) receipt by the company of notice that the shareholding has been sold to a third party in the manner described above; and

    (ii) due compliance to the satisfaction of the company with the s 212 notice.

These sanctions are not included in Table A. Article 41 in Appendix E complies with the Listing Rules and is discussed below.

(14) A power to cease sending dividend warrants by post may not be exercised until either warrants have been returned undelivered or left uncashed on two consecutive occasions or, after one occasion, reasonable enquiries have failed to establish a new address of the registered holder (art 142).

(15) A power to sell the shares of a member who is untraceable may not be exercised unless:

(a) during a period of 12 years, at least three dividends have become payable and no dividend during that period has been claimed; and

(b) on or after the expiry of the 12 years, the company has given notice by advertisements, both in a national newspaper and in a newspaper circulating in the area in which is situated the last known address of the member or the address at which service of notices may be effected under the articles, of its intention to sell the shares and has notified the London Stock Exchange of that intention (art 151).

(16) Although an amount paid up in advance of calls on a share may entitle the holder to interest, it must not entitle him to dividends on that amount. This provision is unlikely to be of practical significance for most listed companies, as it is unusual to have partly paid shares and even more unusual for a shareholder to make a payment in advance of calls, but an appropriate form of regulation is included as art 24 in Appendix E.

(17) A power to forfeit unclaimed dividends must not be exercisable until at least twelve years after the dividend was declared or became due for payment. This requirement accords with reg 108 of Table A (art 143).

(18) If the articles permit the giving of notice by advertisement, the advertisement must be inserted in at least one national newspaper (art 159).

(19) If the articles provide that notices will be given only to those members whose registered addresses are within the UK, a member whose address is not within the UK must be entitled

to name an address within the UK which, for the purpose of notices, will be considered as his address. This is covered in reg 112 of Table A (art 153).

(20) The articles must prohibit a director from voting on a contract, arrangement or other proposal in which he has an interest which (together with interests of persons connected with him) is a material interest other than by virtue of his interests in securities of, or otherwise in or through, the company. Exceptions may be provided, in similar manner to reg 94 of Table A, where the interest arises in respect of a resolution:

(a) relating to the giving of a security, guarantee or indemnity in respect of:

　(i) money lent or obligations incurred by him or by another person at the request of or for the benefit of the company or a subsidiary undertaking; or

　(ii) a debt or obligation of the company or a subsidiary undertaking for which he has assumed responsibility in whole or in part under a guarantee or indemnity or by the giving of security;

(b) where the company or a subsidiary undertaking is offering securities in which offer the director is or may be entitled to participate as a holder of securities or in the underwriting or sub-underwriting of which the director is to participate;

(c) relating to another company in which he and any persons connected with him do not to his knowledge hold an interest in shares (within CA 1985, ss 198–211) representing one per cent or more either of its equity share capital or of its voting rights;

(d) relating to an arrangement for the benefit of the employees of the company or its subsidiary undertakings which does not award him a privilege or benefit not generally awarded to the employees to whom the arrangement relates; or

(e) concerning insurance which the company proposes to maintain or purchase for the benefit of directors or for the benefit of persons including directors.

It is customary to adopt the exceptions specified by the Listing Rules more or less verbatim (see art 122 and the comments on reg 94 in Chapter 2).

(21) A person appointed by the directors to fill a casual vacancy on, or as an addition to, the board must retire at, or at the end of, the next following annual general meeting and will be eligible to stand for election. This is in accord with reg 79 of Table A (art 94).

(22) Where a person, other than a director retiring at the meeting or a person recommended by the directors, is to be proposed for re-election or election as a director, notice (of a period which must be specified in the articles and which must be not less than seven or more than 42 days) must be given to the company of the intention to propose him and of his willingness to serve as a director. This follows reg 76 of Table A except that the length of the period mentioned is extended (art 90).

Further requirements of the Listing Rules are as follows (references to paras are to those in the Listing Rules):

(1) Unless shareholders otherwise agree, a company proposing to issue equity securities for cash must first offer the securities to existing shareholders. In a rights issue, exceptions may be made to deal with fractions and to avoid legal problems under the laws of overseas territories (see paras 9.18 and 9.19 of the Listing Rules and art 9).

(2) To the extent that shareholders authorise the disapplication of the pre-emption rights set out in CA 1985, s 89, issues of equity securities for cash made otherwise than to existing shareholders in proportion to their existing holdings are permitted for a period fixed by the authority. The period must not exceed 15 months from the date of the resolution. The disapplication of s 89 is dealt with further in the commentary on art 9.

(3) A proxy form must be sent with the notice of a meeting to each person entitled to vote at the meeting (para 9.26 and art 75).

(4) To communicate with holders of listed bearer securities, an advertisement must be placed in at least one national newspaper and must give an address from which copies can be obtained (para 9.28 and art 153(3)).

(5) Airmail must be used for sending documents to shareholders outside the member states and first class mail must be used for the others (paragraphs 9.29 and 9.30 and art 153).

(6) Transfers must be registered or rejected within two business days of receipt (para 9.39). This requirement was imposed in 1995 (art 33).

(7) Certificates must be issued without charge within:
  (a) one month of the date of expiration of any right of renunciation
  (b) five business days of the lodgment of transfers (para 9.40 and art 12).

(8) Proxy forms must be sent out with notices of meetings and provide for two-way voting. The form must enable a shareholder to appoint a proxy of his choice and must state that, if the form does not indicate how the proxy is to vote, the proxy will be entitled to exercise his discretion (para 13.28 and art 75).

(9) If more than five directors are standing for re-election, the proxy form must enable the shareholders to cast their votes on an individual basis (para 13.29).

(10) Where there are in issue listed convertible securities convertible into or carrying a right to subscribe for equity shares of the same class as the shares which the company proposes to purchase, the approval by extraordinary resolution of the holders of the securities must be obtained before the purchase (para 15.11 and art 7).

Association of British Insurers

The ABI is a very influential body which seeks to ensure that listed companies observe certain minimum standards. In particular, the ABI makes a number of recommendations as to what should be included in the articles of listed companies, as follows:

(1) The articles should specify both a maximum and a minimum number of directors (art 80).

(2) One-third of the directors should rotate at each annual general meeting (art 86).

(3) If power is taken to appoint divisional or similar directors, there should be a clear provision that they do not have authority to act on behalf of the company as directors (art 107).

(4) The power of the board to dismiss a director should be exercisable only with a majority of at least 75 per cent of the other directors (art 97(1)(e)).

(5) There should be a power to dismiss a director who fails to attend either a specified number of board meetings or any of the board meetings held during a specified period (art 97(1)(f)).

(6) Borrowing powers should be restricted to an amount based on group borrowings (art 103).

The ABI has also published statements setting out its views on the directors' power to allot shares and disapply shareholders' pre-emption rights, purchases of the company's own shares and scrip dividends. These are detailed in the commentary on art 9 in Appendix E which appears below at p 183.

Cadbury and Greenbury Codes

The code of best practice formulated by the committee on the financial aspects of corporate governance (which is generally known as the Cadbury Code) was published in December 1992 and has been adopted by the London Stock Exchange. Although compliance with the Code is not obligatory for listed companies, they are required to state in their accounts the aspects of the Code with which they have not complied and the reasons for the non-compliance.

The Code does not have a direct impact on articles of association but the following recommendations could be expressly covered:

(1) The board should have a formal schedule of matters specifically reserved for its decision.

(2) There should be an agreed procedure for the directors, in furtherance of their duties, to take independent advice at the company's expense when this is necessary.

(3) A removal of the secretary should be a matter for the board as a whole.

(4) The majority of non-executive directors should be independent of management and free from any business or other relationship which could materially interfere with the exercise of their independent judgement.

(5) The appointment of non-executive directors should be a matter for the board as a whole.

(6) Directors' service contracts should not exceed three years without shareholders' approval.

(7) Executive directors' pay should be subject to the recommendation of a remuneration committee made up wholly or mainly of non-executive directors.

(8) The board should establish an audit committee of at least three non-executive directors with written terms of reference dealing clearly with its authority and duties.

It is not current practice to incorporate these recommendations in the articles. This may be because the Code was only recently published and there has not been time for there to be sufficient experience to determine whether it is soundly based or whether it needs to be revised. Until the Code is fully established and, perhaps, until its adoption is obligatory, it would seem to be best not to incorporate its terms into articles which can be changed only by special resolution.

The study group on directors' remuneration (the Greenbury Committee) has also published recommendations which have the support of the London Stock Exchange. The report concentrates on the disclosure of a range of matters relating to directors' remuneration and other benefits. At this stage, none of them gives rise to any special provisions to be included in the articles.

Commentary on long form articles

Appendix E contains a set of long form articles which are suitable for a listed company and comply with the requirements of the London Stock Exchange. As far as possible, the articles are based on Table A and changes to the wording in Table A have been made only where and to the extent that it is felt useful to do so, although the opportunity has been taken to modernise the drafting. In view of this, many of the comments made on the Table A regulations in Chapter 2 are relevant and the following commentary deals only with those articles which do not repeat—either precisely or substantially—the regulations of Table A.

Article 1
An express statement excluding the application of Table A is required because of CA 1985, s 8(2).

Article 2
The definition of 'recognised person' is included because CA 1985, s 185(4) provides that a share certificate does not have to be issued to a

member of the company which is a recognised clearing house or a nominee of a recognised clearing house or of a recognised stock exchange. It is not necessary to define these terms as they are defined in s 185 and art 2 adopts statutory definitions.

The designated nominee of the London Stock Exchange is SEPON Ltd.

An additional clause which often appears in art 2 is:

6.1   Effect of special and extraordinary resolutions

If for any purpose an ordinary resolution is required, a special resolution or extraordinary resolution shall be as effective and, if an extraordinary resolution is required, a special resolution shall be as effective.

This is, however, unnecessary insofar as it refers to an ordinary resolution as the period of notice and requisite majority for the passing of an ordinary resolution are the minimum that have to be satisfied and there is no reason why a longer period or larger majority would not be equally effective. In the case of an extraordinary resolution which is required by statute, a special resolution will not suffice as CA 1985, s 378 provides that an extraordinary resolution requires a 75 per cent majority at a meeting of which notice specifying the intention to propose the resolution as an extraordinary resolution has been duly given.

Article 3

Table A does not include a statement as to the authorised share capital of the company. In long form articles it is the usual practice to include an article which records the share capital at the date of adoption of the articles. This is particularly desirable if the shares are divided into different classes.

If the share capital is altered after the articles as a whole are adopted, it is common practice, although not essential to amend art 3 accordingly. It is, in any case, helpful to attach a note, either here or to the capital clause in the memorandum of association, recording the history of the changes that have taken place.

Article 6

Although this article is based on reg 4 of Table A, it amplifies the regulation by spelling out the power to pay commissions given by CA 1985, s 97. The article also refers to the power which companies have, in the ordinary course of business, to pay fair and reasonable brokerage on the issue of its share capital (*Metropolitan Coal Consumers' Association v Scrimgeour* [1895] 2 QB 604; see also the reference to brokerage in CA 1985, s 98(3) and in reg 6 of Old Table A).

Article 7
This article appears in a different—and, it is suggested, more logical—position than the corresponding regulation in Table A.

The ABI, whilst not publishing formal guidelines, has requested that the power for a company to purchase its own shares should be implemented only with the sanction of a special resolution, and not the ordinary resolution required by CA 1985, s 166. The requirement that the approval of the holders of convertible shares must be obtained at separate class meetings arises under the Listing Rules of the London Stock Exchange, as mentioned above.

Article 8
This article does not appear in Table A. It is based on CA 1985, s 125 and covers much the same ground as regs 4 and 5 of Old Table A.

Article 9
The provisions of ss 80 and 89 of CA 1985 are of considerable importance in relation to listed companies and both the London Stock Exchange and the ABI take an interest in the way companies deal with the rights and powers conferred by the sections.

Section 80 provides that the directors may not exercise the power of the company to allot 'relevant securities' unless authorised by the company in general meeting or by the articles of association. 'Relevant securities' are the shares of the company other than those taken by the subscribers to the memorandum of association and shares allotted under an employees' share scheme (s 80(2); 'employees' share scheme' is defined in s 743). Section 89 requires that 'equity securities' which are to be allotted wholly for cash must be offered pro rata to existing shareholders. 'Equity securities' are essentially shares which are not restricted as to their dividend and capital rights (CA 1985, s 94). Section 95 provides that, where the directors have an appropriate s 80 authority, they may, by special resolution, be given power to allot the shares without regard to s 80.

As mentioned above, the Listing Rules confirm that shareholder approval must be obtained for equity securities to be issued for cash. The Rules also require that a disapplication of the s 89 pre-emption rights must be for a fixed period not exceeding 15 months and special provisions are included to deal with rights issues.

The ABI has issued recommended forms of resolutions to give authority and power under ss 80 and 89 and have indicated that the number of shares covered by the s 80 authority should be the lesser of the unissued ordinary shares of the company and one-third of the issued ordinary shares. It accepts a period of up to five years for a s 80 authority. This is consistent with the maximum period specified by CA 1985, s 80(4). The s 89 power should be limited, in the case of allotments otherwise than in connection with a rights issue, to five per cent of the issued ordinary share capital.

Listed companies normally renew their s 80 authority and s 89 power annually. Article 9 is intended to facilitate the passing of the necessary resolutions by incorporating the substantial amount of detail which would otherwise be required in the annual resolutions.

Article 11

This article takes advantage of CA 1985, s 188 which permits the articles to authorise the issue of warrants. Although, in practice, it is unusual for warrants to be issued, the authority is generally included in articles.

As mentioned above, the Listing Rules of the London Stock Exchange lay down a number of requirements which have to be met if the authority to issue warrants is given.

The power to issue warrants is often contained in an article which is much less detailed than art 11, such as the following:

6.2 General power to issue share warrants

> The directors may determine and vary the conditions on which share warrants to bearer are issued including conditions relating to the issue of a new warrant or coupon in place of one which is worn out, defaced, lost or destroyed (but a new warrant shall not be issued unless the directors are satisfied beyond reasonable doubt that the original has been destroyed), to the entitlement of the bearer to attend and vote at general meetings and to the surrendering of warrants and the entering of the name of the bearer in the register of members in respect of the shares comprised in the warrant. The bearer of a warrant shall be subject to the conditions from time to time in force in relation to warrants. Subject to those conditions and to the provisions of the Act, the bearer of a warrant is deemed to be a member and has the same rights and privileges as if he was registered as the holder of the shares comprised in the warrant.

Article 12

This article largely follows reg 6 of Table A and also complies with the requirements of the London Stock Exchange Listing Rules as described above. The reference to 'recognised persons' arises as a result of CA 1985, s 185(4), which provides that share certificates do not have to be issued to a recognised clearing house or to the nominee of a recognised clearing house or of a recognised investment exchange.

Article 16

The second sentence of this article differs from reg 10 of Table A by providing that the transferee of shares sold in exercise of a lien is not required to see to the application of the purchase money (see the comments on reg 10 of Table A in Chapter 2).

Article 17

The requirement in reg 11 of Table A, that the share certificate must be surrendered before the proceeds of sale are paid to the person whose shares have been sold, is omitted. Once the procedures under the preceding article have been implemented and the transferee registered as holder of the shares, the old share certificate has no value.

Article 18

Unlike reg 12 of Table A, art 18 allows calls to be postponed as well as revoked.

Article 21

This article differs in three respects from reg 15 of Table A. It refers to an instalment as well as a call itself; it provides for the defaulting member to be responsible for the company's costs; and it specifies a rate of interest of 15 per cent which is to apply if the directors do not fix any other rate.

Article 24

This corresponds to reg 21 in Old Table A, which is not duplicated in the present Table A. The wording is in accordance with the requirements of the Listing Rules of the London Stock Exchange referred to above.

Article 27

If a public company forfeits shares, it must cancel them and reduce its share capital accordingly if the shares are not sold within three years of the forfeiture (CA 1985, s 146).

Article 28
This article cross-refers to art 21 in respect to the liability of the defaulting member for interest and costs. The cross-reference should be kept in mind if the numbering of the article is changed as a result of amendments.

Article 31
Paragraph (2) deals in a broad way with the developing procedures for effecting paperless transfers of securities.

Article 32
The reference, in relation to the right to refuse to register transfers of partly paid shares, to dealings on an open and proper basis arises because of the Listing Rules as mentioned above. The reference to recognised persons arises because, as mentioned in relation to art 12, it is not obligatory to issue share certificates to them. The Listing Rules require that a limit on the number of persons who may be registered on joint account must not be less than four.

Article 33
The period of two business days is that required by the Listing Rules, as mentioned above.

Article 37
Although it is unlikely that the company would incur liability as a result of the destruction of documents and records, it is generally accepted that it is desirable to put the position beyond doubt. The various periods specified in art 37 are arbitrary but are commonly accepted as being a fair compromise between protecting the interests of shareholders and avoiding the cost and inconvenience of retaining documents for an unnecessarily long time.

Article 39
This article extends the corresponding provisions in Table A by giving the directors power to require that a person who has a right of election as to who should be registered as holder of the share does not leave the position undetermined for an indefinite period (see also Appendix D, art 15.)

Article 40

The cross-reference to art 39 which appears in art 40 will need to be adjusted if the numbering of the articles is changed.

Article 41

Section 212 of CA 1985 gives a public company a power to require persons to state their interests in shares. The purpose is to enable the company to go behind nominee holdings and find out who are the beneficial owners of shares held in nominee names. The Listing Rules allow sanctions to be imposed on a shareholder who fails to comply with a disclosure request. Article 41 is in accordance with the rules.

A distinction is made in relation to the permitted sanctions between shareholders who have holdings of less than 0.25 per cent of the shares of a class and those who have larger holdings. In the latter case, the sanctions may include, in addition to loss of voting rights, the withholding of dividends and restrictions on transfers. The restrictions may not apply to sales to *bona fide* third parties. The Listing Rules specify a minimum period of 14 days before the sanctions become effective but many long form articles provide that the notice period must not be less than 28 days if the shares in question comprise less than 0.25 per cent of the issued shares of the class. The distinction appears to be made because the Listing Rules used to require 28 days' notice in all cases. In 1989 the London Stock Exchange announced that it intended to reduce the period to 14 days for the larger holdings but, in the event, the 14 day period was introduced for all holdings regardless of size.

The statutory references which appear in art 41 are explained in the footnotes to the article.

Article 42

If a company has major overseas shareholders, it may find that the local jurisdiction seeks to recover from the company amounts attributable to taxation liabilities of a member who lives or dies within that jurisdiction. The recovery of taxes by one state will not, as a matter of general law, be enforced by another state. The collection from the company of sums attributable to liabilities of a member will accordingly be enforceable, if at all, only against assets of the company within that jurisdiction.

Article 42 gives the company the right to recover the sums paid from the member whose liability triggers the claim. It would be most surprising if the laws which made the company liable for the debts of the member did not also give the company a right of recovery from the member. The article is thus unlikely to have real practical significance but it is becoming increasingly common to include such a provision in long form articles.

Article 43

Old Table A contained a similar provision in relation to the creation of stock but these are omitted from the present Table A. Stock offers no advantages as it is now possible to resolve that shares do not bear definitive numbers but it is nevertheless normal practice to include a stock article in long form articles.

Article 50

Paragraph (2) of this article can be omitted in relation to listed companies as it will not in practice be possible to obtain the necessary level of consent for holding the meeting at short notice.

Article 51

The reference in this article to the failure to send out instruments of proxy, which does not appear in reg 39 of Table A, is strictly irrelevant as there is no statutory duty to send out proxy forms. It is merely an obligation under the Listing Rules of the London Stock Exchange (see above). Article 51 covers the point in order to avoid doubts which might otherwise arise.

Article 52

Whereas reg 40 of Table A requires that a quorum is present when business is to be transacted, art 52 merely specifies that the quorum is needed when the meeting begins. This avoids the rather remote possibility of the meeting becoming inquorate because members leave before the meeting has finished and, whilst the distinction is somewhat theoretical, this approach is preferred to that adopted in Table A.

Article 53

This differs from reg 41 of Table A in a number of respects:
  (1) Under art 52, a quorum is required only at the commencement of business; the meeting does not have to be adjourned if the number present falls below the level for a quorum.
  (2) If the meeting is one that was convened by or on the requisition of shareholders and is inquorate, it will be cancelled.

(3) Notice is required if the meeting is adjourned for at least 30 days.

Article 54

Unlike reg 42, art 54 provides that, if the chairman is absent, his place is taken by a director who is nominated by him. Alternatives are to provide for the director to be nominated by the board (as in reg 42) or by the directors who are present (which is effected by replacing 'by the chairman in writing' in art 54 with 'by resolution of the directors present').

Articles 57 and 58

In recent years there have been some bad experiences of shareholders' meetings becoming disorderly and with large attendances making it impossible for everyone to fit in the meeting room for which the meeting was convened. This has resulted in many listed companies adopting articles which provide that:
  (1) the meeting may be adjourned if the shareholders wishing to attend cannot be accommodated or the meeting becomes too disorderly.
  (2) arrangements may be made for an overflow meeting. For a consideration of the factors to be taken into account by the chairman see *John v Rees* [1969] 2 All ER 274 and *Byng v London Life Association Ltd* [1990] Ch 170.

Article 57, unlike reg 45 of Table A, deals with the possibility of the meeting being adjourned indefinitely or, in the words of those who still enjoy Latin tags, *sine die*. No notice of the adjournment is required unless the adjournment is for at least 30 (as opposed to 14) days and the article makes it clear that, in those cases where notice of the adjourned meeting is not required, it is also not necessary to give notice of the business to be transacted.

Article 59

The reference to 'members' in paras (3) and (4) is interpreted as including a single member because of the application of the Law of Property Act 1925, s 61 whereby the plural is deemed to include the singular (see the comment on reg 1 of Table A in Chapter 2). The faint-hearted may nevertheless prefer to replace 'members' with 'a member or members'.

Article 61

This article is largely a statement of the law applicable to permitted amendments to resolutions (*Re Moorgate Mercantile Holdings Ltd* [1980] 1 All ER 40) but is nevertheless helpful in resolving doubts.

Article 66

The reference in art 66 to a member being deemed to be present in person (which does not appear in reg 54 of Table A) relates to the position of corporate members acting by representatives (art 79). Under reg 54, a member who also is the representative of a corporate member nevertheless has only one vote on a show of hands. Article 66 gives him a separate vote for each capacity in which he is present. The second sentence in art 66 is added by way of clarification.

Article 69

In addition to the provisions relating to liens, a member who is in default in relation to the payment of calls on his shares is subject to three sanctions. The first of these is under art 69 which disenfranchises the shares in relation to which the default exists. The second arises under art 135 whereby dividend entitlement is proportionate to the amounts paid up on the shares. Finally, art 137 enables the directors to deduct sums owing to the company from the dividends payable on the shares in relation to which there is a default.

As an alternative to these scattered provisions—which have the merit of appearing in the places where they take effect—a single article could be adopted, as follows:

6.3   Sanctions if calls unpaid

> A member is not entitled to receive a dividend or to be present or vote at a general meeting, either personally (except as proxy for another member) or by proxy, or be included in the quorum or exercise any other right or privilege as a member whilst calls payable on the shares held by him, either alone or jointly with another person, remain unpaid beyond the due date.

Article 73

The first two sentences of art 73 repeat reg 59 of Table A. The second sentence is, in addition, implied by CA 1985, s 372(2)(*b*), which states that a member of a private company is not entitled to appoint more than one proxy to attend on the same occasion unless the articles otherwise provide.

The third sentence is consistent with CA 1985, s 372(1) which states that a proxy need not be a member of the company. The last sentence is a statement of the common law (*Cousins v International Brick Co* [1931] 2 Ch 90).

Article 74

This article is based on reg 60 of Table A but omits the wholly unnecessary form which is included in the regulation. The common requirement that the instrument of proxy given by a company must be signed by an authorised agent of the company or be under the common seal is modified to take account of CA 1985, s 36A. Under this section, a document signed as a deed by two directors or by a director and the secretary is as effective as if executed under the common seal and para (2) of art 74 recognises this possibility.

Article 75

This article confirms the obligation imposed on the directors by the Listing Rules, as mentioned above, to send proxy forms to all members entitled to vote. Section 372(6) of CA 1985 makes directors potentially liable to a fine if proxy forms are sent to some only of the members entitled to vote at the relevant meeting.

Article 77

This deals with the somewhat unlikely occurrence of a number of competing proxy forms being lodged with the company. The applicable common law rule would appear to be that the proxy which is the last to be executed should be the one that is effective. There is, however, a practical difficulty in that the directors will generally not to be able to ascertain with certainty when a particular form was signed and art 77 therefore adopts the different approach of treating the time of deposit as being definitive. Even this is not readily implemented and the directors should seek to arrange that proxy forms are time stamped on receipt if a proxy battle is anticipated. The authority of the directors given by the article which enables them to be flexible is a necessary protection but, in exercising this power, the directors should do so in the manner which is most likely to give effect to the shareholder's wishes.

Article 78

In recognition of practicalities, art 78 modifies reg 63 of Table A by requiring that notice of the determination of the authority of a proxy or corporate representative will not be effective unless it is deposited at the registered office at least three hours before the meeting.

Article 79

The first two sentences of this article repeat the provisions of CA 1985, s 375. An equivalent regulation appeared in Old Table A but has been omitted from the current version of Table A.

Article 80

This corresponds to regulation 64 of Table A but differs because, in accordance with the recommendations of the ABI (see above), a maximum number of directors is specified as well as a minimum.

Article 82

This differs from reg 66 of Table A in three respects. First, an alternate director who is absent from the UK will nevertheless be entitled to receive notice of meetings provided that he leaves an address in the UK for the receipt of notices. Secondly, an alternate does not have a director's power to appoint his own alternate. Finally, the alternate's appointor may surrender part of his own remuneration in favour of his alternate.

Article 83

This corresponds to reg 67 of Table A with the addition of the provision that the alternate director ceases to hold office if events occur which would have caused him to cease to be a director if he had been one. This is strictly unnecessary as art 97, which deals with the circumstances giving rise to the directors losing their office, applies also to alternate directors by reason of art 84. Nevertheless, the additional words clarify the position.

Article 86

The rotation of directors is an important protection for the shareholders of a listed company. Although Table A provides that executive directors are not subject to rotation, there is a developing view that all directors should rotate. It is not yet obligatory to adopt this approach but many companies provide that only the chief executive is freed from the requirement to rotate.

The wording adopted in art 86 for determining how many directors are to rotate each year and which directors are subject to rotation has the same effect as reg 73 of Table A but is thought to be easier to follow.

Article 87

Unlike reg 74 of Table A, this article takes into account, in determining the number and identity of the directors who are to rotate, any director who is resigning but not standing for re-election. The last two sentences have been added in accordance with the comments on reg 74 in Chapter 2.

Article 89

The reference to directors who are deemed to have been re-appointed, which does not appear in reg 80 of Table A, ties in with art 88.

Article 90

The periods for the giving of notice for the appointment of a new director are a minimum of seven (compared with the minimum in reg 76 of Table A of 14) days and a maximum of 42 days (rather than 35). These are in accordance with the periods which are mentioned in the Listing Rules of the London Stock Exchange. In addition, the article provides that the notice regarding the proposed director must be signed by some shareholder other than the nominee.

Article 93

Section 303 of CA 1985 gives the shareholders the power to remove a director by ordinary resolution regardless of anything to the contrary in the articles or any agreement he has. The disadvantage of the statutory procedure is that special notice has to be given of the resolution and, under s 304, the director has the right to protest against his removal. It is therefore customary to include in the articles an alternative, simpler procedure. Very often this requires the passing of a special resolution but there seems to be no reason why the s 303 power should not be supplemented by an alternative one which also needs an ordinary resolution but does not require the giving of special notice. This is the approach adopted by art 93.

Article 95

Section 293 of CA 1985 provides that, in the absence of contrary provision in the articles, a person cannot be appointed as a director of a public company after he has attained the age of 70 and a director must resign at the annual general meeting commencing next after he attains the age of 70. The director may, however, be appointed or re-appointed by ordinary resolution provided that special notice of the resolution has been given to shareholders. A director who is to be appointed or re-appointed at a time when he has attained the age of 70 (or any other retirement age applicable under the articles) must notify the company of his age (CA 1985, s 294).

It is common practice to remove the retirement age entirely from the articles—as does art 95—or rather less frequently to replace the age of 70 by a greater age. If the articles do not have any retirement age, it would appear that s 294 does not apply as there is no retiring age for the director to notify.

If s 293 is not excluded, the following article is useful in setting out the requirements of ss 293 and 294:

6.4   Director over age 70 to retire

(a) A person shall not be appointed as a director if, at the time when the appointment would take effect, he would have attained the age of 70. A director shall vacate his office at the conclusion of the annual general meeting which next follows his attaining that age. But acts done by a person as director are valid notwithstanding that it afterwards discovered that, by reason of this article, he should not have been appointed or his appointment had terminated.

(b) If a person retires under this article, no provision in these articles for the automatic reappointment of retiring directors in default of another applies.

(c) Nothing in this article prevents the appointment of a director at any age, or requires a director to retire at any time, if his appointment is or was made or approved by the company in general meetings; but special notice is required of a resolution appointing or approving the appointment of a director for it to have effect under this paragraph and the notice of the resolution given to the company, and by the company to the members, must state or have stated the age of the person to whom it relates.

(d) A person reappointed director on retiring under paragraph (a), or appointed in place of a director who retires under that paragraph, is to be treated, for the purpose of determining the time at he or any other director is to retire, as if he had become a director on the day on which the retiring director was appointed or last reappointed before his retirement.

Article 96

It is unusual to require directors to hold shares in the company to enable them to act as directors. This is partly because the requirement has no real value as a director can meet the obligation by holding shares as the nominee of a third party. The underlying concept that directors should have a stake in the company can be rendered meaningless.

If a share qualification is required, the following article will be appropriate:

6.5 Share qualification for directors

> The qualification of a director is the holding, either in his own name or by his nominee, of shares of any class which have a nominal value of not less than £   . A person who is appointed may act before acquiring his qualification but it shall be deemed a condition of his election that he acquires the qualification within two months and, in default, his office shall be vacated. A person who vacates office under this article shall not be eligible for re-appointment or re-election until he obtains his qualification.

The period to two months is the maximum time that may be given to a director to obtain his shares (CA 1985, s 291(1)). Although it is not necessary to impose an obligation to hold qualification shares, CA 1985, s 291(3) and (4) provide that a director who does not obtain his qualification shares automatically vacates office and may not be re-appointed until he has obtained the shares.

Article 97

Regulation 81 of Table A sets out a number of grounds for vacation of office by a director and these are normally adopted, with variations of detail, in long form articles. Paragraph (c) commonly takes a number of forms and, apart from the wording in reg 81, two other variations are to be found in the commentary on that regulation in Chapter 2. Article 97 omits para (c)(i) because it is to be anticipated that, if a director is admitted to hospital and is unable to perform his duties, the other directors will exercise their power of removal under para (a). Paragraphs (e) and (f) meet the requirements of the ABI as mentioned in Chapter 6.

If art 96 is amended to impose a share qualification, an additional event giving rise to vacation of office should be added: 'if he ceases to hold the necessary share qualification'.

It should be noted that the amended version of art 96 provides for the director to vacate office if he fails to obtain his qualification within two months of his appointment and the applicable provisions could, alternatively, be included in art 97.

Paragraph (2) of art 97 is a useful provision which minimises the scope for disputes.

Article 98

The arrangements for fixing the remuneration of directors is a topical and sensitive subject. The Cadbury Code (see above) requires the establishment of remuneration committees with a majority of its members being non-executive directors. In *Guinness plc v Saunders* [1990] 2 AC 663, the House of Lords applied an extremely restrictive interpretation to articles of association in holding that, in the absence of totally specific provisions, a committee, even if it has very wide powers, cannot determine the remuneration of its own members as this is a power which must be exercised by the whole board.

It is standard practice for the fees payable to directors to be subject to a stated aggregate limit and sometimes the articles go further and specify the maximum fees payable to directors individually. If, as in art 98, the stated maximum is indexed, the tax legislation provides a useful definition of the retail prices index. The Income and Corporation Taxes Act 1988, s 833(2) defines the retail prices index as 'the general index of retail prices (for all items) published by the Central Statistical Office of the Chancellor of the Exchequer; and if that index is not published [for a relevant month,] any substituted index or index figures published by that Department (*sic*).'

Article 98 is limited to the fees payable to non-executive directors. This is because the remuneration of executive directors is determined by the board (see art 107) and the salary they receive is normally inclusive of directors' fees.

Article 99

A non-executive director may sometimes provide special services which entitle him to an extra fee. This may become more common with the increasing attention being given to the role of non-executive directors, for example in serving on remuneration committees (see the comments on the Cadbury Code, above). The position in relation to executive directors is covered in art 108.

Article 100

This differs from reg 87 of Table A in referring to a body corporate which is a subsidiary undertaking, and not just a subsidiary, of the company. The reason for this change is that, in principle, it is better to widen the scope of the regulation rather than narrow it.

Article 102

The reference to the company's memorandum or association which appears in reg 70 of Table A is omitted as it would be most unusual for the memorandum to restrict the ability of the directors to manage the company. This article also differs from reg 70 in that, as suggested in the commentary on the regulation in Chapter 2, the provision relating to the powers of a quorate meeting is transferred to art 117.

Article 103

It is almost invariable practice for the borrowing powers of listed companies to be restricted and, indeed, as mentioned above, the ABI recommend that they are restricted to an amount based on group borrowings. Nevertheless, for most practical purposes borrowing limits have no real value as a *bona fide* third party will not be affected by the limitations (CA 1985, s 35A). Furthermore, the article restricting the directors' borrowing powers will normally confirm the protection for a third party (see, for example, para (4) of art 103). The directors will, however, be in default if they knowingly allow the limits to be breached and this should ensure that directors are very concerned to avoid an infringement.

Old Table A imposed an unworkable limitation on borrowing powers, whereby borrowings could not, without the sanction of shareholders in general meeting, exceed the nominal amount of the company's issued share capital. It is normal for the borrowing article for listed companies to adopt a different formulation and to be much more detailed. Although the precise wording will vary considerably, there is a well-established format:

(1) The limit is a multiple of the company's share capital and consolidated reserves.

(2) The reserves are determined from the last audited accounts.

(3) Adjustments are made to the amounts shown in the accounts to take account of changes after their date.

(4) There is often a lengthy definition of what constitutes borrowings.

Article 103 sets out a typical long form, and the following comments relate to that article:

Paragraph (1): the directors have implied power to exercise the powers of the company to borrow (*General Auction Estate and Monetary Co v Smith* [1891] 3 Ch 432) and an express statement to that effect is not essential. It is probably for this reason that Table A does not repeat reg 79 of Old Table A which started with wording similar to that of para (1).

Paragraph (2): the restriction is spelled out in general terms and makes use of the commonly adopted concept of 'adjusted share capital and reserves'. For the purpose of art 103, the group includes subsidiaries but it is sometimes provided that the group comprises the company and its 'subsidiary undertakings' (see also para (3)(a)). The widening of the group in this way will tighten the limits if there are subsidiary undertakings which are not subsidiaries and which have incurred heavy borrowings. The converse will be the case if the subsidiary undertakings have a low level of gearing.

Paragraph (3)(b): the purpose of the lengthy definition of adjusted share capital and reserves is to ensure that the borrowing powers are not based on a measure which, if taking place at a time which is significantly later than the end of the last accounting period for which accounts are available, could be very much out of date. Accordingly, numerous adjustments are made to reflect the sort of changes that may have occurred. The most important adjustment is contained in para (3)(b)(ix) which gives the auditors a broad brief to do what they consider appropriate. The preceding paragraphs are almost superfluous as a result but the auditors probably find them helpful because they lay down guide lines for the kinds of adjustments that are suitable.

Paragraph (3)(c): the purpose of this is to make it clear that the basis of the computation of the adjusted share capital and reserves is the figure shown in the consolidated accounts if the company is a member of a group. The consolidation will include subsidiary undertakings which are not subsidiaries and if the approach is adopted, as with this article, of dealing only with subsidiaries, then it is appropriate to make adjustments to the consolidated accounts to exclude any such subsidiary undertakings.

Paragraph (3)(d): the most complicated part of the typical article relating to borrowing powers is that which extends the term 'borrowings' so as to include liabilities in the nature of, although not strictly constituting, borrowings. The objective is to ensure that the borrowing limit is not circumvented by the directors incurring a mixture of liabilities which give rise to the same risks as borrowings but which would not otherwise be restricted. The approach is similar to that adopted in relation to loan facilities where the lenders will have a real concern to restrict the ability of the company to take on competing liabilities. The circumstances are, however, quite different and it is not obvious why the exercise of borrowing powers by directors should be circumscribed whereas their other powers, which can involve the company in greater risk or exposure, are unfettered. The protection for shareholders lies in the directors' duty of good faith and the ability of shareholders to remove directors by special resolution.

The extension of the term 'borrowing' to cover other transactions is particularly pointless and there is no reason why the extended definition in art 103 should be adopted.

As, however, the use of lengthy definitions is probably the norm rather than exceptional, the following comments are given by way of explanation:

(1) The purpose of this is to exclude debentures to the extent that they are held by other group members and, as a subsidiary point, to avoid the argument that debentures issued for a consideration other than cash do not constitute borrowing by the issuer.

(2) An acceptance credit arises where a bill of exchange drawn by a company is accepted by its bankers. Although no liability arises until the bill is due, the effect of the arrangement is similar to a loan from the bank as there will in due course be an obligation to reimburse the bank for payments made under the bill. Bills drawn for ordinary trading purposes are excluded because they represent normal trade credit made available to the company.

(3) A guarantee of an obligation of a third party is treated as a liability of the guarantor.

(4) Preference shares are treated as a form of borrowing as the ordinary shareholders will receive no part of the assets of the company until both borrowings and preference shares have been paid off.

(5) Debentures are often repayable at a premium. The coupon on the debenture and the premium together comprise the return

to the holder and there may be marketing and taxation reasons to split the return in this way.

(6) Borrowings from another member of the group do not affect the risk of ordinary shareholders as investors because, in principle, the liability of the borrower is matched by the asset belonging to the debenture holder.

(7) It is realistic to exclude temporary borrowings which are intended to be applied, and are in fact applied, in repaying other borrowings. The circumstances where this might occur are, for example, where there is a window of opportunity to borrow money on favourable terms to repay existing borrowings even though the existing borrowings have not yet fallen due for repayment. Four months is a typical period for temporary borrowings to be disregarded.

(8) This exclusion is barely necessary as the auditors, in making their adjustments under para (3)(b)(ix), would in any case doubtless disregard a proportion of the borrowings of a partly-owned subsidiary.

(9) If borrowings are incurred to finance a transaction where there is no risk of a default in payment under the transaction, there is no reason to treat the borrowing as giving rise to an exposure for ordinary shareholders. A guarantee by the ECGD should be risk free.

Paragraph (3): To avoid the necessity for the directors to obtain an auditors' certificate whenever there is a possibility of the borrowing limit being exceeded, the directors are allowed to rely on *bona fide* estimates made on a temporary basis. The position will, at latest, become clear when the group accounts are audited.

Article 104

This article is very generally adopted and provides for a particular form of delegation by the directors. In practice, however, the power is utilised only very occasionally and it is of no real benefit to any but the largest of companies. Accordingly, it may normally be omitted.

Article 105

The words 'with such powers, authorities and discretions (not exceeding those vested in the directors)' are added to reg 71 of Table A for clarification and are not essential.

Article 106

There is no reason why all the members of a committee must be directors but it is good practice to provide that directors must be in the majority both as members and as persons attending any particular meeting.

The purpose of para (2) is to overcome the restrictive decision in *Guinness plc v Saunders* (see the comments on art 98).

Apart from the addition of para (2), some minor changes are made to the wording of reg 72 of Table A. These are the references to conditions, to authorities and discretions and to sub-delegation in para (1) and the final words of para (3) dealing with the possibility of the directors changing the regulations relating to the operation of committees. These are mere drafting points and are not significant.

Article 107

The purpose of this article is to enable the company to give senior executive the status of being quasi-directors without giving them the powers and rights which exist with true directors. The objective may not be wholly successful as third parties who have taken these executives to be directors may be able to rely on the concept of holding out. If the company holds out a person as having an office which he does not in fact have, third parties who have taken action in reliance on the holding out may be able to prevent the company denying that the executive has the powers and authorities of a director. The article does, nevertheless, make it clear for internal purposes that the employees are not directors and have no right to attend and vote at board meetings.

The article complies with the requirement of the ABI referred to above that it must be made clear that the executives do not have authority to act on behalf of the company as directors.

Article 108

There is no obligation to provide that the employment of an executive director terminates if he ceases to be a director. Whilst it may be true that an executive director who has been removed from office or is unable to continue as a director is unlikely to be able to perform his executive duties, this will not invariably be the case. In particular a senior employee may be a valued member of the executive team but not be a real contributor to board discussions. In such a case it should be possible for the active directors to agree that he leaves the board but continues as an executive. An alternative and more flexible wording to replace the last sentence of para (1) of art 108 is as follows:

6.6   Circumstances in which executive director's employment ends

Unless the terms of his contract of employment with the company provide otherwise or the directors (excluding the director concerned and, in his capacity as such, any alternate director appointed by him) resolve otherwise, the appointment of a director to an executive office terminates if he ceases to be a director.

Paragraph (2) of the article clarifies the powers that may be conferred on an executive director but it can be omitted without any disadvantage.

Article 109

Section 319 of CA 1985 provides that a director cannot have a contract of employment for a term of more than five years without the approval of an ordinary resolution. The Cadbury Code (see above) recommends a maximum period of three years. As it is not obligatory for listed companies to adopt the Code, it is preferable not to reduce the period stated in the articles to less than the statutory maximum as the articles would have to be changed in the possible but unlikely event of a more relaxed requirement being introduced by future versions of the Code.

Article 110

For the most part, this article is a paraphrase of reg 85 of Table A. Paragraph (2), however, does not appear in Table A although it was included in Old Table A.

Article 111

This article is provided for clarification and is not essential.

Article 112

The provisions of this article track those of CA 1985, s 317, which requires a director to declare an interest in a contract with the company. It should be noted that a declaration is required even if the interest is not material; this is to be contrasted with reg 94 which, subject to specified exceptions, prohibits a director from voting on a transaction in which he is interested provided that the interest is a material one.

Old Table A referred to the statutory obligation to make a declaration but this is omitted from the current Table A. The requirement to make a declaration is, however, of such fundamental importance in seeking to ensure that directors behave, and are seen to behave, with full regard to their fiduciary duties that most long form articles follow the approach

taken in art 112. It is not unusual to find that the article which relates to
the obligation on a director to declare his interests includes an exception
corresponding to para (b) of reg 86 of Table A. This provides that an
interest is disregarded if the director does not know of it and it is
unreasonable to expect him to know of it. As explained in the
commentary on reg 86 in Chapter 2, this exception relates to
reg 85 of Table A which deals with the director's voting rights.
Section 317 does not contain a similar exception and there seems to be
no basis on which it can be implied from reg 86. Accordingly art 112
does not include this paragraph.

The definition of 'connected persons' in CA 1985, s 346, which is
referred to in para (2)(b), is very wide. It includes the person's spouse
and children and trustees of a trust for their benefit. It also includes
companies with which he is 'associated', being companies in which he
and persons connected with him hold at least one-fifth of the equity or
voting capital.

Article 114

It is usual to include, in an article which allows for board meetings to
be held by telephone, a provision as to the location at which the meeting
is treated as having taken place. This is barely necessary although there
is the possibility of a suggestion that, if the meeting is treated as being
held in a place other than that for which it was convened, a director who
was unable to attend was not given proper notice of where the meeting
would be held. For this reason, art 114 deems the meeting to have been
held at the place for which it was convened.

Article 116

Paragraph (1) of this article adopts the approach suggested in Chapter 2
in the commentary on reg 88 of Table A. If it is not intended that a
director who is outside the UK should receive notices of board meetings,
the second and third sentences of art 116 should be replaced by the
wording in reg 88, namely:

6.7   No notice of board meetings to director who is abroad

> It shall not be necessary to give notice of a meeting to a director who is
> absent from the United Kingdom.

If the approach of art 116 is retained, it may be thought desirable to
require that the address to be given must be in the UK. This is achieved

by inserting in art 116, after 'at an address' in the second sentence, the words 'in the United Kingdom'.

Paragraph (2) entitles a director to waive the giving of notice. This is useful where board meetings have to be held urgently and it is not realistic to ensure that all directors receive adequate notice. It seems, however, that a director may not have a general right to waive the giving of notice (*Re Portuguese Consolidated Copper Mines* (1889) 42 ChD 160), but it may be that this rule is subject to contrary provision in the articles. It is certainly clear that there is no principle that all directors must always be given notice of meetings since Table A makes it unnecessary to give a director notice if he is outside the United Kingdom. Paragraph (2) should, therefore, be effective but the position is not free from doubt.

Article 117
The third sentence of this article appears in reg 70 of Table A.

Article 118
This article corresponds to reg 90 of Table A but has a number of differences. Whilst reg 90 refers simply to the number of directors falling below the number fixed as the quorum, the really significant number is the minimum number for the directors, as determined by or under art 81. If, for some reason, there is no minimum number, the quorum becomes important and art 118 therefore refers to both.

The second sentence does not appear in reg 90 and the purpose is to enable a member to call a meeting if there are no directors without having to apply to the court under CA 1985, s 371.

Article 119
The ability to appoint a deputy chairman is useful in the larger companies and art 119 differs from reg 91 of Table A by permitting this. In addition, the chairman is given the power to nominate another director to take the chair in his absence.

Article 122
The Listing Rules of the London Stock Exchange require that articles of listed companies contain provisions limiting the right of directors to vote on resolutions in which they have an interest. As described above, the Rules spell out a number of exceptions which correspond to those contained in reg 94 of Table A. The exceptions are the maximum

concessions which may be given to directors and, whilst their scope may be reduced, it is normal practice—which has been followed in art 122—to adopt the contents of the Rules more or less verbatim.

The differences between the exceptions specified in the Rules and those contained in reg 94 are as follows:

(1) Whereas reg 94 refers to transactions involving subsidiaries of the company, the Listing Rules provide an exemption in relation to subsidiary undertakings. The definition of subsidiary undertakings is contained in CA 1985, s 258 and includes not only subsidiaries but also other entities where there is an appropriate degree of control or influence. As the exceptions are helpful to the board, the same amendment is often made with companies which, although not listed, adopt long form articles with similar restrictions on the directors' voting rights.

(2) Paragraph (a) of reg 94 does not extend to loans made or obligations incurred by persons other than the director.

(3) Paragraph (c) of reg 94, which provides an exemption in the case of the director subscribing for securities of the company or participating in the underwriting of an issue of securities, is replaced by a rather narrower clause, as set out in para (1)(b) of art 122. That paragraph refers to the director being offered securities of another company by reason of his being a holder of securities or a participator in an underwriting. Regulation 94 does not restrict the circumstances giving rise to the subscription.

(4) Paragraphs (1)(c) and (e) do not appear in reg 94. Further comments on para (c) are made below.

(5) Paragraph (d) of reg 94 is narrowly restricted to retirement benefits schemes and the equivalent provision in the Listing Rules was, until recently, broadly similar. The current form of the exemption, which appears in para (1)(d) of art 123, is much wider and more to the point. The purpose of the restriction on the voting rights of the directors is to reduce the scope for them to use their votes for personal advantage. If, however, their interest is no different from that of the employees as a whole, there is no reason in principle to prevent them from voting. This is the approach now taken by the Listing Rules and is one that could reasonably be adopted by all long form articles.

Paragraph (1)(c) of art 122 permits a director to vote in relation to a transaction with another company in which he has a less than one per cent interest. The paragraph refers to the complex provisions of ss 198 to 211 of CA 1985. The broad effect of these sections is as follows:

(1) The sections set out the obligations on persons acquiring interests in shares of public companies to disclose the details to the company.

(2) An interest is notifiable if it relates to at least 3 per cent of 'relevant share capital' (that is, share capital carrying voting rights). The 3 per cent level is to be contrasted with the 1 per cent specified in the Rules.

(3) A person is taken to be interested in shares if his spouse or infant children are interested or if they are held by a company which acts in accordance with his instructions or in which he holds not less than one-third of the share capital (s 203).

(4) Interests which are to be notified include those held as beneficiary of a trust and those which are in the form of options over shares (s 208).

(5) A range of interests is excluded by s 209. This is a fairly complicated section and, instead of merely referring to the section and leaving it to the secretary to work out how it applies to a particular case, the following paragraph can be added to art 122:

6.8   Factors determining whether director has an interest in shares

To determine whether a proposal concerns a body corporate in which the director and persons connected with him hold an interest:

(a) shares held by a person as a bare or custodian trustee and in which he has no beneficial interest shall be treated as not held by him;

(b) shares comprised in a trust in which a person's interest is in reversion or remainder shall be treated as shares in which he is not interested if and so long as some other person is entitled to receive the income of the trust; and

(c) shares comprised in an authorised unit trust scheme (as defined in the Financial Services Act 1986) in which a person is interested only as a unit holder shall be disregarded in relation to that person.

The Listing Rules are rather curiously drafted in referring to ss 198 to 211 because, as the brief summary above shows, most of those sections are not in point. It would be simpler to amend para (c) as follows, so that it refers instead to ss 203 and 208 in defining the interests to be disclosed:

> (c) relates to another company in which he does not, to his knowledge, hold an interest in shares (within the meaning of sections 203 and 208 of the Act) representing one per cent or more either of its equity share capital or of its voting rights;

In addition, the article should set out the main exceptions granted by s 209 in summary form as above.

Regulation 94 treats, for all the purposes of the regulation, interests held by persons connected with the director as his interests. This is unduly onerous and art 122 takes that approach only in relation to para (1)(c).

Paragraph (3) of art 122 differs from reg 95 of Table A in that it excludes a director from being counted in the quorum only if the reason that he is not entitled to vote is because of an interest in the subject matter of the resolution. Directors also lose the right to vote, for example, if they are involved in a question as to whether art 122 applies and in that case there is no reason why the director affected should be excluded in counting the quorum.

Article 125

This corresponds to reg 99 of Table A with the addition of the reference to the secretary's possible right to compensation. This protection is not required for the normal secretarial appointment and is relevant only where the secretary has a formal appointment with a proper employment contract.

Article 127

Regulation 100 of Table A is amended so that the appointments which have to be recorded in minutes are those of directors and members of committees and not of officers.

Article 129

Section 362 of CA 1985 provides that a company whose objects comprise the transaction of business in any of the countries listed in Sched 14 to the Act may keep in that country a branch register of the members who are resident there. The registrar is known as an 'overseas branch register' and Sched 14 lays down a number of requirements that must be met. Advantage of this section will be taken only with the largest companies and then only if they have particular concentrations of shareholders in the country concerned. The right to have an overseas branch register is not dependent on there being a provision to that effect in the articles and accordingly art 129 can safely be omitted.

Article 131
Section 39 of CA 1985 permits the use of a facsimile seal outside the United Kingdom, if authorised by the articles, and s 40 provides that a company which has a common seal may use a facsimile with the word 'Securities' on its face for sealing securities. These are known as 'official seals' and are of reduced significance since the introduction of CA 1985, s 36A provided an alternative form of execution for deeds.

Article 135
The reference to amounts paid up in advance of calls being disregarded for dividend purposes is consistent with art 24. The repetition of the point avoids there being a conflict between the two articles.

Article 136
Most listed companies have taken power to satisfy the entitlement to cash dividends by the allotment to shareholders who agree to the arrangement of additional shares of a value equal to that of the dividends foregone. These issues of shares are known as scrip dividends and are popular with the companies who issue them as they conserve cash resources. From the point of view of the shareholders, scrip dividends are an inexpensive way of acquiring additional shares in the company as they do not have to pay brokerage. It should be noted that scrip dividends do not give rise to a tax benefit as the recipients are treated as if they had received gross income of an amount which, when reduced by income tax at the lower rate, is equal to the value of the shares allotted to them.

The power to issue scrip dividends requires the sanction of an ordinary resolution and the ABI has indicated that the authority should be subject to renewal at intervals of not more than five years (see the statement by the Investment Committee of the ABI dated 24 July 1992). The ABI have also stated that the authority should be related to the net cash dividend payable, that the shares should be subscribed at the full middle market quotation (or, if preferred, an average of, say, five dealing days) following the day on which the ordinary shares are first quoted '*ex*' the relevant dividend. The allotted shares rank *pari passu* with the shares whose dividend is involved except, of course, that they are not entitled to the dividend represented by the bonus shares.

Shareholders are given a right of election so that they can choose either the cash or the scrip dividend. If they are living in a territory where the laws invalidate an offer of shares being made in this way they may be excluded from the right to make an election.

Article 137
This article corresponds to reg 119 of Old Table A but does not appear in the current Table A.

Article 138
A record date is a date upon which the register is read for the purpose of identifying the members who are entitled to receive the dividend, payment or notice in respect of which the members need to be known. It is clearly of practical benefit if the record date can be a few days before the payment has to be made or the document posted and the procedures of the London Stock Exchange for dealing with shares '*cum*' and '*ex*' dividend ensure that appropriate adjustments are made where ownership of shares changes between the record date and the date of payment.

Article 141
The second sentence of this article is referred to in the commentary on reg 107 in Chapter 2. The third sentence is added for clarification.

Article 142
This useful article complies with the requirements of the Listing Rules as set out above. The cross-reference to art 155 will need to be altered if the numbering of the articles is changed.

Article 144
The power of directors to place sums to reserve was expressly confirmed in Old Table A but has been omitted in the present version. This is presumably because the power falls within the general authority of the directors to manage the business of the company as set out in art 102. Nevertheless it is commonly included in long form articles.

Article 145
A few minor alterations to reg 110 of Table A are made in art 145. The reference in para (1) to undivided profits is replaced by undistributed profits (see the comments on reg 110 in Chapter 2) and 'fixed' as well as 'preferential' dividends are treated as having the first call on the distributable reserves. Paragraph (3) allows fractions to be ignored (although this will not be the general practice with listed companies) and para (5) is added to ensure that the directors do not have difficulty in implementing minor administrative arrangements merely because they are not given express power to make them.

Article 146
The obligation to keep accounting records is imposed by CA 1985, s 221. This is such a well understood obligation of any company—and particularly if it is listed—that a reference to it is commonly omitted from the articles. The requirement has not been included in the current Table A although it did appear in Old Table A.

Article 147
The first sentence of this article repeats CA 1985, s 222(1). The second sentence corresponds to reg 109 of Table A.

Article 148
The obligation to send accounts to members is contained in CA 1985, s 238 and, although not included in Table A, is set out in art 148 by way of reminder. Summary accounts may be sent in accordance with the regulations made under CA 1985, s 251 (see the Companies (Summary Financial Statements) Regulations 1995).

Article 149
This article is similar in concept to art 120.

Article 150
This confirms the rights given to auditors under CA 1985, s 390 in relation to attendance and speaking at meetings. The right to receive notices of meetings is covered by art 50.

Article 151
This article is almost invariably adopted by listed companies as it enables them to clear the register of members who have effectively

disappeared. As the effect is to deprive the shareholders of their shares, the London Stock Exchange sets out in the Listing Rules a number of protections for shareholders which must be included in these provisions. The shares must have been held for at least 12 years, at least three dividends must have been payable but not cashed, no communication must have been received from the shareholder, two advertisements must be placed before the shares are sold and the London Stock Exchange must be notified of the intention to sell the shares.

Article 152

This largely corresponds to reg 111 of Table A except that the part of the regulation relating to the giving of notices of meetings of directors has been moved to art 116. Because the article requires that notices must be in writing, it is unnecessary to state elsewhere in the articles where provision is made for giving notices that they must be written.

Article 153

This article is based on reg 112 of Table A but complies with the Listing Rules of the London Stock Exchange in requiring the use of first class post or airmail, although the reference to airmail is barely necessary in view of para (2) which provides that members without an address in the UK are not entitled to received notices. Paragraph (2) adopts the wording suggested in Chapter 2 in the commentary on reg 112. Paragraph (3) also complies with the Listing Rules in relation to advertised notices.

The article provides that, in the case of joint holders, notices may be given to any one of them. A common variation, and the procedure that will in practice be more or less invariably followed, is to require that, if notices are given to one only of joint holders, it must be given to that holder whose name appears first in the register of members.

Article 154

It is an obvious administrative convenience if envelopes for posting documents to shareholders can be prepared on the basis of the names on the register a few days before the actual posting has to take place.

Article 155

This is another protection for the company against having to continue to send communications to shareholders who have disappeared. It is similar to art 142 but is useful for those companies which, for whatever reason, do not pay dividends regularly.

Article 157

Although this article corresponds to reg 114 of Table A, it goes into much more detail. In particular, it deals with the case where, even though the company is aware of the death, bankruptcy or liquidation of the member, notices continue to be sent to the address shown in the register of members. The register is for this purpose conclusive until the procedures for changing the address on transmission has been carried out (art 40).

Article 158

As with reg 115 of Table A, this article deals with the procedure for proving that a notice has been served and for determining the time of service. The article is more detailed than reg 115 as it covers service by means other than posting.

Article 159

The ability to give notices by advertisement if posting is not possible is a useful protection. Some companies go further and permit advertisements to be used generally by means of an article as follows:

6.9   Notice by way of advertisement

> Any notice which the company is required to give to the members may be given by advertisement in at least one national newspaper, unless these articles or the Act expressly provide otherwise.

The reference to one national newspaper is in accordance with the requirements of the Listing Rules of the London Stock Exchange (see above).

Appendix A

Articles of Association of a Private Company

Table A

1 The regulations contained in Table A in the Schedule to the Companies (Tables A to F) Regulations 1985 ('Table A'), apart from regs 26, 41,[1] 44,[2] 60, 61, 64, 65, 67, 73 to 80, 86, 89 and 94 to 98, apply to the company except insofar as they are inconsistent with these articles. A reference in these articles to a 'regulation' of a particular number is a reference to the regulation of that number in Table A.

2[3] *Regulation 1 is amended:

(a) by adding after the definition of 'United Kingdom' the following additional definition ' "Writing" includes any method of representing or reproducing words in a legible and non-transitory form';

(b) by adding at the end of the last sentence the words 'but, if a particular word or expression has more than one definition in the Act, the definition to be adopted is that which has the most general application in the Act'; and

(c) by deleting in the last sentence the words 'but excluding any statutory modification thereof not in force when these regulations become binding on the company'.

Private company

3* The company is a private company. Accordingly, no offer or invitation shall be made to the public (whether for cash or otherwise) to subscribe for shares in or debentures of the company and the company shall not allot or agree to allot (whether for cash or otherwise) shares in or debentures of the company with a view to all or any of them being offered for sale to the public.

Share capital

4 The share capital at the date of the adoption of these articles is £[   ] divided into [   ] ordinary shares of £1 each.

5* Regulation 2 is amended by adding at the end 'or, if there is no relevant resolution or so far as the resolution does not make specific provision, as the directors determine'.

6 Subject to any contrary direction given by the company in general meeting and to the provisions of the Act, the directors are authorised to create, allot, deal with or dispose of the shares which are authorised but unissued at the date of the adoption of these articles to such persons and on such terms as they think fit. The authority given to the directors shall expire five years from the date on which the resolution adopting these articles was passed but the directors may allot or dispose of shares after the expiry in pursuance of an offer or agreement made by the company before the expiry.

7 Section 89(1) of the Act does not apply to the company.

8* Regulation 5 is amended by adding at the end 'or, in the case of a bearer warrant, in the bearer of the warrant'.

Share certificates

9* The first sentence of regulation 6 is amended by replacing 'upon becoming the holder of any shares' with 'within two months after the allotment, or lodgment of a duly stamped transfer, to him of the shares (or within such other period as the terms of issue provide)'.

Lien

10 The lien conferred by regulation 8 attaches to all shares, whether fully paid or not, registered in the name of a person indebted or under liability to the company, whether he is the sole holder of the shares or one of two or more joint holders, and to all distributions and other moneys and property attributable to them. The lien shall be for all sums

presently payable to the company by him or his estate and regulation 8 is modified accordingly.

11* Regulation 10 is amended by adding at the end the following sentence:

'The transferee shall be registered as the holder of the shares comprised in the transfer (whether the share certificate has been produced or not) and he shall not be bound to see to the application of the purchase consideration.'.

12* Regulation 11 is amended by replacing 'to the person entitled to the shares at the date of the sale' with 'to the person entitled to the shares immediately prior to the sale'.

Calls on shares and forfeiture

13* Regulation 12 is amended:
  (a) by replacing 'subject to receiving at least fourteen clear days' notice' with 'subject to being given at least fourteen clear days' notice'; and
  (b) by replacing 'before receipt by the company of any sum due thereunder' with 'before receipt by the company of the sum due thereunder'.

14* Regulations 15 and 21 are amended by adding after 'at the appropriate rate (as defined by the Act)' the words 'or, if higher, at the rate of 15% per annum'.

15* Regulation 18 is amended:
  (a) by adding after 'together with any interest which may have accrued' the words 'and all expenses incurred by the company as a result of the nonpayment'; and
  (b) by adding at the end the following sentence:
      'The directors may accept the surrender of a share which is liable to be forfeited. In that event, references in these articles to 'forfeiture' include 'surrender'.'

16* Regulation 19 is amended by replacing 'all dividends and other moneys payable in respect of the forfeited shares' with 'all distributions attributable to the forfeited share'.

17* Regulation 20 is amended by adding at the end the following sentence:

'The directors may receive the consideration given for the share on its disposal and, if the share is in registered form, may register the transferee as the holder.'.

Transfer of shares

18 (a)(i) A member who wishes to transfer shares or an interest in shares (a 'Vendor') shall give to the directors a notice (a 'Transfer Notice') specifying:

(A) the number of shares (the 'Specified Shares') which, or an interest in which, he wishes to transfer;

(B) the third party (the 'Proposed Transferee') to whom he wishes to transfer the Specified Shares or interest if the Specified Shares are not purchased by members in accordance with this article; and

(C) the price per share (the 'Offer Price') at which he intends to transfer the Specified Shares or interest to the Proposed Transferee.

(ii) The Transfer Notice shall constitute the directors the Vendor's agents for the sale of the Specified Shares. The directors shall, within seven days of receipt of the Transfer Notice, offer the Specified Shares in writing to the other members in proportion to their then holdings of shares, fractions being rounded upwards. Each offer shall specify:

(A) the total number of the Specified Shares;

(B) the number offered to the offeree;

(C) the Offer Price; and

(D) the Proposed Transferee;

and shall provide that, if the offeree does not accept the offer in respect of any of the shares allocated within fourteen days of the offer, he shall be deemed to have declined it. Each offeree shall be asked to state whether he accepts the offer in whole or in part how many shares in excess of his allocation he wishes to purchase and, if he does wish to purchase shares, whether he accepts the Offer Price.

(iii) If the offers are not accepted by each offeree in respect of the whole of his allocation, the unclaimed shares shall be used in or towards satisfying applications for excess shares in proportion to the numbers of excess shares applied for.

Fractions of shares which would otherwise be allocated shall be consolidated and allocated by the drawing of lots.

(iv) If an offeree (a 'Dissenting Offeree') states that he accepts his allocation in whole or in part but does not accept the Offer Price, his acceptance shall be disregarded if acceptances, including excess applications, from offerees ('Assenting Offerees') accepting the Offer Price are received for at least the number of the Specified Shares. A Dissenting Offeree shall otherwise be required to purchase the number of the Specified Shares accepted by him for the Fair Price (determined in accordance with paragraph (vi)) unless the Vendor withdraws the Transfer Notice in accordance with this article.

(v) If the aggregate number of shares for which the offer and the Offer Price are accepted including, to the extent required, excess applications is equal to the number of the Specified Shares, the directors shall as soon as practicable give notice to the Vendor and the Assenting Offerees who shall be required by the directors to complete the sales and purchases within twenty-eight days. If the aggregate number of shares for which the offer is accepted, including excess applications, is less than the number of the Specified Shares, the directors shall as soon as practicable give notice to the Vendor. The Vendor may within seven days of being given the notice withdraw the Transfer Notice and, if he does not do so and all the members accepting the offer were Assenting Shareholders, the directors shall, as soon as practicable after the end of the period of seven days, give notice to the Vendor and the Assenting Shareholders requiring them to complete the sales and purchases of the shares for which the offer was accepted within twenty-eight days.

(vi) Unless under paragraph (v) sales of some or all of the Specified Shares are required to take place or the Vendor withdraws the Transfer Notice, the directors shall, as soon as is practicable, instruct the auditors to determine the fair price of each of the Specified Shares (the 'Fair Price'). The Fair Price shall be determined on the basis of the value as going concerns, as between a willing seller and a willing buyer, of the businesses of the company and any subsidiaries which it has as at the date on which the auditors are instructed to make their determination. The Fair Price shall not be adjusted by reason of the Specified Shares constituting a particular proportion of the issued share capital. In determining the Fair Price, the auditors shall be acting as independent experts and not as arbitrators and their determination shall, in the absence of manifest error, be conclusive. The directors shall notify the Fair Price to the Vendor and the Assenting and Dissenting Offerees within seven days of its determination by the auditors.

(vii)   If the Fair Price is less than 95 per cent of the Offer Price, the fees and expenses of the auditors shall be paid as to one half by the Vendor and as to the other half by the Dissenting Offerees, in proportion to the numbers of the Specified Shares in respect of which they have accepted the offer. In any other case, the fees and expenses shall be paid in full by the Dissenting Offerees in the same proportions.

(viii)   If the Fair Price is less than 95 per cent of the Offer Price, the Vendor may, within seven days of being given notice of the Fair Price, withdraw the Transfer Notice.

(ix)   If the Fair Price is more than 5 per cent above the Offer Price, an Assenting Offeree who does not wish to accept the Fair Price may within seven days of being given notice of the Fair Price withdraw his acceptance. The shares apportioned to him shall, so far as possible, be allocated amongst the offerees who have accepted the offer as if they were unclaimed shares to which paragraph (iii) applied.

(x)   If the above procedure does not result in offers at the Offer Price or the Fair Price, as the case may be, for all of the Specified Shares, the directors shall as soon as reasonably practicable notify the Vendor accordingly. The Vendor may, within seven days of being notified, withdraw the Transfer Notice.

(xi)   If the Vendor withdraws the Transfer Notice in accordance with this article, he shall not be entitled to dispose of the Specified Shares, or any interest in them, or to offer all or any of his holding of shares under this article within six months of the withdrawal.

(xii)   Unless the Transfer Notice is withdrawn in accordance with this article, the Vendor and the accepting offerees who have not exercised a right to withdraw their acceptances shall be required, by notice given by the directors as soon as practicable after the above procedure has been carried out, to complete the sales and purchases within twenty eight days.

(xiii) If the Vendor fails to carry out sales of any of the shares in accordance with this article, the directors may appoint some person to execute appropriate transfers on his behalf and to give a receipt for the purchase price, which shall be paid over to the Vendor.

(xiv) If the directors do not find purchasers for all the Specified Shares under the above provisions and the Vendor has not exercised a right to withdraw the Transfer Notice, the Vendor may sell those of the Specified Shares which are unsold to the Proposed Transferee for a cash price per share which is not less than the Offer Price. The directors may, before registering the transfer, require the production of evidence to enable them to satisfy themselves reasonably that the consideration shown on the instrument of transfer is a cash price and that no circumstances exist in relation to the sale which make that consideration misleading.

(b) Paragraph (a) does not apply to:

(i) A transfer by a member or the personal representatives of a deceased member to a relative of the member or to the trustees of a settlement created by the member or a relative of the member for the benefit of all or any of the member and his relatives. For this purpose, the relatives of a member are his children or remoter issue, spouse, brother, sister, parent or remoter forbear or their spouses;

(ii) A transfer by the personal representatives of a deceased member to a person to whom the shares in question have been specifically bequeathed;

(iii) A transfer for the purpose only of effecting the appointment of new trustees;

(iv) A transfer by an individual member to a company controlled by the member. For this purpose, a company is controlled by an individual if he, together with his relatives within the meaning of paragraph (i), owns shares conferring more than 50 per cent of the voting rights conferred by all the issued shares of that company;

(v) A transfer by a holding company to a subsidiary or by a subsidiary to its holding company or to another subsidiary of its holding company.

If, following a transfer made under paragraph (iii) or (iv) above, the relationship between the transferor and the transferee changes to one not within those paragraphs, the transferee shall as soon as possible transfer the shares either to the transferor or to a person to whom the transferor could have transferred the shares under those paragraphs. The directors may require that the transferee provides them with such information as they from time to time reasonably require to satisfy themselves that the transferee continues to have the same relationship with the transferor.

(c) The directors shall refuse to register a transfer made otherwise than in accordance with paragraph (a) or (b).

19 Regulation 24 is amended:

(a) by adding in the second sentence after 'also refuse to register a transfer' the words 'which is otherwise permitted under these articles'; and

(b) by adding in paragraph (a) after 'it is lodged' the words 'duly stamped (if stampable)' .

20 Regulation 25 is amended by replacing 'two months' with 'fourteen days'.

21 Regulation 28 is amended by replacing 'shall be returned to the person lodging it' with 'shall (except in the case of fraud) be returned to the person lodging it'.

22 Regulation 31 is amended:

(a) by adding at the end of the last sentence 'unless there are no other members'; and

(b) by adding at the end the following sentences:

'When a person becomes entitled to a share by transmission, the rights of the holder in relation to it cease. The person entitled by transmission may give a good discharge for dividends and other distributions in respect of the share.' .

Annual general meetings

23 Unless there is in force an elective resolution under section 366A of the Act to dispense with the holding of annual general meetings, the company shall in each year hold a general meeting as its annual general meeting and not more than fifteen months shall elapse between the date of one annual general meeting and that of the next.

Notices of general meetings

24 (a) The first sentence of regulation 38 is amended by deleting 'or a resolution appointing a person as a director'.

    (b) Notices of meetings need not be given to the directors as such and regulation 38 is modified accordingly.

25 Every notice calling a meeting of the company shall include, with reasonable prominence, a statement that a member entitled to attend and vote is entitled to appoint a proxy to attend and vote instead of him and that a proxy need not also be a member.

Proceedings at general meetings

26* Regulation 40 is amended by replacing 'unless a quorum is present' with 'unless a quorum is present when the meeting commences business'.

27* If, within 15 minutes (or such longer time not exceeding one hour as the chairman of the meeting decides) from the time appointed for the meeting, a quorum is not present the meeting, if convened on the requisition of members, shall be dissolved. It shall otherwise be adjourned to the same day in the next week, at the same time and place, or to such other day and at such time and place as the chairman or, failing him, the directors determine. At the adjourned meeting, the quorum shall be a single member present in person or by proxy.

28 Regulation 42 is amended by replacing 'or in his absence some other director nominated by the directors' with 'or a director nominated by the chairman or, in the absence of the chairman or of the director (if any) nominated by the chairman, some other director nominated by the directors'.

29* Regulation 43 is amended by replacing 'the members present and entitled to vote shall choose' with 'the members present and entitled to vote may choose'.

30* A corporate member may, by resolution of its directors or other governing body, authorise such one person as it thinks fit to act as its representative at general meetings of the company or meetings of any class of members. The authorised person may exercise the same powers on behalf of the grantor of the authority as the grantor could exercise if it were an individual member.

31* The persons entitled to attend and speak at general meetings and at separate class meetings are the directors (even if they are not members), the auditors (but their right to speak is limited to business which concerns them as auditors) and any other person invited to do so by the chairman. A proxy has the same right as the member who appointed him to speak at the meeting which he is appointed to attend and at adjournments of the meeting.

32 Paragraph (b) in regulation 46 is replaced with 'by any member having the right to vote at the meeting;' and paragraphs (c) and (d) are deleted.

33* Regulation 47 is amended:

    (a) by adding after 'Unless a poll is duly demanded' the words 'and the demand is not withdrawn before the poll is taken'; and

    (b) by deleting 'and an entry to that effect in the minutes of the meeting'.

34 *Regulation 48 is amended by deleting 'but only with the consent of the chairman'.

35 *The chairman shall appoint scrutineers if required to do so by the meeting. Regulation 49 is modified accordingly.

Votes of members

36 Regulation 54 is amended by replacing 'on a poll every member shall have one vote' with 'on a poll every member who is present in person, by representative or by proxy shall have one vote'.

37 Regulation 57 is amended:

    (a) by adding after 'in respect of any share held by him' the words 'or to exercise any privilege as holder of the share'; and

    (b) by replacing 'all moneys presently payable by him in respect of that share' with 'all moneys presently payable by him in respect of calls on that share'.

38 Regulation 58 is amended by replacing the first two sentences with the following sentences:

    'An objection to the qualification of a voter or to the counting of, or failure to count, a vote may be raised only at the meeting or adjourned meeting at which the vote is tendered. Unless an objection is made in due time, every vote counted and not disallowed at the meeting or adjourned meeting is valid and every vote disallowed or not counted is invalid.'.

39 Regulation 59 is amended by deleting the second sentence.

40 An instrument appointing a proxy shall be in writing, executed by or on behalf of the appointor, and shall be in any usual form or in a form approved by the directors. The appointment shall be valid for an adjournment of the meeting and the instrument shall be deemed to confer authority to vote on amendments to resolutions put to the meeting for which the authority is given or at an adjournment, unless in each case the instrument of proxy states otherwise. Where it is desired to afford members an opportunity to instruct the proxy how he shall act, the instrument appointing a proxy shall be in any form which enables the members to direct how their votes are to be exercised on each of the resolutions comprised in the business of the meeting for which it is to be used.

Number of directors

41 The minimum number of directors is one and, unless otherwise determined by ordinary resolution, the number of directors is not subject to a maximum. A sole director may exercise all the powers and discretions given to the directors by these articles and the Act.

Alternate directors

42 A director (other than an alternate director) may appoint as his alternate any person who is willing to act and may terminate the appointment.

43 Regulation 66 is amended:

    (a) by replacing 'but shall not be entitled to receive any remuneration from the company for his services as an alternate director' with the following sentence:

> 'An alternate director shall not be entitled to remuneration from the company for his services as an alternate director except that he may be paid by the company such part of the remuneration otherwise payable to his appointor as the appointor specifies by notice to the company.';

and

    (b) by adding at the end the following sentences:

'An alternate director who is also a director or who acts as alternate director for more than one director shall have one vote for every director represented by him in addition to his own vote if he is also a director. An alternate director, in his capacity as such, is not entitled to vote on a resolution on which his appointor is not entitled to vote.'.

44 An alternate director ceases to be an alternate for his appointor when his appointor ceases to be a director.

45 Regulation 68 is amended by adding after 'by notice to the company signed by the director making or revoking the appointment' the words 'and delivered to the office or tendered at a meeting of the directors'.

Delegation of directors' powers

46 Regulation 72 is amended:
  (a) by replacing the first sentence with the following:
      'The directors may delegate any of their powers to a committee consisting of such persons as they think fit provided that a majority of the members of the committee are directors.';
  and
  (b) by adding the following as the second sentence:
      'The power to delegate extends to the power of the directors to fix the remuneration of, or confer other benefits on, the members of the committee (whether in relation to their membership of the committee or in respect of any other office in the company) and is not limited by certain of these articles, but not others, referring expressly to particular powers, authorities or discretions being exercised by the directors or a committee of the directors.'.

Appointment and retirement of directors

47 The directors are not subject to retirement by rotation. The last sentence of regulation 84 is accordingly deleted.

48 The company, by ordinary resolution, or the directors may appoint as a director, either to fill a vacancy or as an additional director, any person who is willing to act, provided that the appointment does not

cause the number of directors to exceed any number fixed in accordance with these articles as the maximum number of directors.

49* A director is not required to hold qualification shares.

Disqualification and removal of directors

50 Regulation 81 is amended:
   (a) by replacing paragraphs (c) and (e) respectively with the following:
        '(c) in the opinion of all the other directors (excluding alternate directors who are not also directors in their own right) he either becomes incapable by reason of mental disorder of carrying out his duties as a director or engages in activities inconsistent with those duties;'
        '(e) he fails to attend three successive board meetings despite a notice being given to him prior to the third meeting that the provisions of this paragraph might apply and all the other directors resolve (the director concerned and, in his capacity as such, any alternate appointed by him being excluded from voting) that his office should be vacated; or';
   (b) by replacing 'by notice to the company' in paragraph (d) with 'by notice delivered to the office or tendered at a meeting of the directors'; and
   (c) by adding at the end the following paragraph:
        '(f) he is served a written notice, signed by or on behalf of the holder of shares conferring a majority of the voting rights conferred by all the shares, requiring him to resign.'.

51 A person is not disqualified from being a director by having attained any particular age.

Remuneration of directors

52 *Regulation 82 is amended:
   (a) by adding after 'entitled to such remuneration' the words 'for their services as such'; and
   (b) by adding at the end the following sentence:
        'A director who has ceased to hold office when the resolution is passed shall, unless it otherwise provides, be

entitled to be paid the appropriate proportion of the remuneration voted to the directors for the period during which he held office.'.

Directors' appointments and interests

53 Regulation 84 is amended by adding after 'Any appointment of a director to an executive office shall terminate' the following:
  '(unless:
    (a) the terms of his appointment provide otherwise; or
    (b) the directors resolve otherwise, the director concerned and any alternate appointed by him being excluded from voting)'.

54 Regulation 85 is amended by deleting 'and provided that he has disclosed to the directors the nature and extent of any material interest of his'.

Proceedings of directors

55 Regulation 88 is amended:
    (a) by replacing 'It shall not be necessary to give notice of a meeting to a director who is absent from the United Kingdom.' with:
        'A director who is or is intending to be absent from the United Kingdom may request the secretary to give him notice of meetings at an address provided by him for that purpose. Notices of meetings of the directors shall be sent to him at that address but, if he does not provide an address, it shall not be necessary to give notice of meetings to him while he is absent from the United Kingdom. The notice calling a meeting of the directors need not be in writing.';
  and
    (b) by deleting the last sentence.

56 The quorum for the transaction of the business of the directors is two except when there is only one director. An alternate director, if his appointor is not present, is counted in the quorum. If he is also a director, he is treated as two directors but at least one other director must be present to constitute a quorum. When there is only one director, he may exercise all the powers conferred on directors by these articles.

57 A director may participate in a meeting of the directors or of a committee of which he is a member by conference telephone or similar communications equipment by means of which all the persons participating in the meeting can hear each other at the same time. Participation in a meeting in this manner is treated as presence in person at the meeting.

58* Regulation 91 is amended by replacing 'The directors may appoint one of their number to be the chairman of the board of directors' with:

'The company may appoint and remove the chairman of the board of directors by ordinary resolution. If and so long as the position of chairman is vacant, the directors may appoint one of their number to be the chairman'.

59 Unless these articles otherwise provide, a director may vote at a meeting of the directors or of a committee on a resolution which concerns or relates to a matter in which he has, directly or indirectly, an interest but he remains obliged in any event to declare his interest in accordance with section 317 of the Act.

Secretary

60* Regulation 99 is amended by adding at the end 'but without prejudice to any right of compensation to which he is entitled.'.

61 A sole director shall not also be the secretary.

Minutes

62 Regulation 100 is amended by replacing paragraphs (a) and (b) with 'of all proceedings of general meetings and meetings of the directors'.

The seal

63* Regulation 101 is amended:

(a) by replacing 'The seal shall only be used' with 'If the company has a seal, it shall be used only'; and

(b) by adding at the end the following sentence:

'A document signed by a director and the secretary or by two directors and expressed to be executed by the company has the same effect as if executed under the seal.'.

Dividends

64* Regulation 106 is amended:
   (a) by adding after 'sent by post' the words 'at the risk of the
       person to whom it is sent'; and
   (b) by adding at the end the following sentence:
       'The company has no responsibility for sums delayed in the
       post or in the course of transfer or where it has complied
       with directions given in accordance with this article.'.

65* Regulation 107 is amended by adding at the end the following
sentence:
   'Unclaimed dividends may be invested or otherwise made use of
   for the benefit of the company until claimed.'.

66* Regulation 108 is amended by replacing 'twelve years' with 'three
years'.

Accounts

67* Regulation 109 is amended by adding at the end 'but they shall at
all times be open for inspection by the company's officers'.

Capitalisation of profits

68* Regulation 110 is amended by replacing 'capital redemption
reserve' in paragraphs (a) and (b) with 'capital redemption reserve or
other reserve or fund'.

Notices

69 Regulation 111 is amended:
   (a) by deleting 'except that a notice calling a meeting of the
       directors need not be in writing'; and
   (b) by adding at the end the following sentence:
       'A notice sent by facsimile transmission is deemed to be in
       writing.'.

70* Regulation 112 is amended:

(a) by adding at the end of the first sentence 'or by facsimile transmission to a number given by the member to the company for that purpose'; and

(b) by replacing the second and third sentences with:
'In the case of joint holders of a share, notices given to any one of them shall be sufficient notice to all of them. If the registered address of a member is, or the registered addresses of joint holders are, outside the United Kingdom, he or they may give the company an address within the United Kingdom at which notices may be given and notices shall be sent to him or them at that address. The member or joint holders shall not otherwise be entitled to receive notices from the company.'.

71* Resolution 115 is amended:

(a) by replacing 'at the expiration of 48 hours after the envelope containing it was posted' with 'at the expiration of 24 hours after the envelope containing it is posted if sent by first class post and at the expiration of 48 hours if sent by second class post'; and

(b) by adding at the end the following sentences:
'A notice which is served by being left at the registered address of the addressee is deemed to be given when it is left there. A notice given by facsimile transmission is deemed to be given when the message is sent.'.

Winding-up

72* Regulation 117 is amended by replacing 'may, for that purpose, value any assets and determine how the division shall be carried out' with 'may, for that purpose and with the like sanction, value any assets and determine how the division shall be carried out'.

Indemnity

73 Regulation 118 is amended:

(a) by adding after 'shall be indemnified out of the assets of the company' the words 'against losses and liabilities which he incurs, otherwise than as a result of his own negligence or default, in connection with the performance of his duties as such and';

(b) by adding after 'in which judgment is given in his favour' the words 'or where the proceedings are withdrawn or settled on terms which do not include a finding or admission of a material breach of duty by him'; and

(c) by adding at the end the following sentence:

'Subject to the provisions of the Act, the directors may purchase and maintain insurance at the expense of the company for the benefit of the directors or other officers or the auditors against liability which attaches to them or loss or expenditure which they incur in relation to anything done or omitted or alleged to have been done or omitted as directors, officers or auditors.'.

---

[1]   If art 27 is omitted, reg 41 should not be excluded.
[2]   If art 31 is omitted, reg 44 should not be excluded.
[3]   Articles marked with an asterisk may generally be omitted.

Appendix B

Articles of Association of a Wholly-Owned Subsidiary

Table A

1 In these articles:

'Parent Company' means a company which is the registered holder of not less than ninety per cent of the issued shares;

'Table A' means Table A in the schedule to the Companies (Tables A to F) Regulations 1985.

A reference in these articles to a 'regulation' is a reference to the regulation of that number in Table A.
2 The regulations contained in Table A, apart from regulations 8–22, 24–26, 64–69, 73–80, 86, 89 and 94, apply to the company except insofar as they are inconsistent with these articles.

Share capital

3 The share capital at the date of the adoption of these articles is £[　] divided into [　] shares of £1 each.

Transfer of shares

4 The directors shall register a transfer of shares which is presented for registration duly stamped.

General meetings

5 Regulation 37 is amended by replacing 'a date not later than eight weeks after receipt of the requisition' with the words 'a date not later than twenty-eight days after receipt of the requisition'.

Notices of general meetings

6 (a) The first sentence of regulation 38 is amended by deleting 'or a resolution appointing a person as a director'.

(b) Notices of meetings need not be given to the directors as such and regulation 38 is modified accordingly.

Proceedings at general meetings

7 If and so long as there is a Parent Company, its representative shall be the only person to constitute a quorum at general meetings. Regulation 40 is modified accordingly.

8 (a) If and so long as there is only one member of the company, a decision taken by the member, which may be taken in general meeting, is as effective as if agreed by the company in general meeting.

(b) A decision taken by a sole member under paragraph (a) (unless taken by way of a written resolution) shall be recorded in writing and a copy shall be provided to the company.

Number of directors

9 The minimum number of directors is one and, unless otherwise determined by ordinary resolution, the number of directors is not subject to a maximum. A sole director may exercise all the powers and discretions given to the directors by these articles.

Alternate directors

10 A director shall not be entitled to appoint an alternate director to represent him at meetings of the directors or of committees. Accordingly:
- (a) regulation 88 is amended by deleting the last sentence; and
- (b) regulation 93 is amended by deleting from and including the words 'but a resolution signed by an alternate director' to the end of the regulation.

Appointment and retirement of directors

11 The directors are not subject to retirement by rotation. The last sentence of regulation 84 is accordingly deleted.

12 Any person who is willing to act may be appointed as a director, either to fill a casual vacancy or as an additional director, by the Parent Company (if there is one) giving notice to the company of the appointment or (if there is no Parent Company) by a resolution of the directors.

13 A director is not required to hold qualification shares.

Disqualification and removal of directors

14 Regulation 81 is amended:
- (a) by replacing 'by notice to the company' in paragraph (d) with 'by notice delivered to the office or tendered at a meeting of the directors'; and
- (b) by adding at the end the following paragraph:
    '(f) he is served a written notice, signed on behalf of the Parent Company (if there is one) or, if there is no Parent Company, signed by or on behalf of the holder of shares conferring a majority of the voting rights conferred by all the shares, requiring him to resign.'.

15 A person is not disqualified from being a director by having attained any particular age.

Directors' appointments and interests

16 Regulation 84 is amended by replacing 'the directors may appoint' with 'the directors may, with the approval of the Parent Company (if there is one), appoint'.

17 Regulation 85 is amended by replacing 'provided that he has disclosed to the directors the nature and extent of any material interest of his' with 'provided that he has obtained the approval of the Parent Company (if there is one)'.

Directors' gratuities and pensions

18 Regulation 87 is amended by replacing 'The directors may provide benefits' with 'The directors may, with the approval of the Parent Company (if there is one), provide benefits'.

Proceedings of directors

19 The quorum for the transaction of the business of the directors is two except when there is only one director. When there is only one director, he may exercise all the powers conferred on directors by these articles.

20 A director may participate in a meeting of the directors or of a committee of which he is a member by conference telephone or similar communications equipment by means of which all the persons participating in the meeting can hear each other. Participation in a meeting in this manner is treated as presence in person at the meeting.

21 Regulation 91 is amended by replacing 'The directors may appoint one of their number to be the chairman of the board of directors' with 'The Parent Company (if there is one) may appoint and remove the chairman of the board of directors by notice to the company. If and so long as the position of chairman is vacant, the directors may appoint one of their number to be the chairman'.

22 A director may vote at a meeting of the directors or of a committee on a resolution which concerns or relates to a matter in which he has, directly or indirectly, an interest but he remains obliged in any event to declare his interest in accordance with section 317 of the Act.

Minutes

23 Regulation 100 is amended by replacing paragraphs (a) and (b) with 'of all proceedings of general meetings and meetings of the directors'.

Dividends

24 Regulation 103 is amended by replacing 'Subject to the provisions of the Act, the directors may pay interim dividends' with 'Subject to the provisions of the Act and with the approval of the Parent Company (if there is one), the directors may pay interim dividends'.

Accounts

25 Regulation 109 is amended by replacing 'No member shall (as such) have any right of inspecting any accounting records' with 'No member, other than the Parent Company (if there is one), shall (as such) have any right of inspecting any accounting records'.

Notices

26 A notice required by these articles to be given by the company may be given by any visible form on paper, including telex or facsimile. A notice given by immediate transmission is deemed to have been given at the time that it is transmitted to the person to whom it is addressed. Regulations 111 and 113 are amended accordingly.

Indemnity

27 Regulation 118 is amended:
  (a) by adding after 'shall be indemnified out of the assets of the company' the words 'against losses and liabilities which he incurs, otherwise than as a result of his own negligence or default, in connection with the performance of his duties as such and';

(b) by adding after 'in which judgment is given in his favour' the words 'or where the proceedings are withdrawn or settled on terms which do not include a finding or admission of a material breach of duty by him'; and

(c) by adding at the end the following sentence:

'Subject to the provisions of the Act and with the approval of the Parent Company (if there is one), the directors may purchase and maintain insurance at the expense of the company for the benefit of the directors or other officers or the auditors against liability which attaches to them or loss or expenditure which they incur in relation to anything done or omitted or alleged to have been done or omitted as directors, officers or auditors.'.

Appendix C

Articles of Association of a Deadlock Company

Table A

1 The regulations contained in Table A in the schedule to the Companies (Tables A to F) Regulations 1985 ('Table A'), apart from regulations 17, 24, 26, 39, 40, 41, 50, 54, 64, 65, 73–80, 81(e), 86, 88, 91 and 94–98, apply to the company except insofar as they are inconsistent with these articles.

2 (a) Definitions adopted for Table A apply in these articles, together with the following definitions:

'Active Member'	the member holding all or a majority of the shares of the other class than those held by the Passive Member;
'A Shares'	the 'A' shares of £1 each;
'A Shareholder'	the holder of an A Share;
'A Director'	a director appointed by the A Shareholders;
'Associated Party'	in relation to a member who is an individual, a Relative or a company Controlled by any combination of the individual and his Relatives; and, in relation to a company, a subsidiary or holding company or another subsidiary of its holding company and a person by whom the company is Controlled;
'B Shares'	the 'B' shares of £1 each;
'B Shareholder'	the holder of a B Share;
'B Director'	a director appointed by the B Shareholders;
'Deadlock Business'	any of the following:
	(a) taking steps for or in connection with the enforcement of a lien on the shares

of a member in circumstances which have not given rise to the existence of a lien on other shares unless the same action is taken in relation to the other shares;

(b) taking steps for or in connection with the enforcement of payment of a call on the shares of a member or the forfeiture of the shares, in circumstances where no calls remain unpaid by other members or the same action is taken in relation to all calls then unpaid, and making a declaration as to forfeiture in accordance with regulation 22;

(c) taking steps for or in connection with the enforcement of the performance by a member of his obligations under article 9;

(d) taking action against a director who any other director believes, or has reasonable grounds to believe, has breached the provisions of article 38;

(e) taking steps for or in connection with the enforcement of any rights which any of the directors believes, or has reasonable grounds to believe, that the company has against a member or an Associated Party of a member;

(f) approving the registration of a transfer of all or a majority of the shares of a class otherwise than to a Permitted Transferee;

(g) approving the registration of a transfer of shares to a Permitted Transferee unless, at the time when approval is sought, replies which are reasonably satisfactory in relation to a request for information under article 9(c) have not been received;

'Fair Price' — in relation to Vendor's Shares, the fair price of each share determined in accordance with article 8;

'Major Transaction' — as defined in article 38;

'Offer Price' — the price, if any, specified by a Vendor in a Transfer Notice;

'Passive Member' — in relation to Deadlock Business:
(a) the member referred to in paragraph (a), (b), (c) or (e) of the definition above;
(b) the member who holds all or a majority of the shares of the class by which the director referred to in paragraph (d) was appointed; or
(c) the member whose Associated Party is referred to in paragraph (e);
(d) the transferor of the shares referred to in paragraph (f);
(e) the holder of all or a majority of the shares of the other class to those to which the transfer referred to in paragraph (g) relates;
as the case may be;

'Permitted Transfer' — as defined in article 10;

'Permitted Transferee' — in relation to a member, a person to whom he may make a Permitted Transfer;

'Proposed Transferee' — a third party to whom a member wishes to transfer the Vendor's Shares or interest in the Vendor's Shares;

'Relative' — in relation to a member, his issue, however remote, spouse, brother, sister, parent or remoter forbear and the spouse of any of the foregoing;

'Transfer Notice' — a notice relating to a transfer of shares given under article 8;

'Vendor' — a member who gives a Transfer Notice;

'Vendor's Shares' — the shares held by a member who gives a Transfer Notice.

(b) For the purposes of this article, a company is Controlled by one or more persons if he or they, in any combination, is or are directly or indirectly the holders of or beneficially interested in shares of the company conferring in aggregate more than 50 per cent of the voting rights conferred by all its shares.

3 A reference to a 'regulation' of a particular number is to the regulation of that number in Table A.

Share capital

4 The share capital at the date of adoption of these articles is £[   ], divided into [   ] 'A' shares of £1 each and [   ] 'B' shares of £1 each. The A Shares and the B Shares constitute different classes of shares but, except as expressly provided in these articles, rank pari passu.

5 The company does not have power to issue share warrants to bearer.

6 (a) Subject to any contrary direction given by the company in general meeting and to the provisions of the Act and of these articles, the directors are authorised to create, allot, deal with or dispose of the shares which are authorised but unissued at the date of the adoption of these articles to such persons and on such terms as they think fit. The authority given to the directors shall expire five years from the date on which the resolution adopting these articles was passed but the directors may allot or dispose of shares after the expiry in pursuance of an offer or agreement made by the company before the expiry.

(b) Section 89(1) of the Act does not apply to the company.

(c) Unless otherwise approved by the company in general meeting, unissued shares which are to be issued shall be offered by the directors on identical terms to all the members in proportion, as nearly as may be with fractions being disregarded, to their existing holdings of shares. The offer shall be in writing and shall state the number of shares which each member is offered, the subscription price to be paid and the period, not being less than 21 clear days, within which the offer, if not accepted, will be deemed to have been declined. If the offers are not accepted in respect of all the shares offered, the directors shall offer the remaining shares to those members who accepted the first offer in proportion to their existing holdings of shares, the new offer being otherwise on the same terms as the first offer. At the expiration of the first offer and, if one is made, the new offer, the accepting members shall pay the subscription price and the directors shall allot the shares accordingly, the shares allotted to each member being designated the same class as the existing shares held by him.

Lien

7 The lien conferred by regulation 8 attaches to all shares, whether fully paid or not, registered in the name of a person indebted or under liability to the company, whether he is the sole holder of the shares or one of two or more joint holders, and to all distributions and other moneys and property attributable to them. The lien shall be for all sums presently payable to the company by him or his estate and regulation 8 is modified accordingly.

Transfer of shares

8 (a) A member who wishes to transfer any shares or an interest in shares shall give to the directors a notice offering to sell all the shares held by him. He may also specify a Proposed Transferee and the price per share at which he intends to sell shares or an interest in shares to the Proposed Transferee.

(b) The Transfer Notice shall constitute the directors the Vendor's agents for the sale of the Vendor's Shares. If the Vendor did not specify or is deemed not to have specified an Offer Price, the directors shall within seven days of the receipt of the Transfer Notice instruct the auditors to determine the Fair Price in accordance with paragraph (i).

(c) The directors shall, within seven days of the receipt of the Transfer Notice if it specified an Offer Price or within seven days of the determination of the Fair Price if the Vendor did not specify or is deemed not to have specified an Offer Price, offer the Vendor's Shares in writing to the other members in proportion to their existing holdings of shares, fractions being rounded upwards. Each offer shall specify:

(i) the total number and class of the Vendor's Shares;

(ii) the number offered to the offeree;

(iii) the Offer Price and the Proposed Transferee, if specified in the Transfer Notice; and

(iv) if an Offer Price was not, or was deemed not to have been, specified in the Transfer Notice, the Fair Price;

and shall provide that, if the offeree does not accept the offer in respect of any of the shares allocated within fourteen days of the offer, he shall be deemed to have declined it but that, if he does accept, he shall not be entitled to withdraw his acceptance except as provided in this article. Each offeree shall be asked to state whether he accepts the offer in whole or in part, how many of the Vendor's Shares in excess of his allocation he wishes to purchase and, if he does wish to purchase shares, whether he accepts the Offer Price, if any.

(d) If there are competing applications for shares, they shall be satisfied in accordance with the following principles:

(i) applications, including applications for excess shares, by holders of shares of the same class as the Specified Shares shall be given priority over applications by the holders of shares of the other class;

(ii) an application up to the number offered to the offeree under paragraph (c) shall be given priority over applications for excess allocations;

(iii) if shares applied for by the holders of a class of shares up to the numbers offered to them under paragraph (c) exceed the number to be allocated to those holders, the shares shall be allocated in proportion to the numbers which they were offered;

(iv) applications for excess allocations shall be satisfied in proportion to the excess numbers applied for.

Fractions of shares which would otherwise be allocated shall be consolidated and allocated by the drawing of lots.

(e) If:

(i) the Transfer Notice specified an Offer Price and the aggregate number of shares for which the offers and the Offer Price are accepted, including excess applications, is greater than the number of the Specified Shares; or

(ii) the Transfer Notice did not specify an Offer Price and the aggregate number of shares for which the offers are accepted, including excess applications, is greater than the number of the Specified Shares;

the directors shall allocate the Specified Shares amongst the accepting members, in accordance with the principles stated in paragraph (d), and paragraph (f) shall then apply.

(f) If:

(i) the Transfer Notice specified an Offer Price and the aggregate number of shares for which the offers and the Offer Price are accepted, including excess applications, is equal to the number of the Specified Shares; or

(ii) the Transfer Notice did not specify an Offer Price and the aggregate number of shares for which the offers are accepted, including excess applications, is equal to the number of the Specified Shares; or

(iii) this paragraph applies under the provisions of paragraph (e);

the directors shall, as soon as practicable give notice to the Vendor and the accepting members who shall be required by the directors to complete the sales and purchases within a period of twenty eight days.

(g) If:

(i) the Transfer Notice specified an Offer Price; and

(ii) an offeree accepted the offer but not the Offer Price; and

(iii) the aggregate number of shares for which the offers were accepted, including excess applications, was not less than the number of the Specified Shares;

but neither paragraph (e) nor paragraph (f) applies, the directors shall, as soon as is practicable, instruct the auditors to determine the Fair Price.

(h) If the aggregate number of shares for which the offers were accepted, including excess applications, was less than the number of the Specified Shares, the directors shall as soon as practicable give notice to the Vendor. The Vendor may within seven days of being given the notice withdraw the Transfer Notice. If he does not do so and all the members accepting the offer accepted the Offer Price (if any) or the Fair Price (if the Transfer Notice did not specify an Offer Price), the directors shall, as soon as practicable after the end of the period of seven days, give notice to the Vendor and the accepting members requiring them to complete the sales and purchases of the shares for which the offer was accepted within twenty-eight days. If the Vendor does not withdraw the Transfer Notice and the Transfer Notice specified an Offer Price which was not accepted by all the accepting members, the directors shall, as soon as is practicable, instruct the auditors to determine the Fair Price.

(i) The Fair Price shall be determined on the basis of the value as going concerns, as between a willing seller and a willing buyer, of the businesses of the company and any subsidiaries which it has as at the date on which the auditors are instructed to make their determination. The Fair Price shall not be adjusted by reason of the Specified Shares constituting a particular proportion of the issued share capital of the company. In determining the Fair Price, the auditors shall be acting as independent experts and not as arbitrators and their determination shall, in the absence of manifest error, be conclusive.

(j) If the Fair Price has been determined because members accepted the offer but did not accept the Offer Price, the fees and expenses of the auditors shall be paid by those members in proportion to the numbers of the Vendor's Shares (including excess applications) in respect of which they accepted the offer. If the Transfer Notice did not specify, or was deemed not to have specified, an Offer Price, the fees and expenses shall be paid by the Vendor.

(k) If the Vendor did not specify, or is deemed not to have specified, an Offer Price, the directors shall notify the Fair Price to the Vendor and those offerees who have indicated their acceptance of the offer within seven days of its determination by the auditors.

(l) If the Vendor specified an Offer Price and the Fair Price is less than 95 per cent of the Offer Price, the Vendor may, within seven days of being given notice of the Fair Price, withdraw the Transfer Notice.

(m) An offeree who, having accepted the Offer Price, does not wish to accept the Fair Price may within seven days of being notified of the Fair Price withdraw his acceptance. If he does so, the shares apportioned to him shall, so far as possible, be allocated amongst the offerees who have accepted the offer as if they were unclaimed shares to which paragraph (d) applied. If he does not withdraw his acceptance, he shall be obliged to purchase the shares allocated to him for the Fair Price.

(n) If the above procedure does not result in offers at the Offer Price or the Fair Price, as the case may be, for all of the Vendor's Shares, the directors shall as soon as reasonably practicable notify the Vendor accordingly. The Vendor may, within seven days of being notified, withdraw the Offer Notice.

(o) If the Vendor withdraws the Transfer Notice in accordance with this article, he shall not be entitled to dispose of the Vendor's Shares, or any interest in them, or to offer all or any of his holding of shares under this article within six months of the withdrawal.

(p) Unless the Transfer Notice is withdrawn in accordance with this article, the Vendor and the accepting offerees who have not exercised a right to withdraw their acceptances shall be required, by notice given by the directors as soon as practicable after the above procedure has been carried out, to complete the purchases within twenty eight days.

(q) If the Vendor fails to carry out the sales of any of the shares in accordance with this article, the directors may appoint some person to execute appropriate transfers on his behalf and to give a receipt for the purchase price which shall be paid over to the Vendor. A share of one class which is transferred to the holder of shares of the other class shall be deemed, on registration of the transfer, to be redesignated as shares of the other class unless, following the redesignation, all the issued shares would be of one class.

(r) If the directors do not find purchasers for all the Vendor's Shares under the above provisions and the Vendor has not exercised a right to withdraw the Transfer Notice, the Vendor may, within three months after being notified as to how many of the Vendor's Shares are unsold, sell the unsold shares for a cash price per share, payable against delivery of an executed share transfer form and the relevant documents of title, which is not less than the Offer Price or the Fair Price, if any. If the unsold shares are sold to the Proposed Transferee, the directors shall register the transfer but if the person to whom it is proposed to transfer the unsold shares is not the Proposed Transferee, the directors may refuse to register the transfer to that person.

9 (a) If a relevant event occurs in relation to a member, he shall be deemed, when the member holding all or a majority of the shares of the other class first becomes aware that the event has occurred, to have given a Transfer Notice to the company in respect of all his shares and not to have specified either a Proposed Transferee or an Offer Price.

(b) For this purpose, a relevant event is:

(i) in relation to a corporate member:

(A) the appointment of a receiver, manager, administrative receiver or administrator over any part of its undertaking or assets;

(B) its liquidation (other than a voluntary liquidation for the purpose of a reconstruction or amalgamation without insolvency);

(C) its making a voluntary arrangement with its creditors; or

(D) a change in the persons by which it is Controlled;

(ii) in relation to an individual member:

(A) his being adjudicated bankrupt;

(B) his making a voluntary arrangement with his creditors;

(iii) in relation to a member holding all or a majority of the shares of either class:

(A) three successive meetings of the members being inquorate because no person who was or represented a holder of shares of the class held by that member was present;

(B) three successive board meetings being inquorate because no director appointed by the holders of shares of the class was present;

(C) a direction (by way of renunciation, nomination or otherwise) being given to the effect that shares to which he is entitled on allotment or transfer should be allotted to another person who is not a Permitted Transferee of the member;

(D) a sale or other disposition of an interest in shares being carried out otherwise than in accordance with article 8 or 10;

and it shall also be a relevant event if a member, or a person connected with the member within paragraph (c), fails, within fourteen clear days, to provide the information required from him under that paragraph or under article 10(c).

(c) To ascertain whether a relevant event has occurred in respect of a member, the directors nominated by the holders of the shares of the other class than those held by the member who nominated them may require the member, or a person connected with him, to provide such information as they reasonably specify. The persons connected with a member are the persons entitled by transmission to his shares, the persons by whom the member (in the case of a corporate member) is or appears to be Controlled and, where the shares held by the member have been the subject of a Permitted Transfer, the parties to the transfer.

10 (a) Article 8 does not apply to any of the following, each being a 'Permitted Transfer':

(i) a transfer to a Relative of the transferor or to the trustees of a settlement whose beneficiaries do not and cannot include any person other than the transferor and his Relatives;

(ii) a transfer by the personal representatives of a deceased member to a person to whom they have been specifically bequeathed or to a Relative of the deceased member;

(iii) a transfer for the purpose solely of implementing the appointment of a new trustee;

(iv) a transfer to a company which is an Associated Party of the transferor;

(v) a transfer by way of charge only;

(vi) a transfer to a member holding shares of the same class as those the subject of the transfer.

(b) If the transferee of shares acquired them as a result of a transfer which was a Permitted Transfer by reason of paragraph (iv) and he ceases to be an Associated Party of the transferor, a relevant event (within the meaning of article 9) shall be deemed to have occurred in relation to the member.

(c) To ascertain whether a proposed transferee is a Permitted Transferee, the directors nominated by the holders of the shares of the other class than the shares to be transferred may require the transferor or the transferee to provide such information as they reasonably specify.

(d) The directors may refuse to register a transfer which purports to be a Permitted Transfer so long as replies which are reasonably satisfactory in relation to a request for information under paragraph (c) have not been received.

11 (a) In this article, the following definitions apply:

(i) 'Majority Member': a member holding all or a majority of the shares of a class;

(ii) 'Stated Price': the price per share specified in the Purchase Notice;

(iii) 'Purchase Notice': the notice given by the Majority Member under paragraph (b);

(iv) 'Recipient Members': the members who hold all the shares of the other class than the shares held by the Majority Member.

(b) A Majority Member may, after the expiration of a period of at least three years from the date of the adoption of these articles, give notice to the Recipient Members (with a copy to the company) requiring that either:

(i) the Recipient Members purchase all the shares held by the Majority Member or, if they do not comprise all the shares of the class and the Recipient Members so elect, all the issued shares of the class which is held by the Majority Member; or

(ii) the Recipient Members sell to the Majority Member all the shares held by them;

in each case for the Stated Price, payable in cash against delivery of an executed share transfer form and the relevant documents of title.

(c) The Purchase Notice shall be deemed to contain a warranty by the Majority Member in favour of the Recipient Members that the Majority Member is not aware of anything relating to the company, or to any subsidiaries that it has, which, to the knowledge of the Majority Member, is not known to the Recipient Members and which, if known, would materially affect their opinion as to the value of the shares of the company. The Recipient Members shall not be entitled to take any action in respect of the warranty after the expiration of twelve months from the date of the registration of the transfer of the shares unless they have commenced proceedings against the Majority Member before the expiration.

(d) Within fourteen clear days of the date of the Purchase Notice, the Recipient Members shall inform the Majority Member in writing as to whether they wish to buy or sell shares. If the Recipient Members do not inform the Majority Member of their wish, they will be deemed to have agreed to sell their shares to the Majority Member.

(e) The relevant members shall be required to complete the applicable sale and purchase within twenty eight days of the notification being given to them under paragraph (c) and the provisions of article 8 shall apply for implementing the transactions as if the Stated Price were the Offer Price and the shares to be purchased were the Vendor's Shares.

12 The directors may refuse to register a transfer unless:

(a) it is lodged at the office or at such other place as the directors appoint and is accompanied by the certificate for the shares to which it relates; and

(b) it is in favour of not more than four transferees;

but shall otherwise register a transfer made in accordance with article 8 or 10.

13 Regulation 25 is amended by replacing 'two months' with 'fourteen days'.

Notice of general meetings

14 Regulation 37 is amended by replacing eight weeks' with 'four weeks'.

15 (a) The first sentence of regulation 38 is amended by deleting 'or a resolution appointing a person as a director'.

(b) Notices of meetings need not be given to the directors as such and regulation 38 is modified accordingly.

16 Every notice calling a meeting of the company shall include, with reasonable prominence, a statement that a member entitled to attend and vote is entitled to appoint a proxy to attend and vote instead of him and that a proxy need not also be a member.

Proceedings at general meetings

17 No business shall be transacted at a general meeting unless a quorum is present. The quorum is one A Shareholder and one B Shareholder,

present in person or by proxy or by duly authorised corporate representative.

18 If a quorum is not present within half an hour of the time appointed for the meeting or if during the meeting a quorum ceases to be present, the meeting shall be adjourned to the same day in the next week, or if that is not a business day to the next following business day, at the same time and place or such other time and place as the directors determine. If, at the adjourned meeting, a quorum is not present within half an hour of the time appointed for the meeting or if during the meeting a quorum ceases to be present, the meeting shall be dissolved.

19 Paragraph (b) in regulation 46 is replaced with 'by any member having the right to vote at the meeting;' and paragraphs (c) and (d) are deleted.

20 On a show of hands or on a poll, the A Shareholders present in person, by proxy or by corporate representative shall together have one vote and the B Shareholders present in person, by proxy or by corporate representative shall together have one vote.

21 If there is a difference between the holders of a class of shares as to how their votes shall be cast, it shall be resolved at a class meeting of the class of shares involved. A holder of the shares on a show of hands shall have one vote and on a poll shall have one vote for each share of the class which he holds.

Appointment and removal of directors

22 Unless otherwise determined by special resolution, the minimum number of directors is one and their number is not subject to a maximum.

23 The A Shareholders may, by majority decision amongst themselves, appoint up to four persons as A Directors and the B Shareholders may, by majority decision amongst themselves, appoint up to four persons as B Directors.

24 A director appointed under article 23 may be removed from office and replaced by the holders of a majority of the shares of the class whose holders appointed him. A director appointed by a Passive Member may be removed from office by the Active Member if taking action against the director would be Deadlock Business.

25 An appointment or removal of a director under article 23 or 24 is effected by a notice, given to the company by being sent to or left at the office or its principal place of business and signed, in a case falling

within article 23, by the holders of all or a majority of the shares of the relevant class or, in a case falling within article 24, by the Active Member. The appointment or removal shall take effect when the notice is received at the office or principal place of business or, if later, with effect from the date and time stated in the notice.

26 The directors are not subject to retirement by rotation. The last sentence of regulation 84 is accordingly deleted.

27 A person is not disqualified from being a director by having attained any particular age.

Alternate directors

28 A director (other than an alternate director) may appoint as his alternate any person who is approved for that purpose by the holders of a majority of the shares of the class by the holders of which he was appointed and may terminate the appointment. An alternate director shall be entitled to receive notice of all meetings of the directors whether he is present in the United Kingdom or not and the last sentence of regulation 66 accordingly does not apply. In the absence of the director appointing him, an alternate director shall (in addition to any voting rights to which he is entitled if he is also a director) be entitled to the same voting rights as his appointor and shall be treated as if he were appointed by the holders of the same class of shares as the shares held by the persons who appointed his appointor.

29 An alternate director ceases to be an alternate for his appointor when his appointor ceases to be a director.

30 Regulation 68 is amended by adding after 'by notice to the company signed by the director making or revoking the appointment' the words 'and delivered to the office or tendered at a meeting of the directors'.

Directors' appointments and interests

31 Regulation 84 is amended by adding after 'Any appointment of a director to an executive office shall terminate' the following:
'(unless:
   (a) the terms of his appointment provide otherwise; or
   (b) the directors resolve otherwise, the director concerned and any
        alternate appointed by him being excluded from voting)'.

32 Regulation 85 is amended by deleting 'and provided that he has disclosed to the directors the nature and extent of any material interest of his'.

Proceedings of directors

33 Subject to the provisions of these articles, the directors may regulate their proceedings as they think fit.

34 A director may, and the secretary at the request of a director shall, call a meeting of the directors.

35 The quorum for the transaction of the business of the directors, other than Deadlock Business, is one A Director and one B Director. If the business of the meeting is, or includes, Deadlock Business, the quorum in relation only to that business is two directors appointed by the Active Member.

36 If a quorum of directors is not present at a meeting of the directors within half an hour from the time appointed for the meeting or if, during the meeting, a quorum ceases to be present, it shall be adjourned to the same day in the next week, or if that is not a business day to the next following business day, at the same time and place. If at the adjourned meeting a quorum is not present within half an hour of the time appointed for the meeting or if, during the meeting, a quorum ceases to be present, the meeting shall be dissolved.

37 The members of a committee to which the directors delegate any of their powers must include at least one A Director and one B Director and Regulation 72 is amended accordingly.

38 A director (including a managing director) shall not have the power, without the prior approval of the board of directors, to commit the company to a Major Transaction. For this purpose, any of the following is a Major Transaction:

> (i) the sale, lease, transfer or other disposal of the whole or a substantial part of the of the undertaking of the company or of a subsidiary of the company;
>
> (ii) engaging an employee at a basic salary in excess of £30,000 per annum or increasing the basic salary of an employee who is, or following the increase will be, entitled to a basic salary in excess of £30,000 per annum;
>
> (iii) dismissing on a summary basis an employee entitled to a basic salary in excess of £20,000 per annum;

(iv) incurring capital expenditure on any one item in excess of £20,000;

(v) entering into or varying the terms of a transaction in which a member, or a person who is known by the director to be an Associated Party of a member, has an interest.

Regulation 70 is amended accordingly.

39 Except in relation to Deadlock Business, at meetings of the directors and of committees of the directors, each of the A Directors present in person or represented by an alternate shall have a number of votes equal to the number of the B Directors present in person or represented by an alternate; and each of the B Directors present in person or represented by an alternate shall have a number of votes equal to the number of the A Directors present in person or represented by an alternate. In relation to Deadlock Business, each of the directors appointed by the Active Member who is present or represented by an alternate shall have one vote and the directors appointed by the Passive Member who are present or represented by their alternates shall together have one vote. A director who is also an alternate shall be treated as an extra person in respect of each director.

40 The chairman of the board, for the period of twelve months following the adoption of these articles, shall be one of the A Directors chosen by the A Directors and for the following period of twelve months shall be one of the B Directors chosen by the B Directors and so on for successive periods of twelve months. The chairman shall preside at every meeting of the directors and of committees of directors at which he is present but he shall not have a second or casting vote.

41 Not less than fourteen clear days' notice of meetings of directors and of committees of the directors shall be given to each of the directors or the members of the committee at his address given for that purpose, whether in the United Kingdom or elsewhere and whether he is present in the United Kingdom or not.

42 The notice of a meeting of the directors or of a committee of the directors shall include an agenda specifying in reasonable detail the matters to be discussed at the meeting. The agenda shall include any item which a director requests the secretary to include in it. No other business shall be discussed at the meeting unless all the directors present otherwise agree. At an adjourned meeting, only business which was specified in the agenda for the original meeting and remains unfinished shall be discussed.

43 A director may participate in a meeting of the directors or of a committee of which he is a member by conference telephone or similar communications equipment by means of which all the persons participating in the meeting can hear each other at the same time. Participation in a meeting in this manner is treated as presence in person at the meeting.

44 A director may vote at a meeting of the directors or of a committee on a resolution which concerns or relates to a matter in which he has, directly or indirectly, an interest but he remains obliged in any event to declare his interest in accordance with section 317 of the Act.

Minutes

45 Regulation 100 is amended by replacing paragraphs (a) and (b) with 'of all proceedings of general meetings and meetings of the directors'.

Accounts

46 Regulation 109 is amended by replacing 'No member shall (as such) have any right of inspecting any accounting records' with 'A member shall be entitled, on giving reasonable notice, to inspect during business hours any accounting records'.

Notices

47 A notice required by these articles to be given by the company may be given by any visible form on paper, including telex or facsimile. A notice given by immediate transmission is deemed to have been given at the time that it is transmitted to the person to whom it is addressed. Regulations 111 and 113 are amended accordingly.

48 A member whose registered address is not within the United Kingdom may give to the company an address either within the United Kingdom or elsewhere at which notice may be given to him and he shall be entitled to have notices given to him at that address. Regulation 112 is amended accordingly.

Indemnity

49 Regulation 118 is amended:
   (a) by adding after 'shall be indemnified out of the assets of the company' the words 'against losses and liabilities which he incurs, otherwise than as a result of his own negligence or default, in connection with the performance of his duties as such and';
   (b) by adding after 'in which judgment is given in his favour' the words 'or where the proceedings are withdrawn or settled on terms which do not include a finding or admission of a material breach of duty by him'; and
   (c) by adding at the end the following sentences:
      'For the purposes of this article, a director who carries out a Major Transaction without the prior approval of the board shall be treated as not having acted, in relation to the transaction, in the execution of the duties of his office. Subject to the provisions of the Act, the directors may purchase and maintain insurance at the expense of the company for the benefit of the directors or other officers or the auditors against liability which attaches to them or loss or expenditure which they incur in relation to anything done or omitted or alleged to have been done or omitted as directors, officers or auditors.'.

Appendix D

Articles of Association Providing Minority Protection

Table A

1 The regulations contained in Table A in the schedule to the Companies (Tables A to F) Regulations 1985 ('Table A'), apart from regulations 17, 20, 24, 26, 40, 41, 64, 65, 73–80, 81(e), 82, 86, 89, 90, 94–98 and 102, apply to the company except insofar as they are inconsistent with these articles.

2 (a) Definitions adopted for Table A apply in these articles, together with the following definitions:

'A Shares'	the 'A' shares of £1 each;
'A Shareholder'	the holder of an A Share;
'A Director'	a director appointed by the A Shareholders;
'Associated Party'	in relation to a member who is an individual, a Relative or a company Controlled by any combination of the individual and his Relatives; and, in relation to a company, a subsidiary or holding company or another subsidiary of its holding company and a person by whom the company is Controlled;
'B Shares'	the 'B' shares of £1 each;
'B Shareholder'	the holder of a B Share;
'B Director'	the director appointed by the B Shareholders;
'Fair Price'	in relation to Specified Shares, the fair price of each share determined in accordance with article 11;
'Offer Price'	the price, if any, specified by a Vendor in a Transfer Notice;

'Permitted Transfer'	as defined in article 12;
'Permitted Transferee'	in relation to a member, a person to whom he may make a Permitted Transfer;
'Proposed Transferee'	a third party to whom a member wishes to transfer the Specified Shares or interest in the Specified Shares;
'Relative'	in relation to a member, his issue, however remote, spouse, brother, sister, parent or remoter forbear and the spouse of any of the foregoing;
'Specified Shares'	the shares specified in a Transfer Notice;
'Transfer Notice'	a notice relating to a transfer of shares given under article 11;
'Vendor'	a member who gives a Transfer Notice.

(b) For the purposes of this article, a company is Controlled by one or more persons if he or they, in any combination, is or are directly or indirectly the holders of or beneficially interested in shares of the company conferring in aggregate more than 50 per cent of the voting rights conferred by all its shares.

3 A reference to a 'regulation' of a particular number is to the regulation of that number in Table A.

Share capital

4 The share capital at the date of adoption of these articles is £[   ], divided into [   ] 'A' shares of £1 each and [   ] 'B' shares of £1 each. The A Shares and the B Shares constitute different classes of shares but, except as expressly provided in these articles, rank pari passu.

5 The company does not have power to issue share warrants to bearer.

6 Regulation 2 is amended by replacing 'ordinary resolution' with 'special resolution'.

7 (a) Subject to any contrary direction given by the company in general meeting and to the provisions of the Act and of these articles, the directors are authorised to create, allot, deal with or dispose of the shares which are authorised but unissued at the date of the adoption of these articles to such persons and on such terms as they think fit. The authority given to the directors shall expire five years from the date on which the resolution adopting these

articles was passed but the directors may allot or dispose of shares after the expiry in pursuance of an offer or agreement made by the company before the expiry.

(b) Section 89(1) of the Act does not apply to the company.

(c) Unless otherwise approved by special resolution, unissued shares which are to be issued shall be offered by the directors on identical terms to all the members in proportion, as nearly as may be with fractions being disregarded, to their existing holdings of shares. The offer shall be in writing and shall state the number of shares which each member is offered, the subscription price to be paid and the period, not being less than 21 clear days, within which the offer, if not accepted, will be deemed to have been declined. If the offers are not accepted in respect of all the shares offered, the directors shall offer the remaining shares to those members who accepted the first offer in proportion to their existing holdings of shares, the new offer being otherwise on the same terms as the first offer. At the expiration of the first offer and, if one is made, the new offer, the accepting members shall pay the subscription price and the directors shall allot the shares accordingly, the shares allotted to each member being designated the same class as the existing shares held by him.

Lien

8 The lien conferred by regulation 8 attaches to all shares, whether fully paid or not, registered in the name of a person indebted or under liability to the company, whether he is the sole holder of the shares or one of two or more joint holders, and to all distributions and other moneys and property attributable to them. The lien shall be for all sums presently payable to the company by him or his estate and regulation 8 is modified accordingly.

9 Regulation 9 is amended by deleting the words 'in such manner as the directors determine' and by adding at the end the following sentence:

'A sale shall be effected by the directors giving a Transfer Notice in respect of the shares without specifying an Offer Price or a third party to whom he wishes to transfer the shares.'.

Calls on shares and forfeiture

10 Subject to the provisions of the Act, a forfeited share may be sold or re-allotted. A sale shall be effected by the directors giving a Transfer Notice in respect of the share without specifying an Offer Price. The share may be re-allotted in accordance with article 7(c).

Transfer of share

11 (a) A member who wishes to transfer shares or an interest in shares shall give to the directors a notice specifying the number of shares concerned. He may also specify a Proposed Transferee and the price per share at which he intends to sell the Specified Shares or interest to the Proposed Transferee.

(b) The Transfer Notice shall constitute the directors the Vendor's agents for the sale of the Specified Shares. If the Vendor did not specify an Offer Price, the directors shall within seven days of the receipt of the Transfer Notice instruct the auditors to determine the Fair Price in accordance with paragraph (i).

(c) The directors shall, within seven days of the receipt of the Transfer Notice if it specified an Offer Price or within seven days of the determination of the Fair Price if the Vendor did not specify an Offer Price, offer the Specified Shares in writing to the other members in proportion to their existing holdings of shares, fractions being rounded upwards. Each offer shall specify:

(i) the total number and class of the Specified Shares;

(ii) the number offered to the offeree;

(iii) the Offer Price and the Proposed Transferee, if specified in the Transfer Notice; and

(iv) if an Offer Price was not specified in the Transfer Notice, the Fair Price;

and shall provide that, if the offeree does not accept the offer in respect of any of the shares allocated within fourteen days of the offer, he shall be deemed to have declined it but that, if he does accept, he shall not be entitled to withdraw his acceptance except as provided in this article. Each offeree shall be asked to state whether he accepts the offer in whole or in part, how many of the Specified Shares in excess of his allocation he wishes to purchase and, if he does wish to purchase shares, whether he accepts the Offer Price, if any.

(d) If there are competing applications for shares, they shall be satisfied in accordance with the following principles:

    (i) applications, including applications for excess shares, by holders of shares of the same class as the Specified Shares shall be given priority over applications by the holders of shares of the other class;

    (ii) an application up to the number offered to the offeree under paragraph (c) shall be given priority over applications for excess allocations;

    (iii) if shares applied for by the holders of a class of shares up to the numbers offered to them under paragraph (c) exceed the number to be allocated to those holders, the shares shall be allocated in proportion to the numbers which they were offered;

    (iv) applications for excess allocations shall be satisfied in proportion to the excess numbers applied for.

Fractions of shares which would otherwise be allocated shall be consolidated and allocated by the drawing of lots.

(e) If:

    (i) the Transfer Notice specified an Offer Price and the aggregate number of shares for which the offers and the Offer Price are accepted, including excess applications, is greater than the number of the Specified Shares; or

    (ii) the Transfer Notice did not specify an Offer Price and the aggregate number of shares for which the offers are accepted, including excess applications, is greater than the number of the Specified Shares;

the directors shall allocate the Specified Shares amongst the accepting members, in accordance with the principles stated in paragraph (d), and paragraph (f) shall then apply.

(f) If:

    (i) the Transfer Notice specified an Offer Price and the aggregate number of shares for which the offers and the Offer Price are accepted, including excess applications, is equal to the number of the Specified Shares; or

    (ii) the Transfer Notice did not specify an Offer Price and the aggregate number of shares for which the offers are accepted, including excess applications, is equal to the number of the Specified Shares; or

(iii) this paragraph applies under the provisions of paragraph (e);

the directors shall, as soon as practicable give notice to the Vendor and the accepting members who shall be required by the directors to complete the sales and purchases within a period of twenty eight days.

(g) If:

(i) the Transfer Notice specified an Offer Price; and

(ii) an offeree accepted the offer but not the Offer Price; and

(iii) the aggregate number of shares for which the offers were accepted, including excess applications, was not less than the number of the Specified Shares;

but neither paragraph (e) nor paragraph (f) applies, the directors shall, as soon as is practicable, instruct the auditors to determine the Fair Price.

(h) If the aggregate number of shares for which the offers were accepted, including excess applications, was less than the number of the Specified Shares, the directors shall as soon as practicable give notice to the Vendor. The Vendor may within seven days of being given the notice withdraw the Transfer Notice. If he does not do so and all the members accepting the offer accepted the Offer Price (if any) or the Fair Price (if the Transfer Notice did not specify an Offer Price), the directors shall, as soon as practicable after the end of the period of seven days, give notice to the Vendor and the accepting members requiring them to complete the sales and purchases of the shares for which the offer was accepted within twenty-eight days. If the Vendor does not withdraw the Transfer notice and the Transfer Notice specified an Offer Price which was not accepted by all the accepting members, the directors shall, as soon as is practicable, instruct the auditors to determine the Fair Price.

(i) The Fair Price shall be determined on the basis of the value as going concerns, as between a willing seller and a willing buyer, of the businesses of the company and any subsidiaries which it has as at the date on which the auditors are instructed to make their determination. The Fair Price shall not be adjusted by reason of the Specified Shares constituting a particular proportion of the issued share capital of the company. In determining the Fair Price, the auditors shall be acting as independent experts and not as arbitrators and their determination shall, in the absence of manifest error, be conclusive.

(j) If the Fair Price has been determined because members accepted the offer but did not accept the Offer Price, the fees and expenses of the auditors shall be paid by those members in proportion to the numbers of the Specified Shares (including excess applications) in respect of which they accepted the offer. If the Transfer Notice did not specify an Offer Price, the fees and expenses shall be paid by the Vendor.

(k) If the Vendor did not specify an Offer Price, the directors shall notify the Fair Price to the Vendor and those offerees who have indicated their acceptance of the offer within seven days of its determination by the auditors.

(l) If the Vendor specified an Offer Price and the Fair Price is less than 95 per cent of the Offer Price, the Vendor may, within seven days of being given notice of the Fair Price, withdraw the Transfer Notice.

(m) An offeree who, having accepted the Offer Price, does not wish to accept the Fair Price may within seven days of being notified of the Fair Price withdraw his acceptance. The shares apportioned to him shall, so far as possible, be allocated amongst the offerees in accordance with paragraph (d). If he does not withdraw his acceptance, he shall be obliged to purchase the shares allocated to him for the Fair Price.

(n) If the above procedure does not result in offers at the Offer Price or the Fair Price, as the case may be, for all of the Specified Shares, the directors shall as soon as reasonably practicable notify the Vendor accordingly. The Vendor may, within seven days of being notified, withdraw the Transfer Notice.

(o) If the Vendor withdraws the Transfer Notice in accordance with this article, he shall not be entitled to dispose of the Specified Shares, or any interest in them, or to offer all or any of his holding of shares under this article within six months of the withdrawal.

(p) Unless the Transfer Notice is withdrawn in accordance with this article, the Vendor and the accepting offerees who have not exercised a right to withdraw their acceptances shall be required, by notice given by the directors as soon as practicable after the above procedure has been carried out, to complete the purchases within twenty eight days.

(q) If the Vendor fails to carry out the sales of any of the shares in accordance with this article, the directors may appoint some person to execute appropriate transfers on his behalf and to give a receipt for the purchase price which shall be paid over to the Vendor. A share of one class which is transferred to the holder of shares of the other class shall be deemed, on registration of the transfer, to be redesignated as shares of the other class unless, following the redesignation, all the issued shares would be B Shares.

(r) If the directors do not find purchasers for all the Specified Shares under the above provisions and the Vendor has not exercised a right to withdraw the Transfer Notice, the Vendor may, within three months after being notified as to how many of the Specified Shares are unsold, sell the unsold shares for a cash price per share, payable against delivery of an executed share transfer form and the relevant documents of title, which is not less than the Offer Price or the Fair Price, if any. The directors shall register the transfer of the unsold shares unless they exercise their power to refuse to register it in accordance with article 13.

(s) If the transferee of the unsold shares is not a Proposed Transferee and the shares are B Shares, the shares shall, on registration of the transfer, be redesignated as A Shares.

12 (a) Article 11 does not apply to any of the following, each being a 'Permitted Transfer':

(i) a transfer to a Relative of the transferor or to the trustees of a settlement whose beneficiaries do not and cannot include any person other than the transferor and his Relatives;

(ii) a transfer by the personal representatives of a deceased member to a person to whom they have been specifically bequeathed or to a Relative of the deceased member;

(iii) a transfer for the purpose solely of implementing the appointment of a new trustee;

(iv) a transfer to a company which is an Associated Party of the transferor;

(v) a transfer by way of charge only;

(vi) a transfer to a member holding shares of the same class as those the subject of the transfer.

(b) If the transferee of shares acquired shares as a result of a transfer which was a Permitted Transfer by reason of paragraph (iv) and he ceases to be an Associated Party of the transferor, the transferee must, without delay, retransfer the shares to the transferor.

(c) To ascertain whether a proposed transferee is a Permitted Transferee, the directors nominated by the holders of the shares of the other class than the shares to be transferred may require the transferor or the transferee to provide such information as they reasonably specify.

(d) The directors may refuse to register a transfer which purports to be a Permitted Transfer so long as replies which are reasonably satisfactory in relation to a request for information under paragraph (c) have not been received.

13 The directors may refuse to register a transfer unless:

(a) it is lodged at the office or at such other place as the directors appoint and is accompanied by the certificate for the shares to which it relates; and

(b) it is in favour of not more than four transferees;

but shall otherwise register a transfer made in accordance with article 11 or 12.

14 Regulation 25 is amended by replacing 'two months' with 'fourteen days'.

Transmission of shares

15 Regulation 30 is amended by adding the following sentence after the first sentence:

'The directors may, by notice given at the registered address of the member, require the person to make his election within twenty-eight clear days of the date of the notice and, if he does not do so, he shall be deemed to have elected to have become the holder of the share.'.

16 Regulation 31 is amended by replacing 'shall have the right' with 'shall (unless and so long as he fails to comply with a notice requiring him to elect under regulation 30) have the right'.

Notice of general meetings

17 Regulation 37 is amended by replacing 'eight weeks' with 'four weeks'.

18(a) The first sentence of regulation 38 is amended by deleting 'or a resolution appointing a person as a director'.

 (b) Notices of meetings need not be given to the directors as such and regulation 38 is modified accordingly.

19 Every notice calling a meeting of the company shall include, with reasonable prominence, a statement that a member entitled to attend and vote is entitled to appoint a proxy to attend and vote instead of him and that a proxy need not also be a member.

Proceedings at general meetings

20 No business shall be transacted at a general meeting unless a quorum is present. Unless all the shares are A Shares, the quorum is one A Shareholder and one B Shareholder, present in person or by proxy or by duly authorised corporate representative. If all the shares are A Shares, the quorum is two A Shareholders, present in person or by proxy or by duly authorised corporate representative.

21 If a quorum is not present within half an hour of the time appointed for the meeting or if during the meeting a quorum ceases to be present, the meeting shall be adjourned to the same day in the next week, or if that is not a business day to the next following business day, at the same time and place or such other time and place as the directors determine. At least three clear days' notice shall be given to the members, specifying the time and place of the adjourned meeting. If, at the adjourned meeting, a quorum is not present within half an hour of the time appointed for the meeting or if during the meeting a quorum ceases to be present, the members present shall form a quorum.

22 Regulation 45 is amended by replacing the last two sentences with the following sentence

'At least seven clear days' notice of the adjourned meeting shall be given, specifying the time and place of the adjourned meeting and the general nature of the business to be transacted.'.

23 Paragraph (b) in regulation 46 is replaced with 'by any member having the right to vote at the meeting;' and paragraphs (c) and (d) are deleted.

24 On a show of hands or on a poll, the A Shareholders present in person, by proxy or by corporate representative shall together have two votes and the B Shareholders present in person, by proxy or by corporate representative shall together have one vote, except that, on a resolution to remove the B Director, the A Shareholders present in person, by proxy or by corporate representative shall together have one vote and the B Shareholders present in person, by proxy or by corporate representative shall together have two votes.

25 If there is a difference between the holders of a class of shares as to how their votes shall be cast, it shall be resolved at a class meeting of the class of shares involved. A holder of the shares on a show of hands shall have one vote and on a poll shall have one vote for each share of the class which he holds.

Appointment and removal of directors

26 Unless otherwise determined by special resolution, the minimum number of directors is one and their number is not subject to a maximum.

27 The A Shareholders may, by majority decision amongst themselves, appoint up to four persons as A Directors and the B Shareholders may, by majority decision amongst themselves, appoint one person as the B Director.

28 A director appointed under article 27 may be removed from office and replaced by the holders of a majority of the shares of the class whose holders appointed him.

29 An appointment or removal of a director under article 27 or 28 is effected by a notice given to the company by being sent to or left at the office or its principal place of business and signed by the holders of all or a majority of the shares of the relevant class. The appointment or removal shall take effect when the notice is received at the office or principal place of business or, if later, with effect from the date and time stated in the notice.

30 The directors are not subject to retirement by rotation. The last sentence of regulation 84 is accordingly deleted.

31 A person is not disqualified from being a director by having attained any particular age.

Alternate directors

32 A director (other than an alternate director) may appoint as his alternate any person who is approved for that purpose by the holders of a majority of the shares of the class by the holders of which he was appointed and may terminate the appointment. An alternate director shall be entitled to receive notice of all meetings of the directors whether he is present in the United Kingdom or not and the last sentence of regulation 66 accordingly does not apply. In the absence of the director appointing him, an alternate director shall (in addition to any voting rights to which he is entitled if he is also a director) be entitled to the same voting rights as his appointor and shall be treated as if he were appointed by the holders of the same class of shares as the shares held by the persons who appointed his appointor. The last sentence of regulation 88 does not apply.

33 An alternate director ceases to be an alternate for his appointor when his appointor ceases to be a director.

34 Regulation 68 is amended by adding after 'by notice to the company signed by the director making or revoking the appointment' the words 'and delivered to the office or tendered at a meeting of the directors'.

Directors' appointments and interests

35 Regulation 84 is amended by adding after 'Any appointment of a director to an executive office shall terminate' the following:

'(unless:
(a) the terms of his appointment provide otherwise; or
(b) the directors resolve otherwise, the director concerned and any alternate appointed by him being excluded from voting)'.

36 Regulation 85 is amended by deleting 'and provided that he has disclosed to the directors the nature and extent of any material interest of his'.

Proceedings of directors

37 Notice of directors' meetings shall be given to a director who is absent from the United Kingdom if he has given an address for the

receipt of notices in such circumstances, whether in the United Kingdom or elsewhere. Regulation 88 is amended accordingly.

38 The quorum for the transaction of the business of the directors so long as there is a B Shareholder is one A Director and the B Director, if appointed. If there is no B Shareholder, the quorum is two A Directors.

39 If a quorum of directors is not present at a meeting of the directors within half an hour from the time appointed for the meeting or if, during the meeting, a quorum ceases to be present, it shall be adjourned to the same day in the next week, or if that is not a business day to the next following business day, at the same time and place. If at the adjourned meeting a quorum is not present within half an hour of the time appointed for the meeting or if, during the meeting, a quorum ceases to be present, the directors present shall form a quorum.

40 The members of any committee to which the directors delegate any of their powers must include the B Director, if appointed, and regulation 72 is amended accordingly.

41 Unless all the shares are A Shares, the directors shall not enter into a Major Transaction without the prior approval of a special resolution or the approval of the B Director given at a board meeting attended by him. For this purpose, each of the following is a Major Transaction:

> (a) creating a mortgage, charge, lien or other encumbrance over any of the assets of the company or any of its subsidiaries, apart from a lien arising by operation of law;
>
> (b) incurring borrowings if the aggregate borrowings of the company and its subsidiaries, as a result, would exceed four times the aggregate of the company's paid-up share capital and reserves as shown in its last published accounts or, if none have been published, would exceed £20,000;
>
> (c) giving credit to any person in amounts or for periods in excess of the company's normal trading terms;
>
> (d) giving a guarantee or indemnity in relation to the liabilities or obligations of another person, not being a wholly-owned subsidiary of the company;
>
> (e) disposing, other than in the normal course of trade, of the whole or a substantial part of the assets or undertaking of the company;
>
> (f) incurring capital expenditure in excess of £10,000 on any one item or in excess of £25,000 in any period of twelve months;

(g) determining the remuneration of directors;

(h) engaging an employee at a basic salary in excess of £20,000 per annum or increasing the basic salary of an employee who is, or following the increase would be, entitled to a basic salary in excess of £ 20,000 per annum;

(i) dismissing on a summary basis an employee entitled to a basic salary in excess of £15,000 per annum;

(j) appointing a managing director or chief executive;

(k) entering into a transaction otherwise than at arm's length;

(l) issuing securities convertible into, or giving a right to subscribe for, shares of the company or granting options in respect of shares of the company;

(m) paying or declaring a dividend on any shares.

Regulation 70 is amended accordingly.

42 When a B Director holds office, not less than fourteen clear days' notice of meetings of directors and of committees of the directors shall be given to each of the directors or the members of the committee, unless the B Director agrees otherwise. There shall otherwise be no minimum period of notice required.

43 When a B Director holds office:

(a) the notice of a meeting of the directors or of a committee of the directors shall include an agenda specifying in reasonable detail the matters to be discussed at the meeting;

(b) the agenda shall include any item which a director requests the secretary to include in it;

(c) no other business shall be discussed at the meeting unless all the directors present otherwise agree; and

(d) at an adjourned meeting, only business which was specified in the agenda for the original meeting and remains unfinished shall be discussed;

unless the B Director agrees otherwise.

44 A director may participate in a meeting of the directors or of a committee of which he is a member by conference telephone or similar communications equipment by means of which all the persons participating in the meeting can hear each other at the same time. Participation in a meeting in this manner is treated as presence in person at the meeting.

45 A director may vote at a meeting of the directors or of a committee on a resolution which concerns or relates to a matter in which he has,

directly or indirectly, an interest but he remains obliged in any event to declare his interest in accordance with section 317 of the Act.

Minutes

46 Regulation 100 is amended by replacing paragraphs (a) and (b) with 'of all proceedings of general meetings and meetings of the directors'.

Dividends

47 Subject to the provisions of the Act and of these articles, the company may declare dividends in accordance with the respective rights of the members but no dividend shall exceed the amount recommended by the directors.

48 Regulation 103 is amended by adding 'and of these articles' after 'Subject to the provisions of the Act'.

Capitalisation of profits

49 Regulation 110 is amended by replacing 'ordinary resolution' with 'special resolution'.

Notices

50 A notice required by these articles to be given by the company may be given by any visible form on paper, including telex or facsimile. A notice given by immediate transmission is deemed to have been given at the time that it is transmitted to the person to whom it is addressed. Regulations 111 and 113 are amended accordingly.

51 A member whose registered address is not within the United Kingdom may give to the company an address either within the United Kingdom or elsewhere at which notice may be given to him and he shall be entitled to have notices given to him at that address. Regulation 112 is amended accordingly.

Indemnity

52 Regulation 118 is amended:
  (a) by adding after 'shall be indemnified out of the assets of the company' the words 'against losses and liabilities which he incurs, otherwise than as a result of his own negligence or default, in connection with the performance of his duties as such and';
  (b) by adding after 'in which judgment is given in his favour' the words 'or where the proceedings are withdrawn or settled on terms which do not include a finding or admission of a material breach of duty by him'; and
  (c) by adding at the end the following sentence:
     'Subject to the provisions of the Act, the directors may purchase and maintain insurance at the expense of the company for the benefit of the directors or other officers or the auditors against liability which attaches to them or loss or expenditure which they incur in relation to anything done or omitted or alleged to have been done or omitted as directors, officers or auditors.'.

Appendix E

Articles of Association of a Listed Company

Table A not to apply

1[1] The regulations contained in the schedule to the Companies (Tables A–F) Regulations 1985 do not apply to the company.

Interpretation

2[2] In these articles—

'Act' means the Companies Act 1985, as modified or re-enacted.
'clear days' in relation to the period of a notice means that period excluding the day when the notice is given or deemed to be given and the day for which it is given or on which it is to take effect.
'holder' in relation to shares means the member whose name is entered in the register of members as holder of them.
'London Stock Exchange' means London Stock Exchange Limited.
'office' means the registered office of the company.
'recognised person' means a recognised clearing house or a nominee of a recognised clearing house or of a recognised investment exchange.[3]
'seal' means the common seal of the company and includes, so far as is applicable, an official seal.[4]
'secretary' means the secretary of the company or other person appointed to perform the duties of secretary, including a joint, assistant or deputy secretary.
'United Kingdom' means Great Britain and Northern Ireland.

'writing' includes any method of representing or reproducing words in a legible and non-transitory form and 'written' is interpreted accordingly.

Unless the context otherwise requires, words and expressions contained in these articles bear the same meanings as in the Act; but, if a particular word or expression has more than one definition in the Act, the definition to be adopted is that which has the most general application in the Act.

Share capital and variation of rights

3[5] The share capital of the company on the adoption of these articles is £[ ] divided into [ ] ordinary shares of £1 each.

4[6] Subject to the provisions of the Act and without prejudice to the rights attached to existing shares, a share may be issued with such rights and subject to such restrictions as the company by ordinary resolution determines or (if there is no relevant resolution or so far as the resolution does not make special provision) as the directors determine.

5[7] Subject to the provisions of the Act, shares may be issued which are to be redeemed, or are liable to be redeemed at the option of the company or the holder, on such terms and in such manner as these articles provide.

6[8] The company may exercise the powers conferred by the Act of paying commissions, and may pay such brokerage as is lawful, as consideration for subscribing or agreeing to subscribe (whether absolutely or conditionally), or procuring or agreeing to procure subscriptions (whether absolute or conditional), for shares. Subject to the provisions of the Act, commissions and brokerage may be satisfied wholly or partly by the allotment of fully or partly paid shares.

7[9] Subject to the provisions of the Act, the company may purchase its own shares (including redeemable shares) but, if there are in issue listed shares convertible into or carrying a right to subscribe for shares of the class proposed to be purchased, a purchase may not be made without prior sanction of an extraordinary resolution passed at a separate meeting of the holders of the convertible shares.

8[10]   (1) If the share capital is divided into different classes of shares, the rights attached to a class of shares may, subject to the provisions of the Act and to the terms of their issue, be varied (whether the company is being wound up or not) with the consent in writing of the holders of not less than three-quarters in nominal value of the issued shares of the class or with the sanction of an extraordinary resolution passed at a separate meeting of the holders of the shares of the class.

(2) The rights attached to shares of a class (unless the rights otherwise expressly provide):

    (a) are deemed to be varied by a reduction of the capital paid up on them or by the creation or issue of further shares ranking in priority for payment of a dividend or in respect of capital or which confer on the holders voting rights more favourable than the voting rights conferred by them;

    (b) are not deemed to be varied by the creation or issue of further shares ranking pari passu with or subsequent to them;

    (c) are not deemed to be varied by a purchase by the company of its own shares.

(3) The provisions of these articles relating to general meetings apply to every separate general meeting of the holders of a class of shares but:

    (a) the quorum is two holders in person or by proxy representing not less than one third in nominal value of the issued shares of the class;

    (b) at the meeting, a holder of shares of the class present in person or by proxy may demand a poll;

    (c) if a quorum is not present at the meeting, one holder of shares of the class present in person or by proxy at an adjourned meeting constitutes a quorum.

9^{11} (1) Subject to the provisions of the Act and of these articles, all unissued shares are under the control of the directors who may allot, grant options over or otherwise deal with or dispose of them to such persons, at such times and on such terms as they think fit.

(2) The directors are generally and unconditionally authorised, under section 80 of the Act, to exercise for each prescribed period all the powers of the company to allot relevant securities up to an aggregate nominal amount equal to the section 80 amount.

(3) In accordance with and within the terms of the above authority the directors may allot equity securities during a prescribed period wholly for cash:

    (a) in connection with a rights issue; or

    (b) up to an aggregate nominal amount equal to the section 89 amount, otherwise than in connection with a rights issue;

as if section 89(1) of the Act did not apply.

(4) The directors may, during the prescribed period, make offers or agreements which require or might require equity securities or other relevant securities to be allotted after the period expires and they may allot the securities in accordance with the offers or agreements as if the prescribed period had not expired.

(5) For the purposes of this article:

    (a) 'rights issue' means an offer of equity securities in favour of ordinary shareholders where the equity securities respectively attributable to the interests of all ordinary shareholders are proportionate (as nearly as may be) to the numbers of ordinary shares held by them, but subject to such exclusions or other arrangements as the directors consider to be necessary or expedient in relation to fractional entitlements or legal, regulatory or practical problems under the laws or regulations of an overseas territory or the requirements of a regulatory body or stock exchange;

    (b) 'prescribed period' means:

       (i) for the purposes of the authority conferred by paragraph (2), the period (not being more than 15 months) for which the authority is given by a resolution stating the section 80 amount for that period; or

       (ii) for the purpose of the power conferred by paragraph (3), the period (not being more than 15 months) for which the power is given by a resolution stating the section 89 amount for the period;

    (c) 'section 80 amount' and 'section 89 amount' for any period are respectively the amounts stated in the appropriate resolution for that period;

    (d) 'relevant securities' and 'equity securities' have the meanings stated in sections 80(2) and 94(2) of the Act respectively.

10[12] Except as required by law, a person shall not be recognised by the company as holding a share on trust. Except as otherwise provided by these articles or by law, the company shall not be bound by or recognise an interest in a share, except an absolute right of the holder, or (in the case of a bearer warrant) of the bearer of the warrant, to the entirety of it.

Share warrants

11[13] (1) The company may issue warrants in respect of fully-paid shares which state that the bearer is entitled to the shares specified in them and may provide, by coupons or otherwise, for the payment of dividends on the shares.

(2) The directors may determine and vary the conditions on which warrants are issued or held and the conditions on which a new warrant or coupon is issued for one which is worn out, defaced, lost or destroyed, or on which a warrant may be surrendered and the name of the bearer entered in the register of members in respect of the shares specified in it. The conditions may provide that evidence other than production of the warrant constitutes proof of the holding. The bearer of a warrant shall be subject to the conditions currently in force, whether made or varied before or after the date of issue of the warrant. Before issuing a new warrant or coupon or other document conferring an entitlement to dividends in place of one which has been lost or destroyed, the directors must be satisfied beyond reasonable doubt that the original has been destroyed.

(3) The bearer of a warrant is not entitled, as bearer, to attend and vote or to exercise in respect of the shares to which the warrant relates rights of a member at general meetings or sign a requisition for a meeting unless:

(a) at least three days before the day appointed for the meeting in the first case or before the requisition is received at the office in the second case, he has deposited the warrant at the office or at such other place as the directors approve or determine, together with a written statement of his name and address; and

(b) the warrant remains there until the meeting and any adjournment of it have been held.

(4) Not more than one person shall be accepted as holder of the warrant.

(5) The directors may require the holder, or person who claims to be the holder, of the warrant to produce his warrant and to satisfy them that he continues to be the holder.

(6) There shall be no liability on the company or its registrar for loss or damage incurred by any person as a result of the name of a person who is not the lawful owner of a warrant being entered in the register of members when the warrant is surrendered.

Certificates

12[14] (1) Every member (other than a recognised person), on becoming the holder of shares, shall be entitled without payment to one certificate for all the shares of each class held by him or, upon payment for every certificate after the first of such reasonable out of pocket expenses as the directors determine, to several certificates, each for one or more of his shares. If a member transfers part of his holding of shares he shall be entitled to a certificate for the balance of his holding without charge.

(2) A certificate shall be issued within one month after the date of expiration of the right of renunciation (or within such other period as the terms of allotment provide) or (in the case of the transfer of shares) within five days after the lodgment with the company of the transfer of the shares, not being a transfer which the company is entitled to refuse to register and does not register.[15]

(3) Every certificate shall be sealed with the seal,[16] or shall be issued in such other manner as the directors determine, having regard to the terms of issue, the Act and the regulations of the London Stock Exchange, and shall specify the number, class and distinguishing numbers (if any) of the shares to which it relates and the amounts paid up on them. A signature on a certificate may be made by such mechanical means as the directors determine.

(4) The company is not obliged to issue more than one certificate for shares held jointly by several persons and delivery of a

certificate for a share to one of several joint holders is sufficient delivery to all of them.

13[17] If a share certificate is defaced, worn out, lost or destroyed, it may be renewed without charge on such terms as to evidence and indemnity and the payment of exceptional out of pocket expenses of the company as the directors think fit and (in case of defacement or wearing out) on delivery up of the old certificate.

Lien

14[18] The company shall have a first and paramount lien on every share (which is not fully paid) for all sums (whether presently payable or not) payable at a fixed time or called in respect of the share. The lien on a share shall extend to all distributions of money and other assets attributable to or in respect of it. The directors may exempt a share wholly or partly from the provisions of this article.

15[19] The company may sell, in such manner as the directors determine, shares on which the company has a lien if a sum in respect of which the lien exists is presently payable and is not paid within fourteen clear days after notice has been given to the holder of the shares, or to the person entitled to it in consequence of the death or bankruptcy of the holder, demanding payment and stating that, if the notice is not complied with, the shares may be sold.

16[20] To give effect to a sale the directors may authorise some person to execute an instrument of transfer of the shares to, or in accordance with the directions of, the purchaser. The transferee shall be registered as the holder of the shares comprised in the transfer (whether the share certificate has been produced or not) and he shall not be bound to see to the application of the purchase money. His title to the shares shall not be affected by an irregularity in or invalidity of the proceedings relating to the sale.

17[21] The net proceeds of sale shall be applied in or towards payment of such part of the amount for which the lien exists as is presently payable. Any residue shall (subject to a similar lien in respect of sums not presently payable as existed upon the shares before the sale) be paid to the person who was entitled to the shares immediately before the sale.

Calls on shares

18^{22} Subject to the terms of allotment, the directors may make calls on the members in respect of sums unpaid on their shares (whether in respect of their nominal value or by way of premium). A call may be made payable by instalments and payment of a call may be wholly or partly postponed. Each member shall (subject to being given at least fourteen clear days' notice specifying when and where payment is to be made) pay to the company as required by the notice the amount called on his shares. A call may, before the company has received the amount called, be wholly or partly revoked or postponed as the directors determine. A person on whom a call is made shall remain liable for it notwithstanding the subsequent transfer of the shares on which the call was made.

19^{23} A call is deemed to be made at the time when the resolution of the directors authorising the call is passed.

20^{24} The joint holders of a share are jointly and severally liable to pay all calls in respect of it.

21^{25} If a call or an instalment of a call is not fully paid by the time when it is payable, the person by whom it is payable shall pay:

(1) all costs, charges and expenses incurred by the company as a result of the non-payment; and

(2) interest on the amount unpaid from the day on which it was payable until payment at the rate of 15% per annum or at such other rate as the directors determine;

but the directors may waive payment wholly or in part.

22^{26} A sum payable in respect of a share on allotment or at a fixed date, whether in respect of its nominal value or by way of premium or as an instalment of a call, is deemed to be a call. If it is not paid, these articles apply as if the sum became payable by virtue of a call.

23^{27} Subject to the terms of allotment, the directors may make arrangements on the issue of shares for a difference between the holders in the amount and timing of calls on their shares.

24^{28} The directors may, if they think fit, receive from a member willing to make the advance all or part of the sums uncalled and unpaid on shares held by him and may pay interest on all or part of the advance (until it would have become payable if it had not been advanced) at such rate as they decide. No part of the advance shall be taken into account in ascertaining the amount of the dividends payable on the shares.

Forfeiture of shares

25[29] If a call or instalment of a call remains unpaid after it has become payable, the directors may give to the person from whom payment is due not less than fourteen clear days' notice requiring payment of the amount unpaid, together with any interest which has accrued and all expenses incurred by the company as a result of the non-payment. The notice shall name the place where the payment is to be made and shall state that, if the notice is not complied with, the shares in respect of which the call was made may be forfeited.

26[30] If the notice is not complied with, a share in respect of which it was given may, before the payment required by the notice is made, be forfeited by a resolution of the directors. The forfeiture shall include all distributions attributable to the forfeited share which have not been paid before the forfeiture.

27[31] Subject to the provisions of the Act, a forfeited share may be sold, re-allotted or otherwise disposed of, on such terms and in such manner as the directors determine, either to the person who was before the forfeiture the holder or to another person. For this purpose, the directors may authorise some person to execute an instrument of transfer of the share. The directors may receive the consideration given for the share on its disposal and, if the share is in registered form, may register the transferee as the holder. The forfeiture may be cancelled before the sale, re-allotment or disposal on such terms as the directors determine. If the share is not sold within three years of the date of the forfeiture, it shall be cancelled and the amount of the share capital shall be diminished by the nominal value of the share.

28[32] A member shall cease to be a member in respect of forfeited shares and shall surrender the certificate for the shares to the company for cancellation, but he shall remain liable to pay to the company all sums which at the date of forfeiture were presently payable by him to the company in respect of the shares, with interest, costs, charges and expenses in accordance with article 21. The directors may waive payment wholly or in part or enforce payment without any allowance for the value of the shares at the time of forfeiture or for any consideration received on their disposal.

29[33] A statutory declaration by a director or the secretary, that a share has been forfeited on a specified date, is conclusive evidence of the facts stated in it as against all persons claiming to be entitled to the share. The declaration shall (subject to the execution of an instrument of transfer if necessary) constitute a good title to the share. The person to whom the share is disposed of or re-allotted shall be registered as the holder of the share and shall not be bound to see to the application of the consideration (if any). His title to the share shall not be affected by an irregularity in or invalidity of the proceedings in reference to the forfeiture, disposal or re-allotment of the share.

30[34] The directors may accept the surrender of a share which is liable to be forfeited. For that purpose, a reference in these articles to 'forfeiture' includes 'surrender'.

Transfer of shares

31[35] (1) A transfer of shares may be effected by a transfer in writing in the usual common form or in any other form approved by the directors. The instrument of transfer shall be signed by or on behalf of the transferor and, in the case of partly paid shares, by or on behalf of the transferee.

(2) Nothing in these articles requires title to securities to be evidenced or transferred by a written instrument if the Act permits otherwise. The directors may implement arrangements as they think fit for securities to be evidenced or transferred in accordance with the Act.

32[36] The directors may, without giving a reason, refuse to register a transfer of shares which are not fully paid (provided that the refusal does not prevent dealings in the shares from taking place on an open and proper basis). They may also refuse to register a transfer unless it is:

(1) duly stamped (if stampable), deposited at the office or such other place as the directors appoint and accompanied by the certificate for the shares to which it relates (except in the case of a transfer by a recognised person, unless certificates have been issued in respect of the shares) and such other evidence as the directors reasonably require to show the right of the transferor to make the transfer;

(2) in respect of only one class of share; and

(3) in favour of not more than four transferees.

33[37] If the directors refuse to register a transfer, they shall within two business days after the date on which the transfer is lodged with the company send to the transferee notice of the refusal.

34[38] The registration of transfers of any class of shares may be suspended at such times and for such periods (not exceeding thirty days in any year) as the directors determine.

35[39] The company is not entitled to charge a fee in respect of the registration of a document relating to or affecting the title to shares.

36[40] The company may retain an instrument of transfer which is registered but a transfer which the directors refuse to register shall (except in case of known or suspected fraud) be returned to the person lodging it when notice of the refusal is given.

Destruction of documents

37[41] (1) The company may destroy:
- (a) a cancelled share certificate after the lapse of one year from the date of cancellation;
- (b) an instruction as to the payment of dividends or other sums in respect of a share after the lapse of two years from the date that the instruction was recorded by the company;
- (c) a notification of change of name or address after the lapse of two years from the date that the change was recorded by the company;
- (d) a transfer or form of renunciation of shares after the lapse of six years from the date of registration; and
- (e) any other document on the basis of which an entry was made in the register of members after the lapse of six years from the date that the entry was made.

The company may, however, destroy a document after a shorter period than that specified above if a copy is retained in permanent form. The copy of a document shall be treated for the purposes of this article as if it were the document.

(2) If the company destroys a document in accordance with paragraph (1) in good faith and without express notice that its preservation was relevant to a claim, it shall be conclusively presumed in favour of the company that the document was valid and that, if it was a share certificate, it was properly cancelled, if it was an instrument of transfer it was properly registered and, if it was any other document, particulars of it recorded in the books or records of the company were

correctly recorded. This article shall not, however, be construed as recognising liability of the company in relation to the destruction by it of a document before the expiration of the relevant period merely because the specified period had not elapsed.

(3) In this article, 'destruction' includes disposal in any manner.

Transmission of shares

38[42] If a member dies, the survivors where he was a joint holder, and his personal representatives where he was a sole or only surviving holder, shall be the only persons recognised by the company as having title to his shares or interest in shares, but the estate of a deceased joint holder shall remain subject to any liability in respect of shares which were jointly held by him.

39[43] A person who becomes entitled to a share in consequence of the death or bankruptcy of a member may, upon production of such evidence as to his title as is properly required by the directors, elect either to be registered himself as the holder of the share or to have some person whom he nominates registered as the holder. If he elects to be registered himself, he shall give to the company notice to that effect. If he elects to have another person registered, he shall sign a transfer of the share in favour of that person. All the provisions of these articles relating to the right to transfer shares and the registration of transfers of shares shall be applicable to the notice or transfer as if the death or bankruptcy of the member had not occurred and the notice or transfer were a transfer signed by him. If the person entitled to the share does not make an election, the directors may give him notice requiring to make the election and, if he fails to do so within ninety days, the directors may subsequently and until the notice has been complied with withhold payment of dividends, bonuses and other sums payable in respect of the share.

40[44] Subject to the provisions of article 39, if a person becomes entitled to a share in consequence of the death or bankruptcy of a member, the rights of the holder shall cease. The person entitled shall have the rights which he would have had as holder of the share and shall be entitled to receive and give a discharge for all benefits attributable to the share, but he shall not, before being registered as the holder of the share, be entitled in respect of the share to receive notices of or to attend or vote at meetings of the company or separate meetings of the holders of any class of shares.

Disclosure of interests

41[45] (1) If a member, or a person appearing to be interested in shares held by a member, has been given a notice under section 212 of the Act and is in default for the prescribed period in supplying the required information to the company, the directors may by a notice (a 'section 212 notice') to the member direct that, in relation to the shares in respect of which the default has occurred (the 'default shares'), the member is not entitled to vote, either personally or by proxy, at a general meeting or a class meeting or to exercise any other right conferred by membership in relation to general meetings or meetings of the holders of any class of shares.

(2) If the default shares represent at least 0.25 per cent of the issued shares of a class, the section 212 notice may also direct that:

(a) dividends and other sums that would otherwise be payable in respect of the default shares shall (in whole or in part) be retained by the company without liability to pay interest on the sum withheld if and when it is paid to the member;

(b) a transfer of the default shares, or of shares which include or might include default shares, which is not an approved transfer shall not be registered unless:

(i) the member is not himself in default as regards supplying the information required; and

(ii) the transfer relates to part only of the member's holding and, when presented for registration, is accompanied by a certificate by the member in a form satisfactory to the directors to the effect that, after due and careful enquiry, the member is satisfied that none of the shares to which the transfer relates is a default share.

(3) The directors shall send a copy of the notice to each other person appearing to be interested in the shares the subject of

a section 212 notice but their failure or omission to do so shall not invalidate the notice.

(4) A section 212 notice shall have effect in accordance with its terms for so long as the default continues and (unless the section 212 notice provides otherwise) for a further period of one week but shall cease to have effect in relation to default shares which are transferred by an approved transfer.

(5) For the purpose of this article:

   (a) a person is treated as appearing to be interested in shares if the member holding the shares has given a notice to the company under section 212 of the Act which either:

      (i) names that person as being interested; or

      (ii) fails to establish the identities of those interested in the shares and (after taking into account the notice and any other relevant notification under section 212) the company knows or has reasonable cause to believe that the person in question is or may be interested in the shares;

   (b) the prescribed period is fourteen days from the date when the section 212 notice is given;

   (c) a transfer is an approved transfer if:

      (i) it is a transfer of shares to an offeror as a result of the acceptance of a take-over offer (as defined in section 428 of the Act[46]); or

      (ii) the directors are satisfied that the transfer is made pursuant to a sale of the whole of the beneficial ownership of the shares to a party unconnected with the member and with the other persons appearing to be interested in the shares; or

      (iii) the transfer results from a sale made through a recognised investment exchange (as defined in the Financial Services Act 1986[47]) or any other stock exchange outside the United Kingdom on which the company's shares are normally traded.

(6) Nothing in this article limits the powers of the directors under section 216[48] of the Act.

42[49] (1) If the law of a country, state or other place imposes or purports to impose an immediate, future or possible liability on the company to make a payment or empowers a government or taxing authority or a government official to require the company to make a payment in respect of shares held either jointly or solely by a member or in respect of dividends or other sums due or payable to the member from or by the company or in respect of shares or for or on account or in respect of the member and whether in consequence of:

(a) his death; or

(b) his failure to discharge a liability to taxation; or

(c) the non-payment of taxation or duty on the death of the member or out of his estate; or

(d) any other act, event or thing;

the company shall be indemnified by the member or his estate in respect of all liability arising as a result of the law and may recover from him or his estate sums paid by the company as a result of the law, with interest at such rate as the directors determine from the date of payment by the company until the date of repayment.

(2) Nothing in this article affects the rights and remedies which the law confers or purports to confer on the company and, as between the company and the member or his estate, they shall be enforceable by the company.

Stock

43[50] (1) The company may, by ordinary resolution, convert paid up shares into stock and reconvert stock into paid up shares of any denomination.

(2) A holder of stock may transfer all or part of it in the same manner and subject to the same provisions of these articles as would have applied to the shares from which the stock arose if they had not been converted, or as near to them as the circumstances permit. The directors may determine a minimum amount of stock which is transferable but the minimum shall not exceed the nominal amount of the shares from which the stock arose.

(3) A holder of stock shall, according to the amount of stock held by him, have the same rights as if he held the shares from which the stock arose but no right shall be conferred by an amount of stock which would not have been conferred if it had existed as shares.

(4) The provisions of these articles applicable to paid up shares shall apply to stock and 'shares' and 'member' shall include 'stock' and 'holder of stock'.

Increase of capital

44[51] The company may by ordinary resolution increase its capital by such sum, divided into shares of such amounts, as the resolution prescribes. Unless otherwise provided by these articles, by the resolution creating the new shares or by the conditions of issue, the new shares shall be subject to the provisions of these articles and shall be unclassified shares.

Alteration of capital

45[52] The company may by ordinary resolution:
   (1) consolidate and divide all or any of its share capital into shares of larger nominal amount than its existing shares;
   (2) subject to the provisions of the Act, sub-divide shares into shares of smaller amount and determine that, as between the shares resulting from the sub-division, some of them have a preference or advantage as compared with the others; and
   (3) cancel shares which have not been taken or agreed to be taken by any person and diminish the amount of its share capital by the amount of the shares cancelled.

46[53] If as a result of the consolidation of shares members would become entitled to fractions of a share, the directors may for the purpose of eliminating the fractions sell the shares representing the fractions for the best price reasonably obtainable and distribute the net proceeds of sale in due proportion among the members who would have been entitled to the fractions. The directors may authorise some person to execute an instrument of transfer of the shares representing the fractions to, or in accordance with the directions of, the purchaser. The name of the transferee shall, upon presentation of the transfer duly stamped, be entered in the register of members as the holder of the shares and he shall not be bound to see to the application of the purchase money. The title of the transferee to the shares shall not be affected by an irregularity in or invalidity of the proceedings relating to the sale.

47[54] Subject to the provisions of the Act, the company may by special resolution reduce its share capital, capital redemption reserve or share premium account.

General meetings

48[55] An extraordinary general meeting is a general meeting which is not an annual general meeting.

49[56] The directors may call general meetings and, on a members' requisition under the Act, shall convene an extraordinary general meeting for a date not later than seven weeks after receipt of the requisition. If there are not within the United Kingdom sufficient directors to call a general meeting, any director or member may call the meeting.

Notice of general meetings

50[57] (1) An annual general meeting and an extraordinary general meeting called for the passing of a special resolution shall be called by at least twenty one clear days' notice. All other extraordinary general meetings shall be called by at least fourteen clear days' notice.

(2) A general meeting may be called by shorter notice with the agreement:

    (a) in the case of an annual general meeting, of all the members entitled to attend and vote at the meeting;

    (b) in the case of any other meeting, of a majority in number of the members having a right to attend and vote at the meeting, being a majority together holding not less than 95 per cent in nominal value of the shares giving the right.

(3) The notice shall specify the time, the day and the place of the meeting and the general nature of the business. In the case of an annual general meeting, the notice shall specify the meeting as such.

(4) Subject to the provisions of these articles and to restrictions imposed on any shares, notices shall be given to all the members (other than members not entitled to receive the

notice), to all persons entitled to a share as a result of the death or bankruptcy of a member, to the directors and to the auditors.

51[58] The accidental omission to give notice of a meeting to, or the non-receipt of notice of a meeting by, or, in cases where instruments of proxy are sent out with the notice, the accidental omission to send an instrument of proxy to, a person entitled to receive notice shall not invalidate the proceedings at the meeting.

Proceedings at general meetings

52[59] No business shall be transacted at a general meeting unless a quorum is present when the meeting proceeds to business. Two persons entitled to vote at the meeting, each being a member or a proxy for a member or a duly authorised representative of a corporation which is a member, constitute a quorum.

53[60] (1) If within 15 minutes (or such longer time not exceeding one hour as the chairman of the meeting decides) from the time appointed for the meeting a quorum is not present, the meeting, if convened on the requisition of members, shall be dissolved. It shall otherwise be adjourned to the same day in the next week, at the same time and place, or to such other day and at such time and place as the chairman or, failing him, the directors determine. If at the adjourned meeting a quorum is not present within fifteen minutes from the time appointed for holding the meeting, the meeting shall be dissolved.

(2) Notice of the adjournment of a meeting need not be given unless it is adjourned for thirty days or more, in which event not less than seven clear days' notice shall be given, specifying the place, the day and the time of the adjourned meeting. It shall not be necessary to specify in the notice the business to be transacted at the adjourned meeting.

54[61] The chairman, if any, of the board of directors, or in his absence some other director nominated by the chairman in writing, shall preside as chairman of the meeting. If neither the chairman nor the nominated director is present within fifteen minutes after the time appointed for holding the meeting, or if neither of them is willing to act as chairman, the directors present may choose one of the directors who is present to be chairman. If there is only one director present and he is willing to act, he shall be chairman.

55[62] If no director is willing to act as chairman or if no director is present within fifteen minutes after the time appointed for holding the meeting, the members present and entitled to vote may choose one of their number to be chairman.

56[63] A director, even if not a member, and any other person invited to do so by the chairman may attend and speak at general meetings and at separate meetings of the holders of a class of shares.

57[64] (1) The chairman may, with the consent of the meeting at which a quorum is present (and shall, if directed by the meeting to do so), adjourn the meeting either indefinitely or to another time or place. The chairman may also, without the consent of the meeting, adjourn the meeting (whether or not it has commenced or is quorate) either indefinitely or to such other time and place as he or the directors decide if it appears to him that:

    (a) the number of persons wishing to attend cannot be conveniently accommodated in the place appointed for the meeting; or

    (b) the unruly conduct of persons attending the meeting prevents or is likely to prevent the orderly holding or continuation of the meeting; or

    (c) an adjournment is otherwise necessary for the business of the meeting to be properly conducted; or

    (d) a proposal of such importance is made that the consideration of a larger number of members is desirable.

    (2) When a meeting is adjourned indefinitely, the time and place for the adjourned meeting shall be fixed by the directors. When a meeting is adjourned for thirty days or more, notice of the adjourned meeting shall be given as in the case of the original meeting. Except where these articles otherwise require, it shall not be necessary to give notice of an adjournment or of the business to be transacted at the adjourned meeting.

    (3) No business shall be transacted at an adjourned meeting other than business left unfinished at the meeting from which the adjournment took place.

58[65] (1) If the chairman considers that the meeting place specified in the notice convening the meeting is inadequate to accommodate all those entitled and wishing to attend, the meeting shall nevertheless be duly constituted and its proceedings valid provided that the chairman is satisfied that adequate facilities are available to ensure that members who cannot be accommodated are able to participate in the business of the meeting and to see and hear all persons present who speak (whether by the use of microphones, loud-speakers, audio visual communications equipment or otherwise), whether in the meeting place or elsewhere, and to be seen and heard by all other persons in the same manner.

(2) The directors may make such arrangements for controlling the level of attendance at each place, whether involving the issue of tickets (on a basis intended to afford all members entitled to attend the meeting an equal opportunity of being admitted to the meeting place specified in the notice) or the imposition of some random means of selection or otherwise, as they consider appropriate. The entitlement of members to attend shall be subject to these arrangements, whether stated in the notice as applying to that meeting or notified to the members after the notice has been given.

(3) The meeting shall be treated for the purposes of this article as having taken place at the meeting place specified in the notice.

59[66] A resolution put to the vote of a meeting shall be decided on a show of hands unless before, or on the declaration of the result of, the show of hands a poll is demanded:

(1) by the chairman; or

(2) by not less than three members having the right to vote at the meeting; or

(3) by members[67] representing not less than one-tenth of the total voting rights of all the members having the right to vote at the meeting; or

(4) by members[67] holding shares conferring a right to vote at the meeting, being shares on which an aggregate sum has been paid up equal to not less than one-tenth of the total sum paid up on all the shares conferring that right.

60[68] Unless a poll is duly demanded and the demand is not withdrawn before the poll is taken, a declaration by the chairman that a resolution has been carried, or carried unanimously or by a particular majority, or lost, or not carried by a particular majority, and an entry to that effect in the book containing the minutes of the meeting shall be conclusive evidence of the fact without proof of the number or proportion of the votes recorded in favour of or against the resolution.

61[69] (1) In the case of a resolution duly proposed as a special or extraordinary resolution, no amendment (other than an amendment to correct a patent error) may be considered or voted on.

(2) In the case of a resolution duly proposed as an ordinary resolution, no amendment (other than an amendment to correct a patent error) may be considered or voted on unless at least forty-eight hours before the time appointed for the holding of the meeting or adjourned meeting at which the resolution is to be proposed notice of the terms of the amendment and of the intention to move it has been lodged at the office.

(3) If an amendment is proposed to a resolution under consideration which in good faith is ruled out of order by the chairman of the meeting, the proceedings on the substantive resolution shall not be invalidated by an error in the ruling.

62[70] If a poll is duly demanded, it shall be taken in such manner as the chairman directs (including the use of ballot or voting papers or tickets). The chairman may, and if required to do so by the meeting shall, appoint scrutineers (who need not be members) and may fix a time and place for the purpose of declaring the result of the poll, which shall be deemed to be the resolution of the meeting at which the poll was demanded.

63[71] A poll demanded on the election of a chairman or on a question of adjournment shall be taken immediately. A poll demanded on any other question shall be taken either immediately or at such time and place as the chairman directs, not being more than thirty days from the date of the meeting or the adjourned meeting at which the poll is demanded. The demand for a poll shall not prevent the continuance of a meeting for the transaction of business other than the question on which the poll was demanded. If a poll is demanded before the declaration of the result of a show of hands and the demand is duly withdrawn, the meeting shall continue as if the demand had not been made.

64[72] The demand for a poll may be withdrawn before the poll is taken, but only with the consent of the chairman. A demand which is withdrawn will not invalidate the result of a show of hands declared before the demand was made.

65[73] Notice need not be given of a poll which is not taken immediately if the time and place at which it is to be taken are announced at the meeting at which it is demanded. In any other case, at least seven clear days' notice shall be given specifying the time and place at which the poll is to be taken.

Votes of members

66[74] Subject to the rights or restrictions attached to any shares, on a show of hands every member who is, or is deemed to be, present in person shall have one vote and on a poll every member who is, or is deemed to be, present in person or by proxy shall have one vote for every share of which he is the holder. A member entitled to more than one vote need not use all his votes or cast all his votes in the same way.

67[75] In the case of joint holders of a share, the vote of the senior who tenders a vote, whether in person or by proxy, shall be accepted to the exclusion of the votes of the other joint holders. Seniority shall be determined by the order in which the names stand in the register of members in respect of the share.

68[76] A member in respect of whom an order has been made by a court having jurisdiction in matters concerning mental disorder may vote, either on a show of hands or on a poll, by the person authorised in that behalf by the court, and the person authorised may, on a poll, vote by proxy. Evidence to the satisfaction of the directors of the authority of the person claiming to exercise the right to vote shall be deposited at the office, or at such other place as is specified in accordance with these articles for the deposit of instruments of proxy, not less than forty-eight hours before the time appointed for holding the meeting or adjourned meeting at which the right to vote is exercised and in default the right to vote shall not be exercisable.

69[77] A member shall not, unless the directors otherwise determine, be entitled to vote at general meetings or at separate meetings of the holders of a class of shares, either in person or by proxy in respect of any share held by him or to exercise any privilege as holder of the share unless all calls and other sums presently payable by him in respect of the share have been paid.

70[78] In the case of an equality of votes, whether on a show of hands or on a poll, the chairman of the meeting at which the show of hands takes place or at which the poll is demanded is entitled to a casting vote in addition to any other votes he has.

71[79] An objection to the qualification of a voter may be raised only at the meeting or adjourned meeting at which the vote objected to is given or tendered. Every vote not disallowed at the meeting is valid. An objection made in due time shall be referred to the chairman of the meeting and his decision shall be conclusive.

72[80] If votes are counted at a meeting which ought not to have been counted or might have been rejected or if votes are not counted which ought to have been counted, the error shall not vitiate the result of the vote unless it is pointed out at the meeting, or at an adjournment of it, and it is in the opinion of the chairman of sufficient magnitude to do so.

73[81] On a poll votes may be given either in person or by proxy. A member may appoint more than one proxy to attend on the same occasion.[82] A proxy need not be a member of the company.[83] The appointment of a proxy shall not preclude the member from attending and voting at the meeting or at an adjournment of it.[84]

74[85] The directors shall send, to all (and not to some only) of the members who are entitled to be sent a notice of the meeting and to vote at it by proxy, instruments of proxy for use at each general meeting or separate meeting of the holders of any class of shares. The instruments:

   (1) shall enable the members to vote for or against each resolution to be proposed at the meeting;[86]
   (2) shall enable the members to appoint persons of their own choice; and
   (3) shall state that, if the instrument does not indicate how the proxy is to vote, the proxy may exercise his right at his discretion.[87]

75[88] An instrument appointing a proxy:

   (1) shall be in writing in any usual or common form, or any other form approved by the directors;
   (2) shall be signed by the appointor or by his agent duly authorised in writing, or if the appointor is a corporation shall be either under its common seal, or signed by two directors or by a director and the secretary, or under the hand of an officer or of an agent authorised in writing;
   (3) shall be deemed (subject to anything to the contrary contained in the instrument) to confer authority to demand or join in demanding a poll[89] and to vote on a resolution or amendment of a resolution put to the meeting for which the authority is given as the proxy thinks fit, but shall not confer any further right to speak at the meeting except with the permission of the chairman; and

(4) unless the instrument provides otherwise, shall be valid for adjournments of the meeting to which it relates.

76[90] The instrument of proxy and any authority under which it is executed, or a copy of the authority certified in a manner approved by the directors, may:

(1) be deposited at the office, or at such other place within the United Kingdom as is specified in the notice convening the meeting or in any instrument of proxy sent out in relation to the meeting, not less than forty-eight hours[91] before the time appointed for holding the meeting or adjourned meeting at which the person named in the instrument proposes to vote; or

(2) in the case of a poll taken more than forty-eight hours after it is demanded, be deposited, at the office or other specified place, after the poll has been demanded and not less than twenty-four hours before the time appointed for the taking of the poll; or

(3) where the poll is not taken forthwith but is taken not more than forty-eight hours after it was demanded, be delivered at the meeting at which the poll was demanded to the chairman or to the secretary or to any director.

An instrument of proxy which is not deposited or delivered in a permitted manner shall be invalid.

77[92] If two or more valid but differing instruments are delivered in respect of the same share for use at the same meeting, the one which is the last to be delivered shall be treated as replacing the others in respect of that share. If the directors cannot readily determine to their satisfaction which was the last to be delivered, they may, in their discretion, determine that any one or none of them shall be treated as valid in respect of the share.

78[93] A vote given or poll demanded by proxy or by the duly authorised representative of a corporation shall be valid notwithstanding the previous determination of the authority of the person voting or demanding the poll unless notice of the determination is received by the company at the office, or at the place (if not the office) at which the instrument of proxy was duly deposited, at least three hours before the commencement of the meeting or adjourned meeting at which the vote is given or the poll demanded or (in the case of a poll taken otherwise than on the same day as the meeting or adjourned meeting) the time appointed for taking the poll.

Corporations acting by representatives

79[94] A corporate member may, by resolution of its directors or other governing body, authorise such person as it thinks fit to act as its representative at a general meeting or at a separate meeting of the holders of a class of shares. The person authorised may exercise the same powers on behalf of his appointor as the appointor could exercise if it were an individual member of the company. An authorised person present at the meeting shall be deemed to be a member present in person. The person who is or claims to be authorised as above may be required by a director or the secretary, or by some other person authorised for that purpose by the directors, to produce a certified copy of the resolution giving him his authority.

Number of directors

80[95] Unless otherwise determined by ordinary resolution, the number of directors (excluding alternate directors) shall not be less than two or more than [   ].

Alternate directors

81[96] A director (other than an alternate director) may appoint another director, or any other person approved by resolution of the directors, to be an alternate director and may remove him from his office of alternate director.

82[97] An alternate director who is present in the United Kingdom shall be given notice of all meetings of directors and of all meetings of committees of directors of which his appointor is a member. He shall be entitled to attend and vote at those meetings if the director appointing him is not personally present and generally to perform all the functions of his appointor as a director in his absence, but not to appoint an alternate. An alternate director who is absent from the United Kingdom shall not be entitled to receive notices unless he leaves with the secretary an address in the United Kingdom for the receipt of notices. An alternate director shall not be entitled to receive remuneration from the company for his services as an alternate director except for any part of the remuneration otherwise payable to his appointor which the appointor by notice to the company directs.

83[98] An alternate director shall cease to be an alternate director on the happening of an event which, if he had been a director, would have caused him to vacate his office or if his appointor ceases to be a director; but, if a director retires by rotation or otherwise but is reappointed, or deemed to have been reappointed, at the meeting at which he retires, an appointment of an alternate director made by him which was in force immediately prior to his retirement shall continue after his reappointment.

84[99] The appointment or removal of an alternate director shall be effected by notice to the company signed by the director making or revoking the appointment and delivered to the office or tendered at a meeting of the directors, or in any other manner approved by the directors.

85[100] Except as otherwise provided in these articles, an alternate director shall be deemed to be a director and shall alone be responsible for his own acts and defaults. He shall not be deemed to be the agent of the director appointing him.

Appointment and retirement of directors

86[101] (1) At each annual general meeting, one-third[102] of the directors who are subject to retirement by rotation or, if their number is not three or a multiple of three, the number nearest to but not exceeding one-third, shall retire from office; but, if the number of directors who are subject to retirement by rotation is two, one of them shall retire and, if there is only one director who is subject to retirement by rotation, he shall retire.

(2) The directors subject to retirement by rotation are all the directors excluding:

(a) directors who hold an executive office, unless their contracts of employment provide that they are subject to retirement by rotation;

(b) alternate directors who are not otherwise subject to retirement by rotation; and

(c) directors who are excluded under any other provisions of these articles.

87[103] The directors to retire by rotation shall include (so far as necessary to obtain the number required) a director who wishes to retire and not offer himself for re-election. Any further directors to retire shall be those of the other directors who have been longest in office since their appointment or last re-appointment but, as between persons who became or were last re-appointed directors on the same day, those to retire shall (unless they otherwise agree among themselves) be determined by lot. The directors to retire shall be determined (both as to number and identity) by the composition of the board of directors at the commencement of business on the day which is fourteen days prior to the date of the notice convening the annual general meeting. A director shall not be required, or be relieved from the obligation, to retire by reason of a change in the board after that time but before the close of the meeting.

88[104] The company, at the meeting at which a director retires by rotation, may fill the vacated office. In default the retiring director, if willing to act, shall be deemed to have been re-appointed, unless at the meeting it is resolved not to fill the vacancy or a resolution for his re-appointment is put to the meeting and lost.

89[105] A director who retires at an annual general meeting may, if willing to act, be re-appointed. If he is not re-appointed or deemed to have been re-appointed, he shall retain office until the meeting appoints someone in his place or, if it does not do so, until the end of the meeting.

90[106] No person other than a director retiring by rotation shall be appointed or reappointed a director at a general meeting unless:

    (1) he is recommended by the directors; or

    (2) not less than seven nor more than forty-two clear days before the date appointed for the meeting notice, executed by a member (not being the person to be proposed) who is qualified to vote at the meeting, has been given to the company of the intention to propose that person for appointment or reappointment together with notice executed by that person of his willingness to be appointed or reappointed.

91[107] A motion for the appointment of two or more persons as directors by a single resolution shall not be made unless a resolution that it shall be made has been first agreed to by the meeting without any vote being given against it. A motion for approving a person's appointment or for nominating a person for appointment is to be treated as a motion for his appointment.

92[108] The company may by ordinary resolution appoint a person to be a director, either to fill a vacancy or as an additional director, and determine in what order additional directors are to retire by rotation. The appointment shall take effect from the end of the meeting at which the resolution is passed.

93[109] Without prejudice to the provisions of the Act, the company may, by ordinary resolution:

(1) remove a director before the expiration of his period of office (but his removal shall be without prejudice to any claim which he has for breach of a contract of employment); and

(2) appoint another person in his place. The person who is appointed shall be treated, for the purpose of determining the time at which he or another director is to retire by rotation, as if he had become a director on the day on which the director in whose place he is appointed was appointed or last reappointed a director.

94[110] The directors may appoint a person who is willing to act to be a director, either to fill a vacancy or as an additional director, provided that the appointment does not cause the number of directors to exceed the number fixed by or in accordance with these articles as the maximum number of directors. The director shall hold office only until the next following annual general meeting and shall not be taken into account in determining the directors who are to retire by rotation at the meeting. If he is not reappointed at the meeting, he shall retain office until the meeting appoints someone in his place or, if it does not do so, until the end of the meeting.

95[111] A director shall not be required to retire from his office and a prospective director shall not be precluded from being appointed or elected to office by reason of his attaining or having attained the age of seventy or any other age. Special notice need not be given of a resolution for the appointment or reappointment or approving the appointment as a director of a person who has attained the age of seventy. It shall not be necessary to give to the members notice of the age of a director or prospective director. Section 293 of the Act does not apply to the company.

96[112] A director does not require a share qualification.

Disqualification and removal of directors

97[113] (1) The office of a director is vacated if:
- (a) he ceases to be a director by virtue of any provision of the Act or pursuant to these articles or he becomes prohibited by law from being a director; or
- (b) he becomes bankrupt or makes an arrangement or composition with his creditors generally or applies to the court for an interim order under s 253 of the Insolvency Act 1986[114] in connection with a voluntary arrangement; or
- (c) an order is made by a court claiming jurisdiction for that purpose on the ground (however formulated) of mental disorder for his detention or for the appointment of a guardian or receiver or other person (by whatever name called) to exercise powers with respect to his property or affairs; or
- (d) he resigns his office by notice sent to or left at the office (unless the terms of his contract of employment preclude resignation); or
- (e) he is requested to resign by a notice (which may consist of several documents each signed by one or more directors) signed by not less than three-quarters of the other directors. In calculating the number of directors who are entitled to make the request, an alternate appointed by the director to whom the request is made shall be disregarded and an alternate director shall be counted as one director with his appointor and may sign the request on behalf of his appointor; or
- (f) he is absent from meetings of the directors for six consecutive months without the permission of the directors, and his alternate director (if any) does not attend in his place, and the directors resolve that his office be vacated.
(2) A resolution of the directors declaring that a director has vacated office under this article shall be conclusive as to that fact and as to the ground of vacation as stated in the resolution.

Remuneration of directors

98[115] The directors (other than directors holding executive office and alternate directors) shall be paid such fees for their services in their offices as directors as are determined by the directors. The aggregate of the fees (excluding amounts payable under any other provisions of these articles) shall not exceed £[100,000] per annum (which figure shall be subject to upward only adjustment in line with any percentage increase in the retail prices index (as defined in s 833(2) of the Income and Corporation Taxes Act 1988) after the date of the adoption of these articles) or such higher amount as is decided by ordinary resolution. The fees shall be divided amongst the directors entitled in such proportions and in such manner as the directors determine or, in default of a determination, equally (except that, if a director holds office for less than the whole of the period to which the fees relate, his share shall be reduced in proportion to the part of the period for which he did not hold office).

99[116] A director who does not hold executive office and serves on a committee or devotes special attention to the business of the company, or otherwise performs services which in the opinion of the directors are outside the scope of the ordinary duties of a director, may be paid such extra remuneration by way of salary, participation in profits or otherwise as the directors determine.

Directors' gratuities and pensions

100[117] The directors may provide benefits, whether by the payment of gratuities or pensions or by insurance or otherwise, for a director who has held but no longer holds an executive office or employment with the company or with a body corporate which is or has been a subsidiary undertaking of the company or a predecessor in business of the company or of a subsidiary undertaking, and for any member of his family (including a spouse and a former spouse) or any person who is or was dependent on him, and may (both before and after he ceases to hold the office or employment) contribute to a fund and pay premiums for the purchase or provision of benefits.

Directors' expenses

101[118] The directors may be paid all travelling, hotel and other expenses properly incurred by them in connection with their attendance at meetings of directors or committees of directors or general meetings or separate meetings of the holders of any class of shares or of debentures of the company or otherwise in connection with the discharge of their duties.

Powers and duties of directors

102[119] Subject to the provisions of the Act and these articles and to any directions given by special resolution, the business of the company shall be managed by the directors who may exercise all the powers of the company. No alteration to these articles and no direction shall invalidate a prior act of the directors which would have been valid if the alteration had not been made or the direction had not been given. The powers given by this article shall not be limited by any special power given to the directors by any other of these articles.

Borrowing powers

103[120](1) The directors may exercise all the powers of the company to borrow money and to mortgage or charge its undertaking, property and assets (present or future) and uncalled capital and to issue debentures and other securities, whether outright or as collateral security for a debt, liability or obligation of the company or a third party.

(2) The directors shall restrict the borrowings of the company, and exercise all other rights and powers of control which the company has in relation to its subsidiaries, so as to secure (but, in relation to subsidiaries, only insofar as the rights and powers of the company enable the board to do so) that the aggregate outstanding principal amount of all borrowings of the group does not, without the sanction of an ordinary resolution, exceed [   ] times the adjusted share capital and reserves.

(3) For the purpose of paragraph (2):

(a) the 'group' at any time comprises the company and its subsidiaries at that time;

(b) the 'adjusted share capital and reserves' at any time is an amount equal to the aggregate of:

    (i)   the amount of the share capital of the company paid-up or credited as paid-up; and

    (ii)   the amount standing to the credit of reserves (including share premium account, capital redemption reserve and profit and loss account) less any debit balance on profit and loss account (except to the extent that a deduction has already been made);

all as shown in the then latest audited balance sheet of the company, but after:

    (iii)   making adjustments to reflect variations in the paid-up share capital or the reserves since the date of the balance sheet and, for this purpose:

        (A)   if the company has issued shares for cash and the issue has been underwritten the amounts (including any premium) to be subscribed within three months after the date of allotment are deemed to have been paid up at the date when the issue was underwritten or, if the underwriting was conditional, on the date when it became unconditional; and

        (B)   share capital (including any premium) shall be deemed to have been paid up as soon as a person has unconditionally agreed to subscribe it or take it up;

    (iv)   making adjustments in respect of variations in the interest of the company in its subsidiaries since the date of the balance sheet;

    (v)   making adjustments in respect of distributions declared, recommended, made or paid by the company or its subsidiaries (otherwise than attributable directly or indirectly to the company) out of profits earned up to and including the date of the balance sheet to the extent that the distributions are not provided for in the balance sheet;

(vi) making adjustments to take account of revaluations of the fixed assets of the company and its subsidiaries made by independent professional valuers;

(vii) deducting amounts attributable to goodwill;

(viii) excluding amounts set aside for taxation; and

(ix) making such other adjustments as the auditors, after consultation with the company, consider appropriate;

(c) the audited balance sheet referred to is the then latest audited balance sheet of the company unless there has for the same period been prepared a consolidated balance sheet of the company and its subsidiaries. In that event the audited balance sheet is the consolidated balance sheet and references to reserves and profit and loss account are to the consolidated reserves and consolidated profit and loss account, amounts attributable to outside interests and to subsidiary undertakings which are not subsidiaries being excluded;

(d) 'borrowings' include the following to the extent that they would not otherwise be taken into account:

(i) the principal amount of debentures of a member of the group, whether or not issued or incurred for a consideration which is wholly cash, which are not beneficially owned by a member of the group;

(ii) amounts outstanding in respect of acceptances by a bank or accepting house under an acceptance credit opened on behalf and in favour of a member of the group, excluding acceptances of trade bills for the purchase of goods in the ordinary course of business;

(iii) the nominal amount of any issued and paid up share capital and the principal amount of any debenture of, or amount borrowed by, any person, which is not owned beneficially by a member of the group but the redemption or repayment of which is the subject of a guarantee or indemnity by a member of the group, or wholly or (to the extent of the part secured) partly secured on the undertaking or assets of a member of the group;

(iv) the nominal amount of any issued and paid up preference share capital of a subsidiary which is not owned beneficially by a member of the group;

(v) any fixed or minimum premium payable on final repayment of any borrowings (within the meaning of this paragraph);

but:

(vi) do not include sums owing by one member of the group to another or (if the creditor is not a wholly-owned member of the group) a due proportion of the sums owing;

(vii) sums borrowed for the purpose of, and within [   ] months of being borrowed applied in, repaying sums previously borrowed by a member of the group are not taken into account pending the application;

(viii) a proportion of the borrowings of a partly-owned subsidiary, which would otherwise be included, corresponding to the proportion of its equity share capital not owned, directly or indirectly, by the company is not taken into account;

(ix) sums borrowed to finance a contract in respect of which the group has the benefit of a guarantee or insurance by the Export Credits Guarantee Department or by another governmental department fulfilling a similar function are not taken into account to the extent of the amount guaranteed or insured;

(e) a sum which is to be taken into account in determining borrowings and which is denominated or repayable (or repayable at the option of a person other than a member of the group) in a currency other than sterling shall be converted for the purpose of calculating the sterling equivalent at the rate of exchange prevailing in London on the day when the amount of borrowings is to be determined or, if the amount of borrowings would as a result be less, at the rate of exchange prevailing in London six months before that date. For this purpose, the rate of exchange on a day is the rate prevailing at the close of business on that day or, if it is not a business day, on the last preceding business day.

(4) A certificate by the auditors as to the amount of the adjusted capital and reserves or the amount of any borrowings is conclusive for the purpose of this article. The directors may act on bona fide estimates of the amounts of the adjusted share capital and reserves and borrowings and, if as a result the limit imposed by this article is exceeded, the excess shall be disregarded until the expiration of six months from the date when the directors, by reason of a certification by the auditors or otherwise, become aware of this.

(5) No debt incurred or security given in respect of moneys borrowed or to be taken into account as moneys borrowed in excess of the limit imposed by this article shall be invalid or ineffectual except in the case of express notice to the lender or the recipient of the security, at the time when the debt was incurred or security given, that the limit had been or would be exceeded. A lender or other person dealing with the company shall not be concerned to see or enquire whether the limit is observed.

Delegation of director's powers

104[121] The directors may establish local boards or agencies for managing the affairs of the company, either in the United Kingdom or elsewhere, and may appoint and remove members of the boards or agencies, or managers or agents, and fix their remuneration. The directors may delegate to a local board, manager or agent any of the powers, authorities and discretions vested in or exercisable by them, with power to sub-delegate, and authorise the members of a local board to fill vacancies and to act notwithstanding vacancies. An appointment or delegation may be made upon such terms and subject to such conditions as the directors determine. The directors may revoke or vary the delegation but a person dealing in good faith and without notice of the revocation or variation shall not be affected by it.

105[122] The directors may, by power of attorney or otherwise, appoint a person to be the agent of the company for such purposes, with such powers, authorities and discretions (not exceeding those vested in the directors) and on such conditions as the directors determine, including authority for the agent to delegate his powers, authorities and discretions.

106[123](1) The directors may, on such conditions as they determine, delegate any of their powers, authorities and discretions (with power to sub-delegate) to committees consisting of one or more directors and (if they think fit) one or more other persons provided that a majority of the members are directors, but a resolution of a committee shall not be valid unless a majority of those present when it is passed are directors or alternate directors.

(2) The power to delegate extends to the power of the directors to fix the remuneration of, or confer other benefits on, the members of the committee (whether in relation to their membership of the committee or in respect of any other office in the company) and is not limited by some of these articles, but not others, referring expressly to particular powers, authorities or discretions being exercised by the directors or a committee of the directors.

(3) The proceedings of a committee consisting of two or more members shall be governed by the provisions of these articles regulating the proceedings of directors, so far as they are capable of applying and are not superseded by regulations made by the directors.

Associate directors

107[124] The directors may appoint a person who is not a director as an associate director or to an office or employment having some other designation or title including the word 'director' and they may attach the designation or title to an existing office or employment with the company. The directors may terminate the appointment or the use of the designation or title. The inclusion of the word 'director' in the designation or title of an office or employment does not constitute the person as a director or empower him to act as, or imply that he is, or is deemed to be, or is empowered to act as, a director for any of the purposes of the Act or these articles. In particular, he is not entitled to receive notice of or, without an invitation, to attend meetings of the directors and, if he does attend, he is not entitled to a vote.

Directors' appointments and interests

108(1)[125] Subject to the provisions of the Act, the directors may appoint a director to an executive office in the company and may enter into an agreement or arrangement with a director for his employment by the company or for the provision by him of services outside the scope of the ordinary duties of a director. The appointment, agreement or arrangement may be made on such terms as the directors determine and they may remunerate the director for his services as they think fit. The appointment of a director to an executive office terminates if he ceases to be a director but without prejudice to any claim which he has for breach of his contract of employment.

(2)[126] The directors may entrust to and confer upon an executive director any of the powers exercisable by them as directors, other than the power to fix the remuneration of the directors or to appointment committees, on such terms as they determine and may revoke or vary his powers.

109[127] A director's contract of employment shall not include a term that it is to be for a period exceeding five years without the approval of an ordinary resolution.

110[128] Subject to the provisions of the Act and provided that he has disclosed to the directors the nature and extent of his interest in accordance with these articles, a director, notwithstanding his office:

(1) may enter into or otherwise be interested in a contract with the company or in which the company is otherwise interested;

(2) may hold any other office in the company (other than the office of auditor) in conjunction with his office of director, and may act in a professional capacity for the company, on such terms as to tenure of office remuneration and otherwise as the directors determine;

(3) may continue to be or become a director or other officer, employee or member of or otherwise interested in, or be a party to a contract with, a company promoted by the company or in which the company is interested, as a member or otherwise, or which is a holding company of the company or a subsidiary of the company or of the holding company of the company;

(4) shall not be liable to account to the company for any profit, remuneration or other benefit he derives from the contract, office or employment;

and a contract shall not be avoided on the grounds of his interest or benefit. For the purpose of this article, 'contract' includes an arrangement, transaction or proposal.

111[129] The directors may exercise the voting power conferred by shares in a body corporate held or owned by the company or exercisable by them as directors of a holding company of the company, or a subsidiary of the holding company, in such manner as they think fit (including voting in favour of a resolution appointing themselves directors or other officers of the body corporate, or voting or providing for the payment of remuneration to the directors or other officers of the body corporate).

112[130](1) A director who is, whether directly or indirectly, interested in a contract or proposed contract with the company shall declare the nature and extent of his interest at a meeting of directors. In the case of a proposed contract, the declaration shall be made at the meeting of the directors at which the question of entering into the contract is first taken into consideration or, if the director was not at the date of that meeting interested in the proposed contract, at the next meeting of directors held after he became interested. If the director becomes interested in a contract after it is made, the declaration shall be made at the first meeting of the directors held after he becomes interested. If the director is interested in a contract which was made before he was appointed a director, the declaration shall be made at the first meeting of the directors held after he is appointed.

(2) A general notice given to the directors by a director to the effect that:

(a) he is a member of a specified company or firm and is to be regarded as interested in any contract which, after the date of the notice, is made with that company or firm; or

(b) that he is to be regarded as interested in any contract which, after the date of the notice, is made with a specified person who is connected with him (within the meaning of s 346 of the Act);

shall (if the director gives the notice at a meeting of the directors or takes reasonable steps to secure that it is brought up and read at the next meeting of the directors after it is given) be deemed a sufficient declaration of interest in relation to the contract.

(3) In this article, a reference to a contract includes a transaction or arrangement, whether or not constituting a contract.

Proceedings of directors

113[131] The directors may meet together for the despatch of business, adjourn and otherwise regulate their meetings as they think fit. A director may, and the secretary at the request of a director shall, at any time call a meeting of the directors.

114[132] A director may participate in a meeting of the directors or of a committee of which he is a member by means of a conference telephone or similar communications equipment which enables all the persons participating in the meeting to hear each other at the same time. Participation in a meeting in this manner is treated as presence in person at the meeting. The meeting is deemed to take place where the meeting was convened to take place or, if there was none, where the chairman of the meeting is present.

115[129] Questions arising at a meeting of the directors shall be determined by a majority of votes. If there is an equality of votes the chairman shall have a second or casting vote. In the absence of the director whom he is representing, a director who is also an alternate director shall have a separate vote on behalf of his appointor in addition to his own vote.

116(1)[133] The notice calling a meeting of the directors need not be in writing. A director who is or is intending to be absent from the United Kingdom may request the secretary to give him notice of meetings at an address provided by him for that purpose. Notices of meetings of the directors shall be sent to him at that address but, if he does not provide an address, it shall not be necessary to give notice of meetings to him while he is absent from the United Kingdom.

(2)[134] A director may, either retrospectively or prospectively, waive the requirement that he is given notice of any meeting.

117[135] The quorum for the transaction of the business of the directors may be fixed by the directors and, unless fixed at another number, is two. A person who holds office only as an alternate director is counted in the quorum if his appointor is not present. A meeting of directors at which a quorum is present may exercise all powers exercisable by the directors.

118[136] The continuing directors or a sole continuing director may act notwithstanding any vacancies in their body, but if and so long as the number of directors is reduced below the minimum number fixed by or in accordance with these articles, or below the number fixed by or in accordance with these articles as the quorum, the continuing directors or director may act only for the purpose of filling vacancies or of calling a general meeting.

119[137] The directors may appoint one of their number to be the chairman, and one of their number to be the deputy chairman, of the board of directors, determine the periods for which they are to hold office and remove them from office. Unless they are unwilling to act, the chairman, or in his absence the deputy chairman (if any) or a director nominated by the chairman for the purpose, shall preside at meetings of the directors. If a chairman is not elected, or if at a meeting neither the chairman, the deputy chairman (if any) nor a director nominated by the chairman is present within five minutes after the time appointed for holding the meeting, or if none of them is willing to act as chairman, the directors present may choose one of their number to be chairman of the meeting.

120[138] Acts by a meeting of directors, or of a committee of directors, or by a person acting as director are, notwithstanding that it is afterwards discovered that there was a defect in the appointment of a director or that any of them was disqualified from holding office, or had vacated office, or was not entitled to vote, as valid as if they had been duly appointed and were qualified and had continued to be directors and had been entitled to vote.

121[139] A resolution in writing signed by all the directors entitled to receive notice of a meeting of directors or of a committee of directors has the same effect as if it was passed at a meeting of directors or (as the case may be) a committee of directors duly convened and held. The resolution may consist of several documents in similar form each signed by one or more directors; but a resolution signed by an alternate director need not also be signed by his appointor and, if it is signed by a director who has appointed an alternate director, it need not be signed by the alternate director in that capacity.

122(1)[140] Except as otherwise provided by these articles, a director may not vote at a meeting of directors or of a committee of directors on a resolution concerning a contract or arrangement or other proposal in which he has a material interest (otherwise than by virtue of his interest in shares or debentures or other securities of, or otherwise in or through, the company) unless the resolution:

(a) relates to the giving of a security, guarantee or indemnity in respect of:

  (i) money lent or obligations incurred by him or by another person at the request of or for the benefit of the company or a subsidiary undertaking; or

  (ii) a debt or obligation of the company or a subsidiary undertaking for which he has assumed responsibility in whole or in part under a guarantee or indemnity or by the giving of security;

(b) relates to an offering of securities by the company or a subsidiary undertaking in which offer he is or may be entitled to participate as a holder of securities or in the underwriting or sub-underwriting of which he is to participate;

(c) relates to another company in which he and persons connected with him do not, to his knowledge, hold an interest in shares (within the meaning of sections 198 to 211 of the Act) representing one per cent or more either of its equity share capital or of its voting rights;

(d) relates to a contract, arrangement or proposal for the benefit of the employees of the company or a subsidiary undertaking which does not award him a privilege or benefit not generally awarded to the employees to whom the contract, arrangement or proposal relates; or

(e) concerns insurance which the company proposes to maintain or purchase for the benefit of directors or for the benefit of persons including directors.

(2)[141] In relation to an alternate director, an interest of his appointor is treated as an interest of the alternate director in addition to any interest which the alternate director otherwise has.

(3)[142] A director shall not be counted in the quorum present at a meeting in relation to a resolution on which he is not entitled to vote under this article.

(4)[143] The company may by ordinary resolution suspend or relax the provisions of this article to any extent, either generally or in respect of a particular matter, and ratify anything done in breach of this article.

123[144] If proposals are under consideration concerning the appointment, the variation of the terms of appointment or the termination of the appointment of two or more directors to offices in or employment by the company or a body corporate in which the company is interested, the proposals may be divided and considered in relation to each director separately. Each of the directors concerned (if not otherwise precluded from voting under these articles) may vote and be counted in the quorum in respect of each resolution except that concerning his own appointment.

124[145] If a question arises at a meeting of directors or of a committee as to the right of a director to vote which is not resolved by his voluntarily agreeing to abstain from voting, the question (except where the director concerned is the chairman of the meeting) may be referred to the chairman of the meeting for his ruling before the meeting concludes. If the question concerns the chairman, it shall be decided by a resolution of the directors, for which purpose the chairman shall be counted in the quorum but he shall not be entitled to vote. The chairman's ruling or the resolution of the directors shall be conclusive unless the nature or extent of the interest of the director or the chairman which is relevant for making the ruling or considering the resolution (so far as it is known to him) has not been fairly disclosed to the meeting.

Secretary

125[146] Subject to the provisions of the Act, the secretary shall be appointed by the directors for such term, at such remuneration and upon such conditions as they think fit. The directors may remove the secretary, but without prejudice to any claim which he has for breach of a contract of employment.

126[147] Anything required or authorised by the Act or these articles to be done by or to the secretary may, if the office is vacant or there is for any other reason no secretary capable of acting, be done by or to an assistant or deputy secretary or, if there is no assistant or deputy secretary capable of acting, by or to an officer authorised generally or specially for that purpose by the directors. If anything has to be done by or to a director and the secretary, it shall not be effectively done if the same person acts both as director and as, or in the place of, the secretary.

Minutes

127[148] The directors shall cause minutes to be made:
  (1) of all appointments of directors and members of committees made by the directors;
  (2) of the names of the directors present at each meeting of directors and committees of directors;
  (3) of all resolutions and proceedings at all meetings of the company, the directors and committees of directors.

128[149] If a minute purports to be signed by the chairman of the meeting at which the proceedings were held, or by the chairman of the next succeeding meeting, it is evidence of the proceedings.

Branch register

129[150] The directors may cause to be kept in any part of Her Majesty's Dominions outside the United Kingdom, the Channel Islands or the Isle of Man in which the company transacts business a branch register of members resident there. The directors may (subject to the provisions of the Act) make and vary such regulations as they think fit respecting the keeping of the register.

Seal

130[151] The seal shall be used only with the authority of the directors or of a committee of directors authorised by the directors. The directors may determine who shall sign an instrument to which the seal is affixed and, unless they determine otherwise, it shall be signed by two directors or by a director and the secretary.

131[152] The company may have official seals under sections 39 and 40 of the Act for use as the directors determine.

132[153] A document signed by a director and the secretary or by two directors of the company and expressed (in whatever form of words) to be executed by the company has the same effect as if it were under the seal. A document which makes it clear upon its face that it is intended by the persons making it to be a deed has effect, upon delivery, as a deed.

Dividends and reserves

133[154] Subject to the provisions of the Act, the company may by ordinary resolution declare dividends in accordance with the respective rights of the members, but a dividend shall not exceed the amount recommended by the directors.

134[155] Subject to the provisions of the Act, the directors may pay interim dividends if it appears to them that they are justified by the profits of the company available for distribution. If the share capital is divided into different classes, the directors may pay interim dividends on shares which confer deferred or non-preferred rights with regard to dividend as well as on shares which confer preferred rights with regard to dividend, but an interim dividend shall not be paid on shares having deferred or non-preferred rights if, at the time of payment, a preferred dividend is in arrear. The directors may also pay, at intervals settled by them, a dividend payable at a fixed rate if it appears to them that the profits available for distribution justify the payment. Provided the directors act in good faith they shall not incur liability to the holders of shares conferring preferred rights for loss which they suffer by the lawful payment of an interim dividend on shares having deferred or non-preferred rights.

135[156] Subject to the rights of persons entitled to shares with preferred or other special rights as to dividends, dividends shall be declared and paid according to the amounts paid up on the shares (otherwise than in advance of calls) on which the dividend is paid. Dividends shall be apportioned and paid proportionately to the amounts paid up on the shares during any portions of the period in respect of which the dividend is paid, except that, if a share is issued on terms that it carries particular rights as to dividend, it ranks for dividend accordingly.

136 (1)[157] The directors may, with the sanction of an ordinary resolution in respect of a dividend which it is proposed to pay or declare, offer the shareholders or any class of them (other than those not entitled to the dividend) the right to elect to receive an allotment of additional ordinary shares, credited as fully paid, instead of the whole or part (to be determined by the directors) of the dividend.

(2) The resolution may specify a particular dividend, whether or not already declared, or may specify all or any dividends declared or payable within a specified period.

(3) The entitlement of each holder to ordinary shares shall be such that the relevant value of the entitlement is, as nearly as possible, equal to but not greater than the cash amount (disregarding any tax credit) of the dividend that the holder elects to forego. In calculating the entitlement, the directors may adjust the figure obtained by dividing the relevant value by the amount payable on the ordinary shares up or down so as to procure that the entitlement of each shareholder to new ordinary shares is represented by a simple numerical ratio. For this purpose, 'relevant value' shall be calculated by reference to the average of the middle market quotations for the ordinary shares on the London Stock Exchange as derived from the daily official list on such five consecutive dealing days as the directors determine (the first day being on or after the day on which the ordinary shares are first quoted 'ex' the relevant dividend) or in such other manner as the directors determine in accordance with the resolution. A certificate of the auditors as to the relevant value is conclusive.

(4) As soon as practicable after announcing that they are to declare or recommend a dividend, the directors, if they intend to offer the opportunity to make an election in respect of the dividend, shall notify the holders of the ordinary shares of the right of election offered to them and specify the procedure to be followed and the place at which and the latest time by which elections must be lodged to be effective. The directors may establish and vary procedures for election mandates, under which holders of ordinary shares may elect to receive ordinary shares credited as fully paid instead of cash in respect of all future rights offered to the holders under this article until the mandates are revoked or deemed to be revoked in accordance with the procedure.

(5) The directors may not proceed with an election unless there are sufficient unissued shares authorised for issue and sufficient reserves or funds that may be capitalised to give effect to it after the basis of allotment has been determined.

(6) The directors may exclude from the offer any holders of ordinary shares where they believe that the making of the offer to them would or might involve the contravention of the laws of any territory or that for any other reason the offer should not be made to them.

(7) The dividend, or that part of the dividend in respect of which a right of election has been offered, shall not be payable on ordinary shares in respect of which an election has been made (the 'elected shares') and instead additional ordinary shares shall be allotted to the holders of the elected shares on the basis of allotment calculated as stated above. For this purpose, the directors may capitalise, out of the amount standing to the credit of reserves (including profit and loss account, share premium account and capital redemption reserve), whether or not it is available for distribution, as they determine, a sum equal to the aggregate nominal amounts of the additional ordinary shares to be allotted and apply it in paying up in full the appropriate number of ordinary shares for allotment and distribution to the holders of the elected shares on that basis.

(8) The additional ordinary shares, when allotted, shall rank pari passu in all respects with the fully paid ordinary shares then in issue, except that they will not be entitled to participate in the dividend or part of a dividend in respect of which the right of election was offered.

(9) The directors may do anything they consider necessary or expedient for giving effect to this article, including making provisions in relation to fractions of ordinary shares resulting either in their being disregarded (so that the benefit of them accrues to the company rather than to the shareholders concerned) or in their being accrued or retained with the accruals or retentions being applied to the allotment of fully paid ordinary shares by way of bonus to, or cash subscription on behalf of, the shareholders.

137[158] The directors may deduct, from dividends and other sums payable to a member on or in respect of a share, any sum payable by him to the company on account of calls or otherwise in relation to shares.

138[159] Notwithstanding any other provision of these articles but without prejudice to the rights attached to any shares, the company or the directors may fix any date as the record date for a dividend, distribution, allotment or issue. The record date may be on or at any time before or after the date on which the dividend, distribution, allotment or issue is declared, paid or made.

139[160] A general meeting declaring a dividend may, upon the recommendation of the directors, direct that it shall be satisfied wholly or partly by the distribution of specific assets and the directors shall give effect to the resolution. If a difficulty arises in regard to the distribution, the directors may settle it as they think appropriate. In particular, they may issue fractional certificates, fix the value for distribution of the assets, determine to make cash payments to members upon the footing of that value, in order to adjust the rights of members, and vest specific assets in trustees upon trust for the persons entitled to the dividend.

140[161](1) A dividend or other sum payable on or in respect of a share may be paid:

    (a) by cheque or warrant sent by post to the registered address of the member or person entitled to it or, if two or more persons are the holders of the share or are jointly entitled to it, to the registered address of any one of them, or to such person and such address as the holder or holders, or person or persons entitled, in writing direct. Every cheque or warrant shall be made payable to the order of the person to whom it is sent or to such other person as the holder or joint holders in writing direct. The cheque or warrant shall be sent at the risk of the person entitled to the moneys represented by it; or

    (b) by any other method (including direct debit or bank or other fund transfer system) which the directors consider appropriate.

The payment of the cheque or warrant or the transfer of funds by the bank or other system shall be a good discharge to the company.

  (2) If several persons are registered as joint holders of a share, any one of them may give effectual receipts for dividends and other moneys payable on or in respect of the share.

  (3) The company shall have no liability in respect of sums lost or delayed in the course of payment by a method selected by the directors in accordance with this article or where they have acted on the directions of the holder or holders or person or persons entitled.

141[162] Dividends and other sums payable on or in respect of a share shall not bear interest as against the company unless otherwise provided by the rights attached to the share. Dividends and other sums payable on or in respect of a share which are unclaimed may be invested or otherwise made use of by the company, at the discretion of the directors, until claimed. The payment into a separate account of an unclaimed dividend or other sum payable on or in respect of a share shall not constitute the company a trustee in respect of it.

142[163] The company may cease to send cheques or warrants by post and may stop the transfer of sums by bank or other fund transfer system in respect of dividends and other sums payable on or in respect of a share which are normally paid in that manner if:

    (1) the cheques or warrants have been returned undelivered or remain uncashed or the transfers have failed:

        (a) in respect of at least two consecutive dividends payable on the share; or

        (b) in respect of one dividend and reasonable enquiries have failed to establish a new address of the holder; or

    (2) the company is not required, by reason of article 155, to send notices to the holder of the share.

The company shall, subject to the provisions of these articles, recommence sending cheques or warrants or transferring funds in respect of dividends and other sums payable on or in respect of the share if the holder or person entitled to the share claims the arrears of dividend.

143[164] A dividend or other sum which remains unclaimed for a period of twelve years from the date when it became payable shall, if the directors so determine, be forfeited and cease to remain owing by the company.

144[165] The directors may before recommending a dividend, whether preferred or otherwise, carry to reserve out of the profits of the company such sums as they think proper as a reserve which shall, at the discretion of the directors, be applicable for any purpose to which the profits of the company may properly be applied and, pending application, either be employed in the business of the company or be invested in such investments as the directors think fit.

Capitalisation of profits and reserves

145[166] The directors may with the authority of an ordinary resolution:

    (1) subject as provided in this article, resolve to capitalise undistributed profits which are not required for paying fixed or preferred dividends (whether or not the profits are available for distribution) or a sum standing to the credit of share

premium account or capital redemption reserve or other reserve or fund;

(2) appropriate the sum resolved to be capitalised to the members who would have been entitled to it if it were distributed by way of dividend and in the same proportions; apply the sum on their behalf either in or towards paying up the amounts, if any, unpaid on shares held by them, or in paying up in full unissued shares or debentures of the company of a nominal amount equal to the sum; and allot the shares or debentures credited as fully paid to those members, or as they direct, in those proportions, or partly in one way and partly in the other. But the share premium account, the capital redemption reserve and any profits, reserve or fund which are not available for distribution may, for the purposes of this article, be applied only in paying up unissued shares to be allotted to members credited as fully paid;

(3) make such provision by the issue of fractional certificates, by ignoring fractions or by the payment of cash or otherwise as they determine in the case of shares or debentures becoming distributable in fractions;

(4) authorise some person to enter, on behalf of and so as to bind all the members concerned, into an agreement with the company providing for the allotment to them, credited as fully paid, of the shares or debentures to which they are entitled on the capitalisation; and

(5) generally do anything required or desirable to give effect to the resolution.

Accounts

146[167] The directors shall ensure that proper accounting records are kept in accordance with the Act.

147[168] The accounting records shall be kept at the office, or (subject to the provisions of the Act) at such other place as the directors think fit and shall at all times be open to inspection by the officers of the company. A member shall not, as such, be entitled to inspect the accounting records, books and documents of the company unless given the right to do so by statute or authorised by the directors or by ordinary resolution.

148[169] (1) Except as provided in paragraph (2), a copy of the reports of the directors and of the auditors, accompanied by the balance sheet (including every document required by law to be annexed or attached to it) and profit and loss account, consolidated balance sheet and consolidated profit and loss account, shall be delivered or sent by post to the registered address of every member and holder of debentures of the company. If securities of the company are listed on the London Stock Exchange, the required number of copies of each of these documents shall at the same time be forwarded to the appropriate department.

(2) The company may, in accordance with section 251 of the Act and regulations made under it, send a summary financial statement to a member instead of or in addition to the documents referred to in paragraph (1).

Auditors

149[170] Subject to the provisions of the Act, all acts done by a person acting as auditor shall, as regards persons dealing in good faith with the company, be valid even if there was a defect in his appointment or if, at the time of his appointment, he was not qualified for appointment or was subsequently disqualified.

150[171] The auditor may attend general meetings and speak on any part of the business which concerns him as auditor.

Untraced Shareholders

151(1)[172] The company may sell shares on behalf of the holder by instructing a member of the London Stock Exchange to sell them if:

(a) the shares have been in issue throughout the qualifying period and at least three cash dividends have been payable on the shares during the qualifying period;

(b) no cash dividend payable on the shares has either been claimed by presentation to the paying bank of the relevant warrant or cheque or been satisfied by the transfer of funds to a bank account designated by the holder during the relevant period;

(c) so far as the secretary at the end of the relevant period is aware, the company has not during the relevant period received any communication from the holder;

(d) the company has caused two advertisements to be published, one in a daily newspaper with a national circulation and the other in a newspaper circulating in the area of the address of the holder shown in the register of members, giving notice of its intention to sell the shares and a period of three months has elapsed from the date of the publication of the advertisements or of the later of the two advertisements if they were published on different dates; and

(e) the company has given notice to the London Stock Exchange of its intention to make the sale.

(2) If, during the relevant period, further shares are issued in right of those held at the beginning of the relevant period and all the requirements of sub-paragraphs (1)(b) to (e) have been satisfied in respect of the further shares, the company may also sell the further shares.

(3) To give effect to a sale of shares under this article, the directors may authorise some person to transfer the shares and an instrument of transfer executed by that person shall be as effective as if it had been executed by the holder of the shares. The purchaser shall not be bound to see to the application of the purchase consideration and his title to the shares shall not be affected by any irregularity or invalidity in the proceedings relating to the sale. The net proceeds of sale shall belong to the company and, on their receipt, the company shall become indebted to the former holder of the shares for an amount equal to the net proceeds. A trust shall not be created in respect of the debt and interest shall not be payable in respect of it. The company shall not be required to account for any sums earned from the proceeds but shall be entitled to use them for the purposes of the company or otherwise as it thinks fit.

(4) For the purpose of this article:

(a) references to the holder of shares include a person entitled to the shares by transmission;

(b) the 'qualifying period' is the period of twelve years immediately preceding the date of publication of the advertisements or the first of the advertisements if they were published on different dates;

(c) the 'relevant period' is the period beginning at the commencement of the qualifying period and ending on the date when all the requirements of paragraph (a) have been satisfied.

Notices

152[173] Except as provided otherwise in these articles, notices to be given to or by a person shall be in writing.

153[174](1) A notice or other document may be given or delivered to a member by the company either personally or by sending it through the post by first class mail or airmail, in a prepaid envelope or cover, addressed to the member at his address as appearing in the register of members, or by leaving it at that address, addressed to the member, or by any other means authorised in writing by the member. In the case of joint holders of a share, the giving or delivery of a notice or other document to one of the joint holders shall be deemed to be giving or delivery to all the joint holders.

(2) If the registered address of a member is, or the registered addresses of joint holders are, outside the United Kingdom, he or they may give the company an address within the United Kingdom at which notices may be given and notices shall be given or delivered to him or them at that address. The member or joint holders shall not otherwise be entitled to receive notices from the company.

(3) A notice which is advertised in at least two daily newspapers with a national circulation in the United Kingdom is effective notice to the holders of bearer warrants and is deemed to be given on the day on which it has appeared in at least two of the newspapers. The advertisement shall give an address in the United Kingdom from which copies of the notice and other documents referred to in the advertisement can be obtained.[175]

154[176] A notice or other document may be given or delivered by the company by reference to the register of members as it stands at any time not more than fifteen days before the date of posting (if the notice or document is posted) or otherwise not more than fifteen days before the date on which it is given or delivered. A change in the register after that time shall not invalidate the giving or delivery of the notice or document.

155[177] If on two consecutive occasions notices have been sent through the post to a member at his registered address or his address for the giving of notices but have been returned undelivered, the member shall not subsequently be entitled to receive notices from the company until he has communicated with the company and supplied, in writing to the office, a new registered address within the United Kingdom for the giving of notices.

156[178] A member present, either in person or by proxy, at a meeting of the company or of the holders of a class of shares shall be deemed to have received notice of the meeting and, where requisite, of the purposes for which it was called.

157[179] A person who by operation of law, transfer or other means becomes entitled to a share shall be bound by a notice in respect of the share which, before his name and address are entered in the register of members, is duly sent to the last registered address of the person from whom he derives his title. A notice or document delivered or sent by post to or left at the registered address of a member in accordance with these articles shall, notwithstanding that the member is then dead, bankrupt, of unsound mind or (being a corporation) in liquidation, and whether or not the company has notice of the death, bankruptcy, insanity or liquidation of the member, be deemed to have been duly given in respect of any share registered in the name of the member as sole or joint holder unless his name has, at the time that the notice or document is given or delivered, been removed from the register of members as the holder of the share. The giving or delivery of the notice or document as above shall for all purposes be deemed a sufficient giving of the notice or document to all persons interested (whether jointly with or as claiming through or under him) in the share.

158[180] Proof that the envelope or cover containing a notice or document was properly addressed, prepaid and posted is conclusive evidence that the notice or document was given or delivered. A notice or other document which is given by post is deemed to be given on the day after the day on which the envelope or cover containing it is posted. A notice given by advertisement is deemed to be given on the day on which the advertisement appears. A notice given by facsimile transmission is deemed to be given (if receipt is acknowledged) when transmitted.

159[181] If, by reason of the suspension or curtailment of postal services within the United Kingdom, the company is unable effectively to convene a general meeting by notice sent through the post, the meeting may be convened by notice advertised in at least two daily newspapers with national circulation. The company shall send confirmatory copies of the notice by post or other means permitted by or in accordance with these articles if, at least six clear days prior to the meeting, the posting of notices to addresses within the United Kingdom again becomes practicable.

Winding up

160[182] If the company is wound up, the liquidator may, with the sanction of an extraordinary resolution and any other sanction required by the Insolvency Act 1986, divide among the members in specie the whole or part of the assets of the company and may, for that purpose, value assets and determine how the division shall be carried out as between the members or different classes of members. The liquidator may, with the same sanction, vest assets in trustees on such trusts for the benefit of members as the liquidator, with the same sanction, thinks fit, but a member shall not be compelled to accept assets in respect of which there is a liability.

Indemnity

161[183] Subject to the provisions of the Act but without prejudice to any indemnity to which a director is otherwise entitled, every director or other officer and auditor shall be indemnified out of the assets of the company against all costs, charges, expenses, losses and liabilities which he sustains or incurs in or about the execution of his office or otherwise in relation to his office, including liability incurred by him in defending proceedings, whether civil or criminal, in which judgment is given in his favour or the proceedings are withdrawn or settled on terms which do not include a finding or admission of a material breach of duty by him, or in which he is acquitted, or in connection with an application in which relief is granted to him by the court from liability for negligence, default, breach of duty or breach of trust in relation to the affairs of the company.

162[184] Subject to the provisions of the Act, the directors may purchase and maintain insurance at the expense of the company for the benefit of the directors and other officers and the auditor against liability which attaches to them or loss or expenditure which they incur in relation to anything done or omitted or alleged to have been done or omitted as directors, officers or auditor.

---

[1]   See the comments in Chapter 6, p 181.
[2]   Corresponding to reg 1 of Table A. See also Chapter 6, p 181.
[3]   See Chapter 6, p 181.
[4]   See art 131.
[5]   See the comments in Chapter 6, p 182.
[6]   Corresponding to reg 2 of Table A.
[7]   Corresponding to reg 3 of Table A.
[8]   Corresponding to reg 4 of Table A. See also Chapter 6, p 182.
[9]   Corresponding to reg 35 of Table A. See also Chapter 6, p 183.
[10]   See Chapter 6, p 183.
[11]   See the comments in Chapter 6, p 183.
[12]   Corresponding to reg 5 of Table A.
[13]   See Chapter 6, p 184.
[14]   Corresponding to reg 6 of Table A. See also Chapter 6, p 185.
[15]   The time limits are in accordance with the Listing Rules of the London Stock Exchange (see Chapter 6, p 173).
[16]   CA 1985, section 40 permits the use of an official seal for sealing documents of title for securities and specific reference is often made to this. The enactment of s 36A has reduced the use of company seals, common and official.
[17]   Corresponding to reg 7 of Table A and complying with the Listing Regulations as discussed in Chapter 6, p 173.
[18]   Corresponding to reg 8 of Table A.
[19]   Corresponding to reg 9 of Table A.
[20]   Corresponding to reg 10 of Table A. See also Chapter 6, p 185.
[21]   Corresponding to reg 11 of Table A. See also Chapter 6, p 185.
[22]   Corresponding to reg 12 of Table A. See also Chapter 6, p 185.
[23]   Corresponding to reg 13 of Table A.
[24]   Corresponding to reg 14 of Table A.
[25]   Corresponding to reg 15 of Table A. See also Chapter 6, p 185.
[26]   Corresponding to reg 16 of Table A.
[27]   Corresponding to reg 17 of Table A.
[28]   This does not appear in Table A. See Chapter 6, p 185.
[29]   Corresponding to reg 18 of Table A with the addition of the reference to instalments of calls and the payment of expenses.
[30]   Corresponding to reg 19 of Table A.
[31]   Corresponding to reg 20 of Table A. See Chapter 2, p 24 and art 27 in Chapter 6, p 185.
[32]   Corresponding to reg 21 of Table A.
[33]   Corresponding to reg 22 of Table A.
[34]   See the comments on reg 18 of Table A in Chapter 2, p 23.
[35]   Corresponding to reg 23 of Table A. See also Chapter 6, p 186.

36 Corresponding to reg 24 of Table A. See Chapter 2, p 27 and art 32 in Chapter 6, p 186.

37 Corresponding to reg 25 of Table A. See also Chapter 6, p 186.

38 Corresponding to reg 26 of Table A and in accordance with the Listing Rules.

39 Corresponding to reg 27 of Table A. The article also meets the requirements of the London Stock Exchange, as discussed in Chapter 6, p 173.

40 Corresponding to reg 28 of Table A.

41 See Chapter 6, p 186.

42 Corresponding to reg 29 of Table A.

43 Corresponding to reg 30 of Table A, but see Chapter 6, p 186.

44 This is a slightly extended version of reg 31 of Table A. See the comments on art 31 in Chapter 6, p 187.

45 See Chapter 6, p 187.

46 A take-over offer is defined in s 428 of the Act as effectively an offer made to all the holders of the shares or a class of shares of the company to acquire those shares.

47 Recognition of an investment exchange as an exempted person in relation to investment business is accorded under s 37 of the Act.

48 This permits the directors to apply to court for an order imposing restrictions on a person who fails to comply with a s 212 notice. The restrictions are set out in s 454 and are similar to those which may be imposed in relation to larger holdings under art 41.

49 See Chapter 6, p 187.

50 See Chapter 6, p 188.

51 This is a slightly extended version of para (a) of reg 32 of Table A.

52 This corresponds to the provisions of reg 32 of Table A, other than para (a), which is dealt with by art 44.

53 Corresponding to reg 33 of Table A, with the addition of the provision requiring the transferee of the fractions to be entered in the register of members.

54 Corresponding to reg 34 of Table A.

55 Corresponding to reg 36 of Table A.

56 Corresponding to reg 37 of Table A.

57 Corresponding to reg 38 of Table A.

58 Corresponding to reg 39 of Table A. See also Chapter 6, p 188.

59 Corresponding to reg 40 of Table A.

60 Corresponding to reg 41 of Table A. See also Chapter 6, p 188.

61 Corresponding to reg 42 of Table A. See also Chapter 6, p 189.

62 Corresponding to reg 43 of Table A.

63 Corresponding to reg 44 of Table A.

64 Corresponding to reg 45 of Table A. See also Chapter 6, p 189.

65 See Chapter 6, p 189.

66 Corresponding to reg 46 of Table A, the last part of which, dealing with the right of the proxy to demand a poll, is included in art 74.

67 See Chapter 6, p 189.

68 Corresponding to reg 47 of Table A.

69 See Chapter 6, p 190.

70 Corresponding to reg 49 of Table A. See the comments on that regulation in Chapter 2, p 43.

71 Corresponding to reg 51 of Table A.

72 Corresponding to reg 48 of Table A.

73 Corresponding to reg 52 of Table A.

74 Corresponding to reg 54 of Table A. See also Chapter 6, p 190.

[75] Corresponding to reg 55 of Table A.
[76] Corresponding to reg 56 of Table A.
[77] See Chapter 6, p 190.
[78] Corresponding to reg 50 of Table A. The position of this article here is more logical than that of reg 50.
[79] Corresponding to reg 58 of Table A.
[80] This is a useful and straightforward provision.
[81] Corresponding to reg 59 of Table A.
[82] This is implied by CA 1985, s 372(2)(*b*) which states that a member of a private company is not entitled to appoint more than one proxy to attend on the same occasion unless the articles otherwise provide.
[83] This is in accordance with CA 1985, s 372(1).
[84] This states the common law position (*Cousins v International Brick Co* [1931] 2 Ch 90).
[85] See Chapter 6, p 191.
[86] This is known as a two-way proxy and the form will be similar to that set out in reg 61 of Table A.
[87] Paras (2) and (3) are as required by the Listing Rules.
[88] See Chapter 6, p 191.
[89] This point is covered by the final part of reg 46 of Table A.
[90] Corresponding to reg 62 of Table A.
[91] Forty eight hours is the maximum permitted time under CA 1985, s 372(5).
[92] See Chapter 6, p 191.
[93] Corresponding to reg 63 of Table A. See also Chapter 6, p 192.
[94] See Chapter 6, p 192.
[95] See Chapter 6, p 192.
[96] Corresponding to reg 65 of Table A.
[97] Corresponding to reg 66 of Table A. See also Chapter 6, p 192.
[98] See Chapter 6, p 192.
[99] Corresponding to reg 68 of Table A.
[100] Corresponding to reg 69 of Table A.
[101] Corresponding to reg 73 of Table A. See also Chapter 6, p 192.
[102] The ABI recommends the one-third proportion (see Chapter 6, p 179).
[103] Corresponding to reg 74 of Table A. See also Chapter 6, p 193.
[104] Corresponding to reg 75 of Table A.
[105] Corresponding to reg 80 of Table A. See also Chapter 6, p 193.
[106] Corresponding to reg 76 of Table A. See also Chapter 6, p 193.
[107] The first sentence of this article substantially repeats CA 1985, s 292(1). The second sentence accords with s 292(3).
[108] The first sentence corresponds to reg 78 of Table A. See also the comments on that regulation in Chapter 2, p 62.
[109] See Chapter 6, p 193.
[110] Corresponding to reg 79 of Table A. See also the requirements of the Listing Rules referred to in Chapter 6, p 173.
[111] See Chapter 6, p 193.
[112] See Chapter 6, p 195.
[113] Corresponding to reg 81 of Table A. See also Chapter 6, p 195.
[114] A voluntary arrangement prevents the taking of bankruptcy proceedings. An interim order can be granted where a debtor intends to make proposals to creditors for a composition in satisfaction of his debts or a scheme of arrangement of his affairs.
[115] See Chapter 6, p 196.

[116] See Chapter 6, p 196.
[117] Corresponding to reg 87 of Table A. Note that references to 'subsidiary' in reg 87 have been replaced by 'subsidiary undertaking'.
[118] Corresponding to reg 83 of Table A.
[119] Corresponding to reg 70 of Table A. See also Chapter 6, p 197.
[120] See Chapter 6, p 197.
[121] See Chapter 6, p 200.
[122] Corresponding to reg 71 of Table A. See also Chapter 6, p 200.
[123] Corresponding to reg 72 of Table A. See also Chapter 6, p 201.
[124] See Chapter 6, p 201.
[125] Corresponding to reg 84 of Table A except that the last sentence of reg 84 has been moved to art 86(2). See also Chapter 6, p 201.
[126] See in Chapter 6, p 201.
[127] See in Chapter 6, p 202.
[128] This is an amplification of reg 85 of Table A. See also Chapter 6, p 202.
[129] See Chapter 6, p 202.
[130] See Chapter 6, p 202.
[131] This article, together with art 115, corresponds to most of reg 88 of Table A.
[132] See Chapter 6, p 203.
[133] Corresponding to part of reg 88 of Table A.
[134] See Chapter 6, p 203.
[135] Corresponding to reg 89 of Table A. See also Chapter 6, p 204.
[136] Corresponding to reg 90 of Table A See also Chapter 6, p 204.
[137] Corresponding to reg 91 of Table A See also Chapter 6, p 204.
[138] Corresponding to reg 92 of Table A.
[139] Corresponding to reg 93 of Table A.
[140] See Chapter 6, p 204.
[141] This follows the final part of reg 94 of Table A.
[142] Corresponding to reg 95 of Table A.
[143] Coresponding to reg 96 of Table A. See also the comments on that regulation in Chapter 2, p 81.
[144] Corresponding to reg 97 of Table A. See also the comments on that regulation in Chapter 2, p 82.
[145] Corresponding to reg 98 of Table A, with amendments as discussed in Chapter 2, p 83.
[146] Corresponding to reg 99 of Table A. See also Chapter 6, p 207.
[147] This article effectively repeats CA 1985, ss 283(2) and 284.
[148] Corresponding to reg 100 of Table A. See also Chapter 6, p 207.
[149] This repeats CA 1985, s 382(2).
[150] See Chapter 6, p 207.
[151] Corresponding to reg 101 of Table A.
[152] See Chapter 6, p 208.
[153] This corresponds to CA 1985, ss 36A(4) and (5).
[154] Corresponding to reg 102 of Table A.
[155] Corresponding to reg 103 of Table A.
[156] Corresponding to reg 104 of Table A. See also Chapter 6, p 208.
[157] See Chapter 6, p 208.
[158] See Chapter 6, p 209.
[159] See Chapter 6, p 209.
[160] Corresponding to reg 105 of Table A, with some minor drafting additions.

[161] Paragraphs (1) and (2) correspond to reg 106 of Table A. See the comments on reg 106 in Chapter 2, p 88, in relation to para (3).

[162] The first sentence corresponds to reg 107 of Table A. See also Chapter 6, p 209.

[163] See Chapter 6, p 209.

[164] Corresponding to reg 108 of Table A but with the addition of the reference to an 'other sum' as well as a dividend.

[165] See Chapter 6, p 209.

[166] Corresponding to reg 10 of Table A. See also Chapter 6, p 210.

[167] See Chapter 6, p 210.

[168] See Chapter 6, p 210.

[169] See Chapter 6, p 210.

[170] See Chapter 6, p 210.

[171] See Chapter 6, p 210.

[172] See Chapter 6, p 210.

[173] Corresponding to reg 111 of Table A. See Chapter 6, p 211.

[174] Corresponding to reg 112 of Table A. See also Chapter 6, p 211.

[175] The second sentence of para (3) complies with the Listing Rules as mentioned in Chapter 6, p 173.

[176] See Chapter 6, p 211.

[177] See Chapter 6, p 211.

[178] Corresponding to reg 113 of Table A.

[179] Corresponding to reg 114 of Table A. See also Chapter 6, p 212.

[180] Corresponding to reg 115 of Table A. See also Chapter 6, p 212.

[181] See Chapter 6, p 212.

[182] Corresponding to reg 117 of Table A. See the comments on that regulation in Chapter 2, p 96.

[183] This is an extended version of regulation 118 of Table A. See Chapter 2, p 97.

[184] See the comments on reg 118 of Table A in Chapter 2, p 97.

INDEX

Page references in italics are to the appendices.

331